Constructing Socialism at the Grass-Roots

Constructing Socialism at the Grass-Roots

The Transformation of East Germany, 1945–65

Corey Ross
Lecturer in Modern History
University of Birmingham

palgrave

Published by PALGRAVE
Houndmills, Basingstoke, Hampshire RG21 6XS and
175 Fifth Avenue, New York, N. Y. 10010
Companies and representatives throughout the world

PALGRAVE is the new global academic imprint of
St. Martin's Press LLC Scholarly and Reference Division and
Palgrave Publishers Ltd (formerly Macmillan Press Ltd).

Outside North America
ISBN 0–333–78980–6

In North America
ISBN 0–312–23041–9

This book is printed on paper suitable for recycling and
made from fully managed and sustained forest sources.

A catalogue record for this book is available from the British Library.

Library of Congress Catalog Card Number: 99–049746

10   9   8   7   6   5   4   3   2
09 08 07 06 05 04 03 02 01

Printed and bound in Great Britain by
Antony Rowe Ltd, Chippenham, Wiltshire

Contents

List of Tables and Figures

Tables

Figures

List of Abbreviations

APuZG   Aus Politik und Zeitgeschichte: Beilage zur
        Wochenzeitung Das Parlament
BGL   Betriebsgewerkschaftsleitung (Factory Union Leadership)
BL   Bezirksleitung (Regional Leadership)
BPO   Betriebsparteiorganisation (Factory Party Organization)
BV   Bundesvorstand (Federal Executive)
CDU   Christlich Demokratische Union Deutschlands (Christian
        Democratic Union of Germany)
DA   Deutschland Archiv: Zeitschrift für das vereinigte
        Deutschland
DBD   Demokratische Bauernpartei Deutschlands (German
        Democratic Farmer's Party)
DfD   Dienst für Deutschland (Service for Germany)
DFD   Demokratische Frauenbund Deutschlands (German
        Democratic Women's League)
DVP   Deutsche Volkspolizei (People's Police)
DWK   Deutsche Wirtschaftskommission (German Economic
        Commission)
FDGB   Freier Deutscher Gewerkschaftsbund (League of Free
        German Trade Unions)
FDJ   Freie Deutsche Jugend (Free German Youth)
GDR   German Democratic Republic
GG   Geschichte und Gesellschaft. Zeitschrift für Historische
        Sozialwissenschaft
GPO   Grundparteiorganisation (Basic Party Organization)
GST   Gesellschaft für Sport und Technik (Society for Sport
        and Technology)
HJ   Hitlerjugend (Hitler Youth)
HO   Handelsorganisation (Trade Organization)
HVDVP   Hauptverwaltung der Deutschen Volkspolizei (People's
        Police Central Administration)
JHK   Jahrbuch für historische Kommunismusforschung
KL   Kreisleitung (District Leadership)
KPD   Kommunistische Partei Deutschlands (German
        Communist Party)
KVP   Kasernierte Volkspolizei (Garrisoned People's Police)

LDPD	Liberal-Demokratische Partei Deutschlands (Liberal-Democratic Party of Germany)
LPG	Landwirtschaftliche Produktionsgenossenschaft (Agricultural Co-operative)
MAS	Maschinen-Ausleih Station (Machine Lending Station)
MdI	Ministerium des Innern (Interior Ministry)
MfS	Ministerium für Staatssicherheit (Ministry for State Security)
MLF	Ministerium für Land- und Forstwirtschaft (Ministry for Agriculture and Forestry)
MO	Mass Organization
MTS	Maschinen-Traktoren Station (Machine and Tractor Station)
ND	Neues Deutschland
NES	New Economic System
NSDAP	Nationalsozialistische Deutsche Arbeiterpartei (Nazi Party)
NVA	Nationale Volksarmee (National People's Army)
SAG	Sowjetische Aktiengesellschaft (Soviet Joint-Stock Company)
SBZ	Sowjetische Besatzungszone (Soviet Occupation Zone)
SED	Sozialistische Einheitspartei Deutschlands (Socialist Unity Party)
SMAD	Soviet Military Administration of Germany
SPD	Sozialdemokratische Partei Deutschlands (Social Democratic Party of Germany)
SPK	Staatliche Plankommission (State Planning Commission)
TAN	Technically-determined norm
VdgB	Vereinigung der gegenseitigen Bauernhilfe (Association for Mutual Farmers' Assistance)
VEAB	Volkseigener Erfassungs- und Aufkaufsbetrieb (People's Own Registration and Purchasing Enterprise)
VEB	Volkseigener Betrieb (People's Own Enterprise)
VEG	Volkseigenes Gut (People's Own Estate)
WPO	Wohnparteiorganisation (Residential Party Organization)
ZfG	Zeitschrift für Geschichtswissenschaft
ZK	Zentralkomitee (Central Committee of the SED)

Preface

This book is the product of a fascination with the history of East Germany that started with my first visit there with friends in Halle in 1991. Of course by that time there was no longer a separate 'East Germany'. But all the same, in those first couple of years after the collapse of the GDR, the history of the communist regime still cast an almost palpable shadow over eastern Germany: the slower pace of life (deriving in part from mass layoffs), the markedly different experiences and political views from what one normally encounters in the West, the neighbourhoods and villages that looked all but untouched since the end of the war, also the rapid transformation of values, orientations, patterns of work and leisure that were currently taking place underneath the often deceivingly sleepy surface.

Although these various remnants of forty years of state socialism were what initially caught my interest, what particularly struck me was how the whole set of fundamental changes taking place in eastern Germany in the early 1990s were in many ways both a result as well as reflection of another set of fundamental changes that had taken place a few decades earlier under communist authority – changes that also must have been similarly fraught with difficulties, disorientation and inauspicious legacies from the past.

Appearing some ten years after the disappearance of the GDR, this book is about some of these earlier changes. It seeks to explore what the socialist transformation of East Germany looked like in the villages, towns and factories, and to connect this story with some of the broader debates about the history of the GDR. Although it is intended as a piece of academic research, evolving as it has from a PhD thesis at the University of London, I nonetheless hope it will be useful for anyone interested in the history of the GDR. Towards this end I have tried my best to include background information wherever necessary, as well as numerous examples that give the story it tells a human face.

I am grateful to many people and organizations that helped me in researching and writing this book. Without the generous financial support of the Berlin Programme of the Social Science Research Council and the German Academic Exchange Service, this project never could have come to fruition. My PhD supervisor, Mary Fulbrook, has been a constant source of insight and encouragement, giving generously of her time despite her many commitments. Sebastian Simsch and Judd Stitziel also deserve special thanks for their comments on earlier versions of the text and for the many profitable conversations I have enjoyed with them. I am likewise grateful to the many archivists at the *Stiftung Archiv der Parteien und Massenorganisationen der ehemaligen DDR*, the *Bundesarchiv Berlin-Lichterfelde*, the *Brandenburgisches Landeshauptarchiv*, the *Landesarchiv Berlin* and the *Bundesarchiv-Militärarchiv* who patiently entertained my questions and opened up to me the vast world of paper produced in the GDR. My thanks also to colleagues in Liverpool and Birmingham for providing such a congenial environment in which to work, and perhaps more importantly for giving me (so far, at least . . .) a rather light administrative load. As helpful as all of this has been, none of it, of course, makes any of these people or organizations responsible in any way for the contents of this book.

As always, my greatest debts of gratitude are emotional, and go to my wife, Deborah Smail, for agreeing to shuttle between the UK and Germany for a number of years, and to my parents, who have supported me in every way from beginning to end.

Birmingham   COREY ROSS

1
Introduction

East Germans and the history of the GDR

The East German Socialist Unity Party (SED) had a remarkably ambitious social and political agenda. This included not only revolutionary changes in the macro-structures of society – in patterns of ownership, wealth distribution, social hierarchy and political organization – but also, in accordance with Marxist-Leninist theory, revolutionary changes at the grass-roots, even in the very people themselves, their attitudes and values. The Soviets and German communists wasted little time in working towards these goals after the end of the Second World War. Former elites in industry and agriculture, especially those with Nazi ties, were rapidly dispossessed, the state administration and economy were within only a couple of years brought into line with SED and Soviet goals, and there was a massive 're-education' and propaganda campaign to try to convince Germans that the future lay with socialism. The two decades after the defeat of the Third Reich was a period of extraordinarily rapid social change in eastern Germany, during which the SED attempted within a generation to realize the basic elements of its social-political programme, forcing East German social structures into a new and in many ways ill-fitting mould, coaxing and coercing East Germans themselves into accepting the roles the SED had assigned to them and at the same time trying to 'win them over' and turn them into 'socialist personalities'. How 'ordinary'[1] East Germans reacted to this ambitious attempt of social engineering and how it was implemented at the grass-roots level are the central questions of this study.

Despite the huge popular and scholarly interest in the history of the Soviet Occupation Zone (SBZ) and German Democratic Republic (GDR) since 1989, these questions have as yet received relatively

1

little attention. For a number of reasons, there has been a tendency in the wake of the regime's collapse to concentrate on the history of the regime *per se*, on processes of political decision-making, dictatorial control and the organs of coercion that helped sustain party rule. First of all, there has been an understandable curiosity finally to cast a glance 'behind the scenes' of the East German dictatorship on the basis of the radically improved availability of sources and to fill in the many 'blank spots' so long hidden by their inaccessability. More importantly, the fact that the regime collapsed so unexpectedly and so rapidly once the Soviet props were pulled out almost inevitably led to a re-emphasis on repression and control in order to explain its longevity. Certainly the political-moral mood in Germany since 1989 has tended to represent the history of the GDR in terms of the unchecked power of Ulbricht, Honecker and especially the *Stasi vis-à-vis* the East German populace – an interpretation that not only serves to legitimate the democratic and capitalist order of its erstwhile western rival, but which also makes it easier for at least some East Germans to remember the years before 1989 as a passive history of victimization and to avoid the unpleasant question of what part they played in constructing and sustaining the East German dictatorship.

To be sure, there are good reasons for emphasizing repression, control and the unchecked power of this dictatorship. In the pursuit of its social and political agenda, the SED's self-styled exclusive understanding of the course of history did not allow for significant digressions from the official line, whether based on older traditions, a different ideology or on the contradictions and wayward effects of its own policies. The claims it made on East German society and individuals were therefore unlimited and absolute: a new society, a new morality, a 'new man'. These claims and their consequences have been described in numerous variants of the theory of totalitarianism, which has witnessed a remarkable renaissance in academic debate since the dramatic events of 1989. The essence of the modern 'totalitarian' regime, so the classic argument runs, lies precisely in its claims to absolute, universal validity, in its undivided control of communication, production, legislation and its enforcement, whatever residual 'islands of separateness' there may have been.[2] Scholars have recently used this basic model in different ways to view the history of the GDR, some stressing structural features such as the SED's 'unlimited and exclusive access to power', and others more socio-psychological aspects such as the mobilization of the masses through a mixture of indoctrination and control.[3] Although most of this literature has limited itself to describing the formal structures of political power, Sigrid Meuschel has offered a more sociological and systems-theoretical concept which stresses the lack of socio-structural autonomy in the GDR.[4] The end result of the claims of the total state was, in this view, a far-reaching 'shutdown' (*Stillegung*) and functional 'non-differentiation' (*Entdifferenzierung*) of social institutions and a *de facto* fusion of politics, economics, law, art, even leisure as the state extended and consolidated its control over these various spheres of what is commonly called 'society' in western liberal polities. Common to all these views is the tendency to deal only with the formal system of power and thus the adoption of a 'top-down' perspective. What got decided at the 'top' was quickly put into practice on the ground by a mixture of supervision and seduction, indoctrination and repression, and was forced on to a populace too scared or fragmented to do much about it. Hence the focus on the regime *per se*, its structures, organs of repression and the leaders who controlled it as the *dramatis personae* in the history of the GDR.[5]

This study examines the socialist transformation of East Germany from the opposite direction. It is about the popular reception and implementation of policy instead of its formulation. It is about how political intervention 'from above' into the structures of East German society was converted and realized at the grass-roots. Above all it is about how ordinary East Germans responded to the various politically-induced intrusions into their lives during the construction of East German socialism, and about how their responses in turn affected the actual outcome of what was decided in the halls of power. As the following chapters show, when one looks more closely at what was happening 'on the ground' in the GDR during its formative years, there emerges a rather more complicated picture than the 'top-down' scenarios just mentioned. The monolithic image of the East German regime – generally considered the most stable and efficient in the entire Soviet bloc – is rapidly displaced by one of unreliable local functionaries, petty corruption, informal 'arrangements' and internal contradictions. The common contradictory image of the East Germans themselves – on the one hand of a wholly disaffected population held in check only through force and on the other of quiescent, obedient subjects complicit in their own domination – also gives way to a more complex picture of ordinary people trying to utilize various regime policies to their own advantage, not so much resisting or complying (to use the conventional dichotomy) as extracting what they could from the circumstances.

The upheavals of autumn 1989 have to some degree enhanced the status of human agency, however constrained by continuing pressures, as a factor in the history of state socialism, or more precisely in the history of its demise. This study seeks to explore some of the possibilities and consequences, as well as the very real limits, of human actions and decisions *during the construction* of state socialism in the GDR, long before the collective political actions of 1989 that helped bring it down. This is by no means to deny the crucial effects of societal pressures in what was, after all, a very restrictive and dictatorial system. As Jürgen Kocka has suggested: 'What will matter is to explore the changing interrelations between dictatorial authority and the manifold ways in which people dealt with it – from supportive cooperation to apathy and retreat into the private sphere all the way to resistance and opposition'.[6] It is precisely this interplay between regime policies and popular responses, this overlap between political and social history, which this study deals with. How were political decisions made at 'the top' realized on the ground? What was the popular response to the constant political interventions of the SED into the lives of East Germans, how did this affect their concrete realization, and (how) did this differ in different groups or on different issues? Simply put, what happened at the grass-roots when the regime tried to mobilize and control ordinary East Germans for the 'construction of socialism'?[7]

Subjects of enquiry, methods, aims

These questions are of course very broad, and various aspects have been dealt with in studies on topics ranging from industrial relations to the land reform.[8] Yet the question of grass-roots responses to central SED policies has not actually been a central focus of study. The bulk of work to date on popular responses and opinions towards the regime has focused almost exclusively on major political flashpoints – 17 June 1953, autumn 1956, the Prague Spring of 1968 – whereby the emphasis inevitably, and somewhat one-sidedly, is placed on discontent and conflict.[9] A number of studies have also taken popular opposition as their subject, which has had the highly beneficial effect of drawing attention to the fact that 'dissent' in the GDR was not merely confined to a few critical intellectuals already well known in the West before 1989, but which has also tended to paint a somewhat one-sided and static picture of popular political behaviour in the GDR, obscuring both the scope and effects of indifference and apathy as well as the very important modes of *interaction* between rulers and ruled.[10]

This study does not focus exclusively on major political flashpoints (although they do feature in it) and intentionally does not take opposition and dissent as a starting point, but rather focuses on precisely this interplay and overlap. In so doing, however, it does not make the attempt to achieve a 'thick' description of how authority was exerted and reproduced on an everyday basis. To attempt this with any degree of empirical detail would involve an examination of a number of issues too extensive to be covered here.[11] While this study is thus in some ways narrower in focus than these 'everyday-historical' approaches, it is at the same time broader in seeking to pull together, compare and contrast some of the ways in which East Germans perceived, dealt with, conformed to and/or opposed the regime's attempts to mobilize and control them for its cause, and what effects these had for the face of East German socialism. In other words, it is not about how SED authority was maintained and reproduced on an everyday basis, but rather about what happened at the grass-roots when the leadership tried to force major changes by exerting it.

It does this by focusing on a selected number of points where the personal lives and interests (broadly defined) of ordinary East Germans intersected most closely and were confronted most immediately by the total claims of the SED. The bulk of the study deals with what I view as the three principle thrusts of the 'construction of socialism' in East Germany during the first two decades after the war: (1) increasing industrial productivity, especially in raw materials and heavy industry; (2) dispossessing old agrarian elites and gaining state control of agriculture; and (3) mobilizing and 'educating' the youth into their future role as socialist citizens. The effects of these policies on the lives of 'ordinary' East Germans were manifold and profound. Increasing work-productivity meant disciplining workers to produce more as well as a concentration of investment in heavy industry at the expense of consumption and wages. Farmers were asked to expropriate the land of traditional rural elites and were later coaxed and coerced into amalgamating their land into large collective farms. And, finally, East German youths were asked to sever their ties with the churches, to spend their free-time in socialist organizations and to perform their 'patriotic duty' of protecting the GDR and its 'socialist accomplishments' from the perceived military threat of the West by participating in paramilitary training and/or joining the armed forces.[12] The popular reaction towards these policies, the manner and extent of their realization at the grass-roots level and the main points of friction and conflict which they called forth form the three main lines of enquiry that run throughout the book. These are accompanied for the period before 1961 by a fourth: the problem of *'Republikflucht'* ('fleeing the republic', or illegal emigration to the West), that unique and most conspicuous popular response to the transformation of East Germany which placed constraints on the entire process of 'constructing socialism' until the sealing of the border around West Berlin.

These are of course only some of the themes that could be addressed. A number of other aspects of the attempt to transform East German society at the grass-roots – in particular the attempt to create a 'new intelligentsia' to administer the schools, hospitals and factories, as well as the social and political profile of local functionaries and officials, who they were and how this changed over time – are dealt with only briefly throughout the text. Such a study inevitably necessitates a certain selection of topics for emphasis. The broad approach I have chosen is intended to be illustrative, not definitive. Yet it nonetheless sheds some important new light on developments in the SBZ/GDR even beyond the primary aim of situating 'ordinary' East Germans in the socialist transformation of East Germany.

First, and most importantly, there are a number of reasons why the focus is on the grass-roots – that is, not on either 'the regime' or 'the populace', but somewhat on both. As I have already remarked, there has been a general tendency in the literature on the history of the GDR to treat regime and populace separately, or at the very least conceptually to keep the two clearly divided. While this cleft is of course undeniable, much of the material presented here suggests that an equally important cleft in the GDR was that between leadership and grass-roots, or in other words between 'centre' and 'periphery'. Unreliable factory managers, local officials and low-level functionaries were, if not exactly the rule throughout the entire period covered, by no means exceptional. Often there was precious little to distinguish them from 'ordinary' East Germans in terms of their political opinions and loyalties, especially during the early years. Because these people represented 'the regime' at the grass-roots, their reliability or otherwise was of central importance to the attempt to create a new socialist society. Yet their role in conveying policies to the grass-roots has as yet received little attention. In trying to understand the regime's ability to control society and push through its plans for a 'new Germany' at the grass-roots, this kind of focus seems more useful than one that keeps 'regime' and 'populace' rigidly separate.

Second, this grass-roots emphasis also offers new perspectives on the themes covered by the various chapters. The material in some of these will be more familiar to students of GDR history than that in others. The literature on industrial workers and shopfloor disputes in the GDR has grown especially rapidly in recent years.[13] Although I draw quite explicitly on this literature, this study places particular emphasis on the interaction between workers, managers and local functionaries in the factories and also attempts to go beyond the prevailing emphasis on material interests and economic disputes to discuss also various non-economic sources of friction on the shopfloor. Processes of social transformation in the countryside have also attracted considerable scholarly attention, though the rather heated debates in the wake of German unification about the question of restitution for those who were dispossessed in the land reform has led to a concentration of recent research on these early years that has tended to eclipse the process of agricultural collectivization that followed.[14] The few studies to date on agricultural collectivization have in any event tended to focus on the political decisions that led up to it and Soviet influence on these decisions.[15] This book examines both of these developments in terms of how they were received, refashioned and implemented in the villages, and lays particular emphasis on the role of rural functionaries in conveying official policies to the grass-roots. Similarly, although SED policy towards youth has been the subject of considerable interest, its transmission and effects on the ground have taken a back seat, and certain issues like the recruitment and responses of would-be rank-and-file soldiers have not yet been a subject of research at all.[16] And as for the problem of *Republikflucht*, most recent research has dealt with refugee and immigration policies in the Federal Republic – not surprising given the ongoing debates about this issue in Germany.[17] This book focuses instead on various aspects of *Republikflucht* within East Germany: from motives for flight to rifts between local functionaries and central authorities over the treatment of former refugees to the ways ordinary East Germans used the threat of flight to extract concessions from state authorities.

Third, there has been a tendency in historical research on the GDR to limit the focus of individual studies to rather small thematic topics or to brief spans of time. There are of course good reasons for this, above all the huge amounts of documentation produced by the East German bureaucracy which itself tends to gravitate against broader studies. It also has to do with the general reluctance to take on broader themes before the empirical basis is more fully developed, as well as with the current aversion among many social and cultural historians towards 'megatheories' and larger structures of interpretation in principle. Fully aware of the problems of taking on as wide an array of themes and social groups as is done here, I nonetheless think that the forest is gradually being eclipsed by so many trees in GDR historiography, and that any attempt, however provisional, to pull various histories together and trace broad developments over a substantial stretch of time is a worthwhile venture.

Finally, the book also attempts to draw some connections between the ongoing conceptual and theoretical discussion on the GDR and the empirical basis available – two distinct discourses which have tended to run parallel to each other since 1989 but whose paths have rarely seemed to cross. By its very focus on the 'periphery' of the communist dictatorship, where the inevitable social proximity of 'ordinary' East Germans and local representatives of the regime often hindered the leadership's attempts to control East German society as it wished, it inherently questions the limits of such notions as the 'undifferentiated' and *'durchherrschte'* (or 'ruled through and through') society of the GDR which have moulded the parameters of debate thus far.

The argument and its structure

The basic argument is straightforward. The socialist transformation of East Germany was an extremely difficult and conflict-ridden process at the grass-roots, where the SED's ambitious attempts to create a 'new society' and 'new man' were hindered, diluted and refracted by a range of problems. Quite obviously, it could not carry out all of its plans unchallenged, as if the society and people over which it governed were a mere *tabula rasa* awaiting organization into a new social system. 'Ordinary' East Germans had their own interests and concerns – most commonly referred to in recent years as '*Eigen-Sinn*', or a sense of one's interests[18] – which sometimes overlapped and often collided with the SED's policies. Most people tried to extract what they could from the circumstances of East German socialism, which, depending on the particular situation, could mean protest, opposition or conformity, but which for most of the populace most of the time did not mean positive support. Making use of the circumstances was often made easier by the fact that the policies that constituted the socialist transformation of East Germany were in many cases not completely converted at the grass-roots in the first place, largely for three reasons: (1) the persistence of older structures, mentalities, and social networks that survived the supposed socialist 'zero hour' after the war and which proved remarkably resilient, (2) the inner contradictions of official policies and between different elements of the regime, and (3) resulting from both of these factors, the unreliability of many of its representatives at the local level. The general unwillingness of most East Germans to assume the social roles the SED had assigned to them, the resilience of local social networks and the inertia of traditional mentalities – together with the unreliability of many local functionaries and the inner contradictions of official policies themselves – meant that the SED's various political interventions into East German society were significantly reshaped at the grass-roots, often to become at least partially compatible with existing social structures, popular wishes and attitudes. Yet it was arguably this very reshaping and dilution that made the rapid socialist transformation of East Germany a viable project at all by allowing for a certain degree of social autonomy at the grass-roots. From the more heavy-handed 1950s to the less ideological 1960s there developed a kind of tacit and pragmatic, if rather unenthusiastic, coexistence between the party leadership which had learned to tolerate this and a populace that increasingly came to take its authority for granted.

The organization of the book follows both a chronological as well as thematic format. The separate sections develop the argument in chronological stages, and each is subdivided into thematic chapters that cover the issues already mentioned. The first section surveys the years up to 1952 during which the East German regime was established, and focuses on the effects of the communists' policies of agricultural and industrial reform in the villages and on the shopfloor. The second section focuses on the period from the summer of 1952 to summer 1953, a crucial year in the history of the

GDR which saw the first campaign for agricultural collectivization, the first open attacks on the churches, the first large military recruitment push as well as the attempt to raise industrial productivity by fiat which led to the tumultuous events of 17 June 1953. Section three covers the years between 1953 and 1961, from the fallout after the debacle of 17 June to the construction of the Berlin Wall. Despite slowly regaining the ground it had lost after the setback of summer 1953, the party leadership nonetheless eventually saw itself forced to lock in its subjects after millions had decided to flee the 'construction of socialism' in East Germany. As the last section demonstrates, the sealing of the border was only a partial caesura in the history of the GDR in terms of its effects at the grass-roots. The changing patterns of social and political relations in the early 1960s were interwoven with tenacious threads of continuity, many of which reached all the way back to the problems that characterized the understandably chaotic years immediately after the war.

Sources, geographic scope

The primary sources I have used are the internal correspondence and information reports of the SED, mass organizations (especially the trade union league, or FDGB) and East German state ('People's Police' and various ministries), all of which present a number of methodological problems. The internal reports of the East German party-state apparatus are politicized through and through, and by no means can be taken to 'speak for themselves'. The ideologized language and conceptual categories in which they increasingly came to be couched over the years present a curious mixture of German bureaucratic euphemism and SED jargon in which such vague terms as 'ideological unclarities' and 'hostile arguments' could denote either insignificant digressions from the party line or seething beds of discontent. The problems run in two different directions. The inflationary use of such terms as 'enemy elements' and 'reactionary forces' must be taken with a pinch of salt if one wants to avoid overemphasizing signs of conflict and dissent. At the same time, there was also a certain tendency towards *Schönfärberei* – watering-down or beautifying reports to one's superiors. The party leadership thus often only heard what lower-level functionaries wanted them to hear. After all, what they reported reflected on their performance. However, once one reads through the formulaic slogans and obvious political bias, these reports contain a wealth of information on popular opinion, the activities of local functionaries, as well as social and economic conditions more generally. Despite the tendency towards 'beautification', most reports seem to attempt to describe the situation on the ground more or less soberly or even pessimistically after a customary paragraph or two on 'positive' developments. Moreover, the voices of 'ordinary' East Germans frequently come through loud and clear; expressions of dissent in particular are often conveyed quite fulsomely and in fascinating detail. So despite their obvious shortcomings, these reports – in conjunction with letters of complaint, petitions, oral history and survey information[19] – are highly useful in evaluating popular responses to various regime policies.

Reports were produced at a number of levels in the party, mass organizations and state apparatus, from the individual factory to the local district (*Kreis*), regional (*Bezirk*) and central levels. It has been suggested that, because of the problem of 'beautification' and filtering at each level, reports from the lowest (usually *Kreis*) level present the most accurate picture of 'reality' at any given time.[20] Although this may often be the case, and although I draw quite extensively on SED district leadership (*Kreisleitung*) reports, I would argue that this assertion is overstretched for two reasons. First, in reading through reports at the different levels, it becomes clear that most beautification that takes place begins at the source and often does not change considerably on the way to the top unless edited as part of a summary. There is therefore not so great a difference between reports at the local and central levels as one might at first think. Secondly, because the party leadership was arguably more interested in receiving accurate information than local functionaries were in producing it, and was in any event fully aware of the problems of report-beautification, it regularly deployed its own *Instrukteure* (instructors, or plenipotentiaries) from the Central Committee to report directly on special problems or matters of interest. These reports, written by true party professionals, are often the most informative of all and serve as a foil to the regular reports from lower levels.

Internal reports in any state bureaucracy, especially dictatorial regimes, tend to focus on problems, difficulties and failures, and the historian who uses them as sources runs the risk of over-emphasizing these at the expense of what *did* work and what was successful from the regime's point of view. The same is of course true of petitions and letters of complaint, which tend to give a one-sided view. Because of this emphasis on problems and failures in the internal communication of the regime, no news can to a certain degree be regarded as good news. I have tried to keep these dangers in mind while reading through stacks and stacks of files in the East German archives. But in the process what struck me most about these reports, petitions and letters of complaint is their sheer and overwhelming profusion. Insofar as no news was good news, the GDR had a lot of problems. While one cannot, of course, simply extrapolate from the particular to the general – for instance, take a complaint about corruption involving the land reform in a certain village or a report on poor work-discipline in a certain factory and claim that it was a general phenomenon – the huge volume of such reports, together with the fact that not all such problems could possibly be registered in the first place, conveys the very strong impression that they were more the rule than the exception. Thus the examples I use throughout the text are, unless otherwise noted, illustrative of fairly common occurrences.

Before proceeding, a brief word on the geographical scope seems necessary. Although this study is intended to address issues and developments affecting the GDR as a whole, it is nonetheless regionally based in order to achieve a higher degree of analytical detail than would otherwise be possible. In order to examine sources from the various levels of the regime's information apparatus, it concentrates on East Berlin and Brandenburg (after 1952, the four administrative *Bezirke* East Berlin, Potsdam, Frankfurt/Oder and Cottbus),[21] though not exclusively and to varying degrees in the different chapters. The regional focus is far more exclusive in the chapters on the factories and villages than in the other two, primarily because of the sheer volume of material on these topics, but also because the actual places themselves – the factories and villages – play a more integral role to these chapters than to the others. In other words, the regional focus here is not intended as an analytical confinement, but rather as a means of examining how directives from the centre were received at the grass-roots.

Of course no regionally-based study can claim to be wholly representative of the entire GDR. Despite being a truncated 'half-nation-state', East Germany still possessed a hearty measure of the regional diversity so characteristic of Central Europe – from the vast expanses of lakes and plains in Mecklenburg to the quaint half-timbered towns of the Harz mountains to the industrial centres of Saxony. Clearly, a local or regional study of any one area of the GDR would invariably run up against the problems of typicality and representativeness. But it is not at all certain that a study executed at the level of the entire GDR would necessarily be preferable or even, for that matter, more 'representative' of developments at the grass-roots given the degree of abstraction this would entail. Moreover, although regional variations undoubtedly existed, these were variations on a common theme.

For a number of reasons, East Berlin and Brandenburg together seemed a particularly promising region to focus on. Besides being the region most immediately affected by the existence and eventual sealing off of West Berlin, its socio-economic structure was quite diverse, presenting a fairly even balance between urban/industrial and rural/agricultural milieux.[22] The region as a whole boasted both long-established urban industrial centres with a commensurately 'traditional' working-class milieu (above all in East Berlin and the industrial penumbra surrounding it) as well as a number of provincial industrial centres such as the steel and chemical plants in Brandenburg/Havel and the extensive collieries of the Niederlausitz region near Cottbus. It was also the site of some of the largest industrialization projects of the 1950s and 1960s – most notably the steel works at Stalinstadt/Eisenhüttenstadt and the petrochemical plants at Schwedt – that radically changed many rural areas and that attracted hundreds of thousands of expellees from the former eastern territories of the Reich into the world of the industrial worker with relatively high wages and the promise of housing. Yet Brandenburg was still predominately rural and its economy overwhelmingly agricultural at the end of the war. In 1950, approximately 33 per cent of Brandenburg's population was still engaged in agriculture.[23] Of the five initial federal states (*Länder*) of the GDR, only Mecklenburg-Vorpommern had a more agrarian economy or was more strongly characterized by the traditional Prussian – or better, *Junker* – pattern of large aristocratic landholdings (*Großgrundbesitz*). In 1939, large estates with more than 100 hectares comprised merely 1.1 per cent of the total number of agricultural enterprises in Brandenburg, but 31 per cent of the land.[24] In terms of farming practices and patterns of ownership, the region itself showed more variegation than the other federal states. Whereas the northern and eastern areas of Brandenburg were dominated by large-scale landholding, the southern area around Cottbus was characterized more by mid-sized (5–20 hectares) and large (20–100 hectares) peasant farms, accounting respectively for 25 per cent and

38 per cent of agricultural acreage in Brandenburg as a whole, as well as widespread second-occupational farming in the villages near the large collieries.

East Berlin and Brandenburg, like the other regions of the SBZ, were not very attractive places to live at the end of the war. At the time, few places in Germany were. The task facing the Soviets and East German communists was immense: building up a disjointed and war-torn economy, integrating hundreds of thousands of refugees, constructing a new apparatus of power and generating a modicum of popular approval for their authority. Let us now turn to what happened at the grass-roots when they tried to solve these problems and build a new society in East Germany.

Part 1

Laying the Foundations, 1945–52

The problems facing the Soviets and German communists after the war were myriad. At a very basic level there was widespread apprehension and dislike towards the Soviet occupation regime and the communist-led German authorities that carried out its wishes. After all, anti-communism and the idea of German cultural (not to mention racial) superiority over the Slavic peoples were central to Nazi teachings, and had numbered among the more integrative aspects of Nazi ideology. More importantly, the destruction caused by the war, above all the collapse of the zone's infrastructure and the desperate shortages of basic necessities, tended to favour a localization, not centralization, of organization and control. The unprecedented confusion and uprooting of millions of people, the political collapse and economic chaos by and large escaped central control in the immediate post-war years. Yet it was during these difficult years that the groundwork was laid for subsequent developments in East Germany, not only in terms of political decisions – the 'Stalinization' of the political system and mass organizations, the exchange of elites, the restructuring of patterns of ownership and the general economic divergence from the western occupation zones – but also the many wayward and unintended effects that resulted on the ground.

Apart from the process of denazifying the zone's administration and security apparatus and the merger of the workers' parties, the two other primary concerns for the Soviets and German communists were to reform and gain control over industry and agriculture, issues that affected most of the population in some way. This section

15

surveys some of the changes this entailed and the problems encountered, first from the perspective of the villages and then from
the factories. As we will see, although this political intervention
into East German society in the years following the war undoubtedly brought about far-reaching structural changes, they were not
flawlessly realized at the grass-roots. The socialist 'zero hour' was
only a partial new-beginning, and the ability to effect radical changes
and exercise strict control at this level was by no means complete
– not in the villages, not in the towns and factories, and above all
not in people's heads.

2
The Land Reform and its Effects

Though neither the Soviets nor German communists had any master plan for rural society in 1945, it was generally agreed that patterns of land ownership in the countryside had to be reformed. Worked out over the summer of 1945 and officially launched in September, the land reform was the first major intervention by the Soviets into the social structure of eastern Germany. Its aim was not just to punish supporters of the Third Reich, but also to help integrate the flood of refugees streaming in from the East, create a more egalitarian structure of land ownership and thereby to gain a rural clientele and expand the influence of the KPD in the countryside. The land reform statutes mandated the expropriation of the *Junker* landlords, viewed by the victorious Allies and the German bloc parties alike as the major social bulwark of German militarism, as well as Nazi war criminals and any other large landowners with Nazi ties. The confiscated land was to be distributed above all to land-poor peasants, landless farm labourers and refugees from the eastern territories – the so-called 'new farmers' – in plots of five to ten hectares, depending on its quality. The land reform was thus a two-sided process: first, to get rid of the traditional rural elites and their estates; and second, to establish a patchwork of small new farms in their place. Although clearly communist-inspired, the transformation of the countryside was also supposed to have a popular and spontaneous character as the expression of the will of the rural populace. For both legitimatory and organizational purposes, it was necessary to enlist the help of the rural farming populace itself in carrying out both of these steps at the grass-roots. But farmers had their own interests, agendas and ideas about the land reform which only partially overlapped – and partially collided – with those of

17

the Soviets and German communists. This affected not only *how* the land reform was carried out at the grass-roots, but also *what* it accomplished. And as we will see, all of this was more easily said than done in the political collapse and economic chaos of the post-war years.

Confiscation, redistribution and the village milieu

The attempt to transform the villages and farms of the East German countryside faced a number of serious difficulties. Given the collapse of the zone's infrastructure, the logistical problems of maintaining authority in the countryside in the chaos of the immediate post-war years were legion. Despite the massive social and demographic upheavals during the closing stages of the war, the close-knit web of rural social relations had not collapsed along with the Reich, and if anything had gained in importance during the years of scarcity as local solidarity had to take over where state services no longer existed. Even the dissemination of information in the countryside was relatively difficult; the rural populace was less likely to own a radio or television, had less access to the cinema or theatre and were also far more difficult to reach via visual propaganda (posters, billboards, etc.) than city-dwellers. Other problems had to do with the very character of rural society itself. The rural populace remained the least educated and most religious segment of East German so-ciety. Farmers tended to be more closely bound to the church than to any political party, and the old networks of kinship and social relations in the villages were difficult to penetrate. The resilience and impenetrability of what might be called the 'village milieu' had proved an irritating hindrance to the Nazis' attempts to mobilize peasants, who by and large were uninterested in the *Volksgemeinschaft* so long as it did not directly affect their religious sensibilities or farming interests. By comparison, the Soviets and German commu-nists were further handicapped by the fact that most farmers saw the single greatest threat to these interests in the prospect of ex-propriation under a socialist regime – an apprehension which had helped the Nazis in rural areas in the first place.

To be sure, many of the initial signs were promising from the communists' point of view. The land reform quickly led to a fun-damental transformation of the structure of land ownership in the Soviet Zone as a whole and in Brandenburg and Mecklenburg in particular. According to official statistics, by November 1945 41 per cent of all agricultural land in Brandenburg had been confiscated and distributed to some 82 810 families, with smaller amounts going to a number of local communities and state enterprises.[1] During the course of the autumn of 1945 the centuries-old dominance of large estates in the Brandenburg countryside was largely replaced by a new agrarian structure characterized by small- and mid-scale enterprises. The *Junker* landlords who had dominated Germany east of the Elbe for centuries indeed lost the social and economic basis of their power – some even lost their lives at the hands of Soviet soldiers, former Russian and Polish forced labourers or in miserable detention camps on the Baltic.[2] But the official statistics on the land reform tend to hide the many difficulties and distortions of the process at the grass-roots, where older social relations and mentalities remained largely intact despite the chaos and destruction during the closing stages of the war.

In many local communities, older habits of social deference proved a persistent obstacle to the drive to dispossess the large landlords. Although the land reform clearly corresponded to the needs and wishes of most land recipients to secure an economic existence in the scarcity and chaos immediately following the war, in many villages the communists found it difficult to mobilize the landless farm labourers and refugees to expropriate the local *Junker* suzerains. While the re-distribution of land in some areas was indeed carried out in a spirit of spontaneity and occasionally even accompanied by festivities, most often the would-be new farmers were rather reluctant to take land from local elites whose authority had rarely been challenged up until then. According to a 1946 year-end report on the land reform in Brandenburg 'the new farmers only went about their work hesistantly during their initial period of getting settled, and did not show absolute trust that the political circumstances would not change'.[3] Little wonder, for there are numerous reports complaining of former estate owners frightening the new farmers from taking control of their plots by telling them that the land reform would be overturned later on. Local land commissions responsible for the re-distribution of land and inventory were only very slowly organized in the autumn of 1945, and many of the landowners whom these commissions were charged to expropriate managed to retain small portions of their property well into 1946. Moreover, many of the refugees expelled from the eastern provinces of the Reich hoped that they would quickly be able to return to their homes and for this reason were hesitant about applying for land.

This reluctance to accept land expropriated from *Junker* estates was not based solely on fear and uncertainty. The paternalistic orientation of many former farm labourers and small tenant farmers, their persisting loyalties *vis-à-vis* their former landlords and the deeply-rooted orientation towards large estate farming prevalent especially in northern and eastern areas also hindered the land reform. Many new farmers were reluctant to break up the large estates given the grim prospects of farming such small plots with little livestock, equipment or, particularly among former farmhands and industrial workers who had received land, little agricultural expertise. There were numerous cases of former landowners managing to retain a piece of land or drifting back to their estates in the course of the winter of 1945–46 and hiring their former employees to the satisfaction of both parties. According to a January 1946 report from the Brandenburg provincial administration, 'in a number of cases the distribution of confiscated estates to land-poor, landless farmers, farmhands and refugees exists only on paper... In some cases the applicants for land are still treated like farmhands and still work for wages or payment in kind... The commissions or authorities often refuse to distribute sown land in order to maintain the unity of the large estates. They justify this failure with the intention to continue working cooperatively or collectively'.[4] Local disregard or transformation of directives against amalgamating plots or distributing amounts of land over 10 hectares was the only way to sustain the new farms at all in some areas.[5] In fact, in many previous manorial villages the new farmers only gradually began working their plots individually in the autumn of 1946, after numerous Soviet threats of sanctions for non-compliance.[6] That these were not merely isolated cases is indirectly evidenced by the Soviet Order 6080 of August 1947 removing all former land owners at least 50 kilometers from their previous estates. According to statistics from the Brandenburg Ministry of Agriculture and Forestry, of the total of 2080 families whose property had been expropriated through the land reform, 798 still had to be expelled from their estates in 1947 on the basis of Order 6080.[7]

The demolition of the old manor houses in 1947 – in the Soviets' and German communists' eyes the very embodiment of *Junkertum* – and their replacement with new farming settlements faced many of the same difficulties. Many locals, even ranking SED members, thought they were of too great historical value to be pulled down or thoroughly altered. But more problematic was the fact that the new farmers themselves were less than enthusiastic about it. Most were still afraid that if the political circumstances changed they would be blamed by the owners of the houses and possibly punished; there were still reports of agitators sent across the border by former estate owners threatening new farmers with revenge should they tear down their houses.[8] Furthermore, many former refugees still hoped to be able to return to their previous homes east of the Oder/Neisse border and therefore showed little desire to take permanent ownership of new buildings. As one report complains, 'for these reasons the farmers can only be persuaded to change the estate character of the houses with great difficulty or with coercion'.[9] This presented not only a political problem, but also a material one; without the construction material acquired from the demolition of the stately homes there was no chance of fulfilling the construction plans for new houses and barns. Eventually, the demolition of some 2000 manorial buildings in Brandenburg in 1948 was carried out against the wishes of many new farmers and local functionaries.

Even with the estate owners gone and their property confiscated, however, the old networks of social relations in the villages presented a number of problems to the land reform, above all in lending themselves to corruption in the distribution of land and inventory. The Soviets and German authorities had early on recognized the potential for local distortions of the land reform measures and introduced a number of controls against it. The local land commissions (*Gemeindebodenkommissionen*) responsible for confiscating and distributing land were to be comprised solely of landless labourers and farmers with less than five hectares of land, thus supposedly ensuring their political reliability. Furthermore, the commissions' expropriation plans had to be ratified by a district commission (*Kreiskommission*), which was in turn controlled by a regional land commission. Nonetheless, the sheer volume of complaints of petty corruption in the archives strongly suggests that minor abuses were more the rule than the exception.

For one thing, the loose definition of who was a Nazi and who was not presented immense opportunities to settle old scores in the villages, and a number of local land commissions confiscated land from persons whom they rather arbitrarily designated as Nazis.[10] Far more common, though, were cases where members of local land commissions tried to enrich themselves, their relatives or their friends over newcomers or rival families in the distribution of confiscated property. One rather spectacular case of corruption was uncovered in 1948 in the village of Kattlow in *Kreis* Cottbus, where the former manager of the estate 'Schönigsche Stiftung', Herr Hendrisch, had distributed the entire estate to members of his family, each of whom received 10 hectares under the land reform statutes. The fact that two of these family members had been members of the SS and three of them still lived in the western zones was, curiously, no hindrance to their receiving land or even to the cultivation of their plots. As the report notes, the 'new farmer' Hendrisch was no new farmer at all, but was actually running the estate much as he always had in his former capacity as estate manager, hiring 25 to 30 seasonal workers from Cottbus for harvesting and sowing. As was often the case, the entire situation was made possible by the fact that Hendrisch had the 'best support from the side of the authorities', namely the local council chairman Schuster, who spent his holidays at the estate and who vouched for Hendrisch as an active anti-fascist, which had led to earlier complaints about him being brushed aside. Schuster was also apparently instrumental in allocating 100 tons of lime (in desperately short supply at the time) to Hendrisch, putatively for revitalizing the fish stock in the estate's lake, but which was actually used to renovate the villa.[11]

Though perhaps an extreme case, Kattlow was by no means the only instance of corruption and collusion with local authorities. There were literally thousands of instances of what one report called the 'peculiar application of the land reform ordinance', usually in the form of family members working the land of a relative who actually lived elsewhere, several members of the same household acquiring land with the tacit approval or indifference of local authorities, officials favouring themselves, their relatives or acquaintances in the allotment of livestock and equipment, etc.[12] Indeed, Kattlow was not even the only case in *Kreis* Cottbus. There was a similar incident in Laubsdorf, where the former manager of an estate, Herr von Schoen, had managed to distribute 400 acres of land exclusively among his family. Nor was simple greed the only motive. In yet another case in *Kreis* Cottbus the former refugee Seifert was given two young cows, one good milk cow, a hog and some field equipment by a suspiciously generous local agricultural official, Herr Böttcher, who reportedly had 'very close relations with the daughter of this new farmer' and was apparently trying to ingratiate himself with the father of his sweetheart. As the report notes, the other new farmers in the village had nothing against a new farmer being helped, 'but this case shows that acquaintances and friends are privileged and enjoy certain advantages from the local council. This is not taken to be the only case; rather, it is said that this department is one big swamp of corruption'.[13]

Herr Seifert was fortunate, for in the majority of cases it was new farmers, and especially former refugees and single women, who suffered most from such nepotism and collusion. As outsiders to the villages in which they lived they were often given the poorest plots from the land-fund, and there were even a number of isolated cases of land commissions refusing to grant land to refugees at all.[14] Even when refugees acquired decent plots of land, they were generally dependent on the native farmers, who often resented their presence in the villages and were of little help. The local VdgBs (*Vereinigungen der gegenseitigen Bauernhilfe*, or Associations for Mutual Farmers' Assistance) that were originally set up in 1945 to support the new farmers by coordinating the use of equipment and storage space were usually taken over by the more established farmers, especially the powerful big farmers, who often manipulated the VdgB resources to their own advantage. According to the 1946 year-end report of the German Administration for Agriculture and Forestry:

> The relations between the old farmers and new farmers in the Province Mark Brandenburg are generally characterized as not good. The new farmers do not assert themselves enough because of their labile economic situation, the old farmers exploit their economic predominance to create for themselves a dominant position in the local executives of the VdgB. The old farmers have recognized that the VdgB is an excellent instrument for realizing their own interests ... Mutual assistance is often only given from old farmer to old farmer. The new farmers reconcile themselves to this situation because they are dependent on the old farmers for many of their daily requirements'.[15]

To be sure, the antagonism between natives and newcomers had to do with more than material interests. Cultural, confessional and even linguistic differences between Brandenburg villagers and refugees were also important factors behind the poor relations in many villages. Refugees from the eastern territories were often looked down on as quasi-racial-inferiors, and were frequently subjected to such epithets as '*Polacken*', '*Spitzbubenbande*', '*verlaustes Russenpack*', or '*polnische Sau*' – insults that were all the more infuriating to people expelled from their homes precisely because they were 'German'.[16] The relatively high percentage of Catholics among the refugees also contributed to the cleft between newcomers and natives in the predominately Lutheran Brandenburg countryside, a region where the word '*katolsch*' was a synonym for 'bogus' or 'treacherous'. The refugees were broadly viewed as intruders in the villages, their presence regarded as desirable only at sowing and harvest time, when they were a source of cheap labour. As refugees in Ostprignitz were told by natives: 'you ought to be plowed under in the autumn and only dug up again in the spring'.[17]

Yet the social and cultural front between newcomers and natives was only as impermeable as seemed profitable. New farmers were also widely involved in petty corruption, though this, too, was usually at the expense of other new farmers. To offer merely one example, in the village of Gersdorf, *Kreis* Oberbarnim the VdgB chairman Balitz, a former refugee and new farmer, saw to it that the VdgB first and foremost assisted the old farmers in the village in return for tacit approval from the native *Bürgermeister* Peter to work several acres of land illegally and sell the produce for profit. Another former refugee in the village, Bruno Rostock (who spoke better Polish than German, the report notes), had also managed to acquire land illegally and apparently ran two or three farms through land-pooling. According to the other new farmers in the village, Rostock was a kind of 'untouchable' whose activities – which also included illegal slaughtering – were covered up by the local authorities. As the report concludes, 'this village is dominated by a nepotism that pushes more or less weak refugees and farmers against the wall and produces a level of dissatisfaction that results in constant letters of complaint'.[18]

From hope to disappointment: the new farmers

Despite all of these hindrances, setbacks and distortions, the land reform met, at least initially, with approval by the majority of farmers, especially the new farmers who directly gained from it and the many refugees for whom a plot of land meant nothing less than a new home and a fresh start. It was hoped – indeed, assumed – that the land reform would give the communists a popular basis in the countryside. The results of elections to the regional parliaments, district and local councils in September and October 1946 showed considerable support for the SED (although recent evidence showing that many older 'native' farmers also voted for the communists suggests that the land reform was not the only factor,[19] and it should also be noted that the Soviets gave the SED certain advantages in terms of campaign resources). In the communal elections it received 59.8 per cent of the vote, and in the regional elections 43.9 per cent (compared to 47.5 per cent in the SBZ as a whole). As for party membership, it was estimated that by 1946 the SED had some 2000 local groups, although it is clear that farmers remained underrepresented in the party rank-and-file, constituting only 9.8 per cent of its membership. In winning the allegiance of farmers the SED's toughest opponent was the CDU. The Christian Democrats were particularly strong in Brandenburg, especially in the eastern regions where the DNVP (*Deutsch-Nationale Volkspartei*, or German National People's Party) and regional farmers' parties had been dominant in the 1920s and early 1930s.[20] In the regional elections in 1946 it received 30.6 per cent of the Brandenburg vote compared to only 24.6 per cent in the SBZ as a whole.[21]

But these election results, however interesting in their own right, do not fully capture the political landscape in the villages of the SBZ. For one thing, after the war the communists were confronted with the daunting task of trying to 're-educate' the many small- and mid-sized farmers who had been ardent Nazis. There were numerous villages in which 95 per cent and even 100 per cent of the farmers had been members of the NSDAP, among them also land-poor and landless farmers applying for plots.[22] Communist functionaries sent into the countryside from Berlin frequently reported of the 'downright catastrophic political situation among the rural populace', of 'widespread reactionary and Nazi attitudes' and of a general atmosphere of rejection and hostility.[23] More importantly, whatever the short-term political credit the SED extracted from the land reform, it was not long before the good feelings about it dissipated.

The new farmers, around one quarter of them trying their hand at farming for the first time, suffered particularly from the economic chaos and shortages in the countryside, above all from the lack of farm labour. Most small and mid-level male farmers had been drafted into the army and many were not able to return home immediately after the cessation of fighting. In May 1946 there were still only 100 men to 170 women in the Provinz Brandenburg as a whole, and in the countryside the ratio was even lower. Of the approximately 620 000 refugees who had reached Brandenburg by the summer of 1946, most of whom were housed in rural areas, only 20 per cent were men capable of physical work.[24] Thus a high proportion of farmers in Brandenburg, and especially new farmers, were women, many of them without their menfolk or adequate help on the farm.[25] The Polish and Russian forced labourers who had kept the farms going during the war had already left for home in their thousands in the summer of 1945, many of them further compounding the problems in the East German countryside by looting villages and taking livestock on the way.[26] Because of the general shortage of seed and fertilizer, even when the new farmers managed to get livestock they often had to sell the animals again because they were not able to produce enough to feed them through the winter.[27] The rapid break-up of the large estates also meant that many of the new farmers' plots had no houses, barns or machinery. Circumstances were particularly bad in the eastern areas of Brandenburg, where large swathes of countryside had been destroyed during the Red Army's drive for Berlin. While roughly 9 per cent of the houses and flats registered in Brandenburg in 1939 had been damaged and 20 per cent destroyed, in some eastern *Kreise* the scope of destruction was well over 30 per cent, in *Kreis* Lebus even 44 per cent.[28] What little accommodation that could be found for the new farmers was often extremely rudimentary; some even resorted to making huts out of clay and any other discarded material they could find.[29] Requests for aid sent by new farmers to the state administration and mass organizations portray the conditions in the new settlements in the starkest of terms. One such request from a new farmer in Altzechdorf, *Kreis* Lebus, speaks of a profound sense of 'despair' (*Mutlosigkeit*), of children without milk living merely on potatoes and salt and of women pulling farm machinery because no draft animals were available.[30]

Much of this could not be helped given the destruction and massive population movements resulting from the war. But in a number of ways Soviet actions only worsened the new farmers' problems, and in the process turned many formerly sympathetic refugees and farmhands against the occupation forces that had been so instrumental in giving them land. The insistence on the break-up of the large estates, against the arguments of many Soviet requisitions officers and German communists, inevitably led to a decrease in agricultural productivity, which the Soviet reparations brigades in turn only exacerbated by hauling off what little chemical fertilizer and farm machinery that was left in the countryside. The forced requisitioning of grain and animal products by the Soviets also embittered German farmers, who were occasionally forced to thresh wheat when they should have been harvesting potatoes, to turn over valuable bread grains in order to fulfil their feed grain quotas or in some cases even to slaughter breeding cattle to fulfil meat quotas.[31] Delivery quotas often seemed to take little account of soil or weather conditions such as the floods on the Oder in 1946 or the droughts of 1947 and 1948, and, given the stiff penalties for failure to fulfil them, were a source of profound bitterness and constant complaint.[32] Corruption and abuses by local commandants were rife, and to make matters even worse, the Soviet authorities were unable to keep their own soldiers from regularly raiding chicken coops and curing-houses.[33]

The German authorities, for their part, were in little doubt about the direct connection between Soviet requisitioning and the ever-increasing numbers of new farmers abandoning their plots. In its 1946 year-end report, the German Administration for Agriculture and Forestry complained that, 'through the actions of the commandants of the Red Army, who have undertaken mass penalties and incarcerations of new farmers without regard to the actual circumstances, a situation has emerged which places the very livelihood of the new farmers in question . . . A portion of the flight from the fields is due to the actions of the agencies of the Red Army in charge of requisitioning'. But as the report goes on to note, the German authorities were of little help to the new farmers, and by and large failed to confront the Soviets on the issue: 'It is noteworthy that the entire German administration from the provincial administration down to the *Bürgermeister* puts up no resistance to the harmful manner of enforcement of the orders of the occupation agencies, but rather carries out all of these orders to the letter and without any objection whatsoever'.[34]

In some villages the local German authorities were themselves part of the new farmers' problems, and the fact that most positions in the state structure were filled by SED members hardly gravitated in the party's favour. The countless complaints among the upper echelons of the SED of incompetence, corruption and inappropriate behaviour on the part of local officials highlight how tenuous was the control of the central authorities at the local level during these early years. It was difficult to train new cadre, and in the meantime the party had to make do with the material at hand – the occasional respected village leader, the scoundrel feathering his own nest and that of friends and relatives, and the hundreds of 'little Stalins' keen to exert their new authority. In Batzlow, *Kreis* Bad Freienwalde, the SED *Bürgermeister* Böhm and his wife reportedly ruled the village as miniature 'dictators', alienating the other villagers from the SED. According to a SED instructor's report: 'Because B. threatened to have the villagers "locked up" every time he wanted to push something through, the complainants sought protection and found their way to the CDU, which wanted to help them. This development was confirmed to me on 17 January by the local councillor Herr Dr. Althoff of the CDU. He told me verbatim: "Herr Jahnke, believe me, it is thanks to the SED mayor Böhm that the CDU has a local group here"'.[35] Overzealous officials were, however, far less common than corrupt ones. Among the many problematic villages was Löwenbruch, *Kreis* Teltow, where the SED mayor Scheu, a new farmer, was neither immune to corruption nor much of a socialist. According to a SED instructor's report, Scheu had apparently managed to procure for himself enough lime and cement (again, both in desperately short supply) to repair his livestock stalls to a condition better than that of most houses in the village. When asked by party instructors where he had acquired it and why he had not allocated it for housing repairs, he merely responded that he had 'got the lime and cement himself'. Scheu was also farming six acres which he had registered as *Neuland* (previously uncultivated land, for which there was no delivery quota) that the other farmers in the village swore had been cultivated for at least 30 years. To make matters worse for the SED in Löwenbruch, the local party chairman, Herr Gotsch, was even less respected than the mayor. Gotsch was not only farming four acres of bogus '*Neuland*' himself, but had also already been fined DM 300 for illegal distilling, had been the subject of a police search for stolen geese and was currently suspected of illegal slaughtering. The result of such behaviour on the part of SED functionaries was typical: nine of the 27 village party members left the party. As the report succinctly notes, 'The CDU has the majority in the village. When functionaries of this sort are active, the regrettable decline is understandable'.[36]

Although a particularly bad case, Löwenbruch was not a spectacular exception in terms of the immense personnel problems the SED faced in building up its grass-roots organization in the countryside during the years following the war. As late as 1949 the SED *Kreisvorstand* in Oberbarnim complained that: 'The greatest weaknesses are presented by the insufficient ideological clarity of the functionaries. This is the case in general in the entire party organization . . . From time to time it is hardly possible to find functionaries who are in a position to perform the functions conferred upon them'.[37] While the problem in many villages consisted of finding enough interested persons, in others it consisted rather of keeping out political trimmers, drunks (generally referred to in the reports as 'morally depraved elements') and other characters with questionable intentions. A report on the collapse of the local SED group in Görlsdorf, *Kreis* Angermünde, illustrates just how difficult this could be:

> The local group in Görlsdorf, which from the beginning was a rather small one because the overwhelming majority of the populace supports the CDU, had in fact essentially fallen apart. After committing a number of thefts, the chairman of the local group disappeared to the West and took all of the party files and catalogue cards with him. We next tried to set up the local group again via the shop-group Landesgestüt Görlsdorf. This seemed to be crowned with success at first, but as it transpired the chairman of the shop-group was also involved in a corruption affair and the shop-group has also fallen apart.

In the end it was decided that the nine remaining members in the village be placed provisionally under the special supervision of the *Kreisvorstand*.[38]

Given this backdrop it is little wonder that the SED was widely perceived as corrupt in the countryside, much as the NSDAP previously. Little wonder as well that by 1947 at the latest, many new farmers felt forgotten and left in the lurch by the Soviet and German communists who had promised them so much in 1945. Returning from a trip to Kremmen, a SED functionary in Berlin reported that

> All [of the new farmers] make no bones about their dissatisfaction. They showed me their houses, and I must say that I can understand their dissatisfaction . . . They pointed out that their potatoes and turnips had frozen, but that the nearby distillery is constantly making schnapps and that there must be potatoes there. There isn't enough feed for the livestock . . . All in all they are very disappointed with the land reform, they had pictured it much better to themselves. The discussions culminated in their blaming the Russians for everything.[39]

Yet the SED came in for its own share of the blame as well. As one Brandenburg farmer put it in a letter to the Central Committee, 'One can only be amazed that the new farmer can muster up the energy to stick at it. But that is because from time to time a party functionary appears in the villages and encourages him to do it. Promises are made that remain only empty phrases, because for the most part the new farmers' situation does not improve. How long will things go on like this? he asks himself'.[40] By the time the GDR was founded in 1949, thousands of new farmers in the SBZ had already stopped asking themselves this question and left their small, unviable plots untilled, many of them to engage in more profitable black market activity.[41]

The new village elite and the path to collectivization: the *Großbauern*

The upshot of these various problems associated with the land reform was that, contrary to all intentions, it effectively benefitted the old farmers, especially the powerful *Großbauern*, more than the new farmers. The old farmers largely controlled the local VdgB executives. In November 1948 there were 6179 established farmers compared to only 4476 new farmers on the local executives in Brandenburg. Moreover, the economic strength of the *Großbauern* had escaped the land reform essentially unscathed, and to a certain extent was even augmented by the dissolution of the aristocratic estates. Many possessed relatively large livestock herds and the majority were well-equipped with outbuildings, tractors and other agricultural machinery. Most therefore had little trouble producing '*freie Spitzen*' in excess of their compulsory delivery quotas which they could sell at higher market prices. Furthermore, because many of the smaller farmers were still dependent on them for machinery and storage space, *Großbauern* were able to achieve a considerable addition to their incomes through lending out buildings and equipment. While the small new farms created by the land reform were struggling to make ends meet, and while thousands of refugees from the former eastern territories were still living in miserable conditions on makeshift settlements or in lice-ridden barns, most *Großbauern* were able to secure a comfortable income and if anything were getting richer. Worst of all from the perspective of the SED leadership, the unpopularity of Soviet requisitioning and the many cases of corruption and misuse of office by local SED officials were enhancing the big farmers' political influence in the villages by driving many formerly sympathetic farm labourers and refugees into the arms of the *Großbauer*-dominated CDU or the church. The introduction of the DBD (*Demokratische Bauernpartei*, or Democratic Farmers' Party) in the spring of 1948 did little to dilute the influence of either in the countryside, and even the carefully controlled VdgB elections in the spring of 1949, accompanied by a massive campaign against the *Großbauern*, only achieved a 12 per cent decrease in the number of positions they held on the local VdgB councils in Brandenburg.[42]

By this time it was clear that the land reform had crippled agricultural production and hampered the economic recovery in the SBZ. Even many higher SED agricultural functionaries had begun to think that it had been managed poorly.[43] But rather than admitting their mistakes and policy shortcomings, the Soviets and SED blamed others instead. The *Großbauern* were the obvious scapegoats, and in 1948 and 1949 the 'class struggle in the countryside' was extended beyond the large landholders to include them as well. This campaign consisted of a number of measures designed to weaken the political and economic power of the large farmers (who were now redefined from anyone possessing more than 50 hectares to anyone with more than 20 hectares of land) and to drive a wedge between them and their poorer neighbours. Taxes and delivery quotas were differentiated more stringently according to farm sizes in 1948 and 1949, *Großbauern* were forced to pay higher fees for equipment and spare parts and were also only allowed to borrow equipment at the MAS after all other classes of farmers had done so.[44] When the compulsory delivery quotas for large farms were once again increased in the early 1950s, the economic burden for many became unsustainable as debts mounted and net profits dropped. To make matters worse, anyone not fulfilling his or her quota ran the risk of being accused of 'sabotage' and arrested.[45]

All of this contributed to a steadily increasing number of big farmers simply giving up their farms, many of them leaving for the West. From 1950 to 1952, a total of 5000 *Großbauern* in the GDR abandoned their farms, which amounted to approximately 10 per cent of all agricultural enterprises between 20 and 100 hectares in size. Thousands of small- and mid-sized farmers also fled the burdens of increasing quotas.[46] This of course entailed a further decrease in agricultural production, and in order to counter the losses the state began in 1951 to confiscate abandoned farms and hand them over to small farmers or to the state-run VEGs. This process was given added impetus in March 1952 when the definition of 'devastated' farms was extended to include not only those abandoned by their owners, but also those with exceptionally low production levels.[47] Yet it was still difficult to maintain production levels as the overall shortage of labour in agriculture did not allow for efficient usage of the abandoned and confiscated land.[48] And despite the weakening of the economies of the *Großbauern* via punitive taxes and discrimination at the MAS, the fact remained that without an all-out attack their influence would continue to be felt in the villages.

It was in this context of a looming agrarian crisis that the SED leadership announced the formation of collective farms, or 'agricultural production cooperatives' (*Landwirtschaftliche Produktionsgenossenschaften*, or LPGs) at the Second Party Conference in July 1952. The new LPGs were to fall under three separate categories ranging from Type I, in which only land was tilled and equipment used collectively, to Type III, in which everything including land and machinery was used and owned collectively. Although a small number of LPGs had already been established earlier that year, the sudden move to agricultural collectivization caught many farmers by surprise. Only seven months earlier, at the Third German Farmers' Congress in December 1951, Grotewohl himself had stuck to the position maintained by the SED since 1945, proclaiming that the government still had no intention of collectivizing agriculture in the GDR.[49] Whether or not this assurance was given in good faith at the time, in the summer of 1952 the government made its new intentions known in no uncertain terms. A mass publicity campaign was launched in support of the formation of LPGs and on 24 July the Council of Ministers decreed a package of tax-breaks and lower delivery quotas for anyone who joined them. The 'construction of socialism' in the GDR meant collectivization for farmers.

3
Recasting the Factories after the War

At the end of the war East Germany was a shambles. Food and fuel were scarce, and much of its housing had been either destroyed or seriously damaged by Allied bombing. A large proportion of its infrastructure and industrial stock had also been destroyed, and much of what was left was either worn out from around-the-clock war production or being dismantled and hauled off to the Soviet Union as reparations. It was clear from the outset that reviving industrial production was a must for both the German and, perhaps more importantly, for the Soviet economy. However, the Soviets and German authorities were finding it hard enough simply to feed, clothe and house the civilian populace, and there were precious few resources left over for investing in new industrial stock. Further hampering economic recovery in the zone were the dire supply problems resulting from the zonal division of Germany and the policy of reparations in kind from running production. The expropriation of large factory owners and the creation of 'Soviet Joint Stock Companies' (SAGs) and 'People's Own Enterprises' (VEBs) may have succeeded in revolutionizing patterns of industrial ownership in the Soviet Zone, destroying the economic foundations of bourgeois power and securing production for key Soviet needs, but it did little to improve the health of the economy. Productivity gains would initially have to come from the workers themselves.

Towards this end, the solutions devised by the Soviets and German communists all ran in the same basic direction. The self-defensive inclinations of the industrial workforce under capitalism had to be overcome through the introduction of a new culture of work and new structures of authority in the factories, most of them imported from the Soviet Union. This had both ideological as well as economic

33

aspects. It was not merely a matter of creating new material incentives geared towards enhancing productivity and work-discipline. There was also the broader attempt to secure the political loyalty of the industrial workforce, to transform them into 'socialist personalities' and mobilize them via various forms of 'socio-political activity' (*gesellschaftspolitische Tätigkeit*). To be sure, the idea of building a socialist future was attractive to many Germans after the horrors of the war, the experiences of mass unemployment during the Weimar years and the heavy-handed labour relations under the Nazis. But under the circumstances of acute material deprivation, it was asking a lot of industrial workers' 'class consciousness' to work harder in the here and now for an occupying power that removed the country's wealth and for an uncertain future that still existed only in the promises of communist political leaders. And combined with the unorthodox opinions and self-interested behaviour of many local functionaries and factory managers, workers' aversion towards both the ever-increasing regimentation of work as well as the constant efforts to mobilize them resisted and refracted the SED's attempts to transform and gain control of the industrial shopfloor.

The problem of productivity and the effects of Order 234

Though the goal of winning the hearts and minds of industrial workers was never entirely disregarded, given the state of the zone after the war purely material considerations were the most pressing at first. Despite the widespread destruction in eastern Germany, it was generally assumed that the SBZ had certain advantages over other areas of Soviet-occupied Europe. Not only was it a highly industrialized region, it also possessed a highly skilled workforce blessed by the traditional 'German' virtues of diligence and discipline, an image widespread in the Soviet Union itself. Whatever the truth or otherwise of this picture for the period before 1945, the orientation and behaviour of German workers was a far cry from this ideal under the impact of post-war deprivation and the Soviet plundering of German industry. In the years following the war, discipline was lax and productivity well under half its prewar level. This had less to do with any conscious opposition to Soviet occupation or labour policies than with more basic problems, foremost among them sheer hunger. The average daily caloric intake of manual labourers hovered at around 65 per cent of the recommended daily requirement during the first two years after the war, increasing only gradually in the two years that followed.[1] This not only sapped workers of much of their strength, it also led to high rates of absenteeism through illness. To make matters worse, the lack of goods available for purchase rendered monetary wages rather ineffective as a means of raising productivity or labour discipline. Under the circumstances, it was often far more profitable for workers to spend several hours trading on the black-market or several days roaming the countryside for food than to go to work, let alone to be more productive. A group of East Berlin workers explained to a SED functionary 'that they have no desire to work under the current circumstances. If they go foraging (*hamstern*) merely once a month they have more than if they worked the entire month'.[2]

Getting workers to be more productive was thus only part of the problem. As the economic impact of dismantling, reparations and the land reform sent workers' morale spiralling during the excessively harsh winter of 1946–47, rates of absenteeism soared out of control, even surpassing 20 per cent in such basic industries as coal, machine building and metallurgy. Soviet data from the summer of 1947 reported absentee rates of 24 per cent in factories working for reparations, 14 per cent in the SAGs and 19 per cent in factories producing for domestic consumption.[3] During the initial years after the war much of the problem was to get workers to show up at all. But even when they did show up, the deleterious effects of hunger and the lack of a wage incentive (coupled, of course, with factory damage and shortages in supply) meant that worker productivity was still some 50–70 per cent below the pre-war level. By 1947 at the latest the initial Soviet image of the legendary German work ethic had all but completely dissolved. Up until then they had been too busy with the land reform, the expropriation of industry and the SED merger to do much about it, but all of this began to change with the downturn in East–West relations. By 1947 it looked as if the SBZ might remain in the Soviet orbit for some time to come and that some form of economic integration into the 'socialist camp' therefore seemed necessary.

Basically, the answer to the productivity and indiscipline impasse was to transfer Soviet-style labour relations to the factories of the SBZ. The main tool used to accomplish this was SMAD Order 234 on 'Further Measures for Increasing Work-Productivity and for the Further Improvement of the Material Situation of Workers and *Angestellte*', commonly referred to as the *Aufbaubefehl* (construction order). The purpose of the order and the reasoning behind it were clear in its preamble: 'The increase of work-productivity and the conscious unfolding of the independent initiative of the workers for the economic upswing in the SBZ presently comprises the main link in the economic system and the key to solving all other economic problems'.[4] It called for a range of social measures to address the most immediate needs of workers, such as improved housing, better wages for women, factory clinics and industrial safety. But the principle aim of Order 234 was to get workers to produce more, and towards this end it established a set of incentives to improve productivity in key enterprises (especially coal, steel and machine building) such as differential wages, promises of clothing, shoes and a hot lunch above and beyond one's rations, accompanied by various sanctions aimed to punish unexcused absenteeism and so-called 'slackers' such as the withdrawal of ration cards or deployment for rubble-clearing at bomb sites.[5] Soviet-style 'socialist competitions' were also to be employed as a means of raising production, and those workers who performed best were to be honoured as 'activists' and also receive monetary awards. Most important of all, it called for the reintroduction of piecework-wages and other forms of productivity-enhancing remuneration throughout industry.

It was one thing to decide to raise factory discipline, but it was quite another to put these new measures into practice. The actual implementation of Order 234 ran into a host of problems right from the start, including such technical problems as confusion over who was responsible for administering the measures, managers drowning in a 'flood' of uncoordinated questionnaires, inability to assess progress at the centre, etc.[6] But the greater problem, and one which promised further difficulties in the future, was the icy reception that met it on the shopfloor.

The idea of raising work discipline and productivity in the current material circumstances of the SBZ understandably found little resonance among the bulk of workers with far more immediate concerns. Reports clearly showed that raising work-productivity was the last thing on most workers' minds at the time: 'The discussion [at employee assemblies] revolved first and foremost around the question of provision with potatoes, which was undoubtedly one of the primary concerns of the workers. The provision of work-clothing, durable shoes as well as the necessary material for repairs, bicycles and tires for them . . . these were the main features of the discussions. The attendance rates at the assemblies can be estimated at 40 to 50 per cent at best, only a few could report attendence rates of 60 to 70 per cent'.[7] Although FDGB chairman Herbert Warnke himself addressed the employee meeting at the Rüdersdorfer Kalkwerke, still only around 40 per cent of the workers showed up, and even among them 'one sensed at first a kind of passive resistance (*passiven Widerstand*)'.[8]

Another hindrance to the 'positive' reception of Order 234 in the factories was the unique culture of work that had developed in the factories after the war. The widespread hunger and deprivation – the same things that made increasing industrial production so imperative – had produced a kind of '*Notgemeinschaft*', a heightened sense of solidarity and mutual assistance on the shopfloor. This '*Gleichmacherei*', as frustrated economic officials called it, was not so much a romantic holdover of self-defensive egalitarianism under capitalism as it was a logical response to the challenges of survival after the war. The idea of individual workers being singled out of the ranks for extra pay, food and other benefits offended this cooperative ethic.

What is more, although the older independent workers' organizations were precluded from organizing after the war, the *Betriebsräte*, or shop councils, that supervised production in many factories across the GDR proved a significant hindrance to raising work-productivity.[9] Up until 1947 they were grudgingly tolerated by the Soviet authorities so long as they were useful in helping to expropriate ex-Nazis and keep production running. But it was simply not realistic to expect shop councils comprised overwhelmingly of Social Democratic and Communist workers to implement differential pay rates and other means of increasing labour discipline that they had opposed for decades. Getting rid of piecework, punch clocks and other instruments of work acceleration from the capitalist past was in fact one of the first things many had done after the war.[10] Whereas 80 per cent of German workers had been on piecework wages before 1945, by 1947 the number had decreased to merely 25 per cent.[11] Reversing this trend fuelled feelings of exploitation, no longer at the hands of capitalist entrepreneurs, but at the hands of the Soviet authorities. Despite the official SED argument that piecework and wage differentials were not the same in a 'democratic economy' as in a capitalist system 'because the piecework system can no longer be used as a means of exploiting the workforce and because the increase in production that is its aim will be used for the benefit of all', workers remained sceptical. Demands such as 'Let's eat first, then we'll produce' were common; even the old working-class slogan '*Akkord ist Mord*', or 'piecework is murder' was resurrected.[12]

Viewed in purely economic terms, the Soviet insistence on raising productivity was quite correct, and might have been more convincing under different circumstances. But it was introduced into a broader political context that prompted widespread resentment and gravitated against its implementation on the shopfloor. For one thing, the absence of truly independent interest representation by the unions meant that any wage and productivity settlement would be regarded by workers as suspect, in the worst case as a 'Russian' imposition. Moreover, the continued dismantling and reparations to the Soviet Union were also a crucial backdrop to the introduction of Order 234. Even among those workers who were in principle in favour of increasing productivity, 'the general opinion and discussion is that producing more through working more "only benefits the Russians"'.[13] Although many Germans assumed that they would have to pay reparations for the war that had been launched from German soil, and therefore grudgingly accepted the first wave of reparations in 1945 and early 1946, the Soviet failures to keep its promises regarding the end of dismantling in 1946 and 1947 were arguably more irritating than the deed itself. As an opinion report from Berlin put it: 'One asks how it happens that, in spite of Marshall Sokolovski's declaration that the dismantling is finished, factories are still being dismantled. One cannot believe a thing the Russians say when one sees how their promises are "kept"'.[14] Combined with the often careless and sometimes brutal 'smash and grab' tactics of the Soviet trophy brigades, such broken promises nourished a broad and diffuse anti-Soviet attitude among many Germans, in particular the industrial workers most immediately affected.[15] Indeed, the very 'Sovietness' of Order 234 was recognized by the FDGB leadership as a potential hindrance from the start. Herbert Warnke, then chairman of the commission on the implementation of Order 234 in the FDGB, was concerned enough to instruct union functionaries to stress the point that the German authorities were intimately involved in formulating Order 234, even adding that one 'should not speak of an order at all, but rather of a measure *per se* for increasing work productivity and improving the situation of workers and salaried employees'.[16]

Judging from the opinion reports at the time, Warnke had good reason to be concerned. The hope cherished by many Germans that it would be possible to overcome the post-war misery through hard work was undermined by both a widespread fear of Soviet reparations making this impossible as well as the more general prospect of a Soviet-style dictatorship being installed in the zone. A report of 7 July 1948 from Berlin-Prenzlauer Berg quoted the following comment as typical of a broad swathe of popular opinion: 'One thing we cannot understand is why one so often reads in your (SED) press of the fulfilling and overfulfilling of such huge plan targets in industry, agriculture, etc.. How then is it possible that we don't get to see even the smallest trace of it? Where is it all? Sometime we eventually ought to see something of it! . . . There are only two possibilities: either your figures are pure illusions or what is generally spoken around is true, namely that the Russians are hauling it all out of Germany!' This latter suspicion was almost universal. As another report from April explained: '. . . they tell themselves that things will only get better with us once the Russians are out of Germany again . . . The number of people who think this is immense (*riesengroß*)'.[17]

SED officials were in little doubt about the ramifications Soviet actions had on the political sympathies of industrial workers, however much support there may have been for socialism in principle: 'It is downright tormenting to have to realize what deep aversion not only women, but also workers have *vis-à-vis* the Russian occupying power. The workers characterize the American occupiers as gangsters, the Russians as plunderers. The workers are above all scared of a Russian dictatorship . . . The parties are only shoved into the foreground in order to disguise the foreign control. The workers are very much for socialism and are also convinced that the new form of society will prevail, but not under Russian authority'.[18]

Yet the 'Sovietness' of Order 234 was not actually the main problem. At a more basic level, it was viewed as divisive and unfair. There were vast differences between its effects in different branches of industry and different factories. While the distribution of extra goods and hot lunches was understandably welcomed and reportedly had positive effects on morale in the enterprises that benefitted most (above all energy and raw materials), there was also bitterness among those workers left out of the social measures of Order 234. Construction and transport workers in particular were angry that they received neither extra food nor extra clothing despite working outside; the pressure on the unions for improvements was described as 'naturally extraordinarily strong'.[19]

Such resentment was also by no means limited to workers. Many of the local union functionaries who were supposed to be helping implement the measures often spent more time criticizing working conditions in their factories and arguing that their own branches of industry – especially transport, construction and textiles, relatively low-skilled industries with high percentages of refugees and women – should not be left out. This was the case, for instance, at the textile enterprises in Forst, Cottbus, Brandenburg and Luckenwalde, where the predominately female workforce worked long hours under notoriously poor conditions for low pay.[20] Here it was reported that

> there was very strong criticism of . . . 'Order 234' which one can almost characterize as direct opposition and which cannot be left unheeded . . . The arguments that were offered were the most inauspicious and stupid ones conceivable . . . 'You should be ashamed of yourselves for explaining Order 234 like that, with the additional provision [for other factories] we have less in our pot than before', 'We're not going to have anything more to do with it', 'Why are we working at all anymore?' . . . Unfortunately, it is clear that it is precisely our SED functionaries who offer this kind of criticism, while the politically unorganized do not get so carried away.[21]

Other reports similarly complain of 'ideological unclarity' among union functionaries in the factories, concluding that they 'do not recognize the dialectical interaction that raising production at the same time means more to eat'.[22] The problem with this assessment was that from the perspective of the factory floor there was no 'dialectical interaction' taking place. The food situation did not improve as was originally promised, and with the continuing removals of grain and sugar to the Soviet Union it remained to be seen whether higher work-productivity would lead to an improved living standard.[23]

Against the backdrop of removals and reparations, the upshot of the increasing regimentation on the shopfloor was widespread grumbling and shirking in factories across the Soviet Zone. This placed factory directors, many of whom felt a greater obligation towards their workers than towards the occupying powers, in an impossible position. Pressured on the one hand by the Soviet-led authorities to implement Order 234 and by their own workers to ignore it, they could, as Jeffrey Kopstein has recently shown, do little else but steer a middle course.[24] There was widespread foot-dragging, most clearly manifested in the fact that by April 1948, six months after Order 234 was announced, there had been only a 3 per cent rise in piecework and performance-related pay.[25] Despite press reports of rates of performance-related pay reaching 70–80 per cent, party investigations in the factories found that the percentage was more like 25–30 per cent.[26]

Of course managers were eventually forced to introduce performance-related wages in some form or another, but even when it was successfully introduced it accomplished little except raising wages. Without a pool of unemployed, and operating in a system in which enterprises were under pressure to produce as much as possible regardless of the cost, managers in effect found themselves in competition for scarce labour: hence it was only logical to regard the transition from hourly to piece-rate pay as a chance to raise wages and make their enterprises more attractive on the labour market. The welfare measures of Order 234 presented certain opportunities to do this, and within months of its introduction, the Soviets and SED began worrying out loud that the so-called '*Aufbaubefehl*' was being turned into an '*Essenbefehl*' (eating order). But the easiest and most common way to retain an adequate workforce was to fudge work norms. A June 1948 investigation of wage trends in 208 Brandenburg factories found that most of the firms that had already gone over to piece-rate wages had based their wage calculations on outdated productivity averages that kept norms low, resulting in a pattern of wage rises which 'could not be reconciled with Order 234'.[27] The payment of extra bonuses was also common. At the Deko-Pneumatik factory, for example, workers were not only paid the standard 15 per cent piece-rate bonus, but also an extra 10 per cent for dirty work; at the sugar refinery in Thöringswerder bonuses amounted to around 50 per cent of total wages.

Instead of seeking the reasons for the problems in their own planned economic system, the effects of reparations and the lack of a wage incentive, the Soviets instead blamed the German administration: 'All of these facts show that neither the Ministry for Labour, nor the Ministry for Economic Planning, nor the Central Administration of the people's own enterprises are earnestly dealing with the wage question'.[28] In its 1948 year-end report on the implementation of Order 234, the German Economic Commission took these criticisms on board: 'Through the failure to draw up work norms or intentionally setting them too low, the existing work in the enterprises is drawn out and labour is hoarded, mostly resulting from a shortage of raw materials'.[29] This tendency to raise wages without raising norms, it complained, needed to be countered by stronger controls on the shopfloor. In other words, it was no longer just a matter of managing workers, but also managing managers. But this, too, proved more easily said than done, mostly because of the difficulty in finding appropriate personnel to do it. As the Economic Commission lamented one year after Order 234 was launched, 'For the necessary inspection of the enterprises in this regard, only a completely insufficient total of 65 revisers ... have as yet been trained in the entire zone'.[30]

While there is some evidence that Order 234 did help improve discipline in the factories in terms of decreasing rates of absentee-ism and 'loafing', by December 1948 the Soviets were nonetheless complaining of the 'indiscriminate introduction of progressive per-formance-related pay and bonus systems' by German factory directors despite the fact that such systems raised wages faster than produc-tivity and were only intended for a tiny circle of the most important enterprises.[31] Although the initial plan was for production to rise twice as fast as wages, workers' opposition to increasing regimenta-tion in the factories and the willingness of local functionaries and managers to succumb to it ensured that just the opposite was the case.

Workers and the Hennecke movement

This left the Soviets puzzled for a time, but never at a loss for ideas they again looked to their own experience of industrializa-tion for a solution and found it in the invigoration of the activist movement and so-called 'socialist competitions'. Although formally initiated under Order 234 for the purpose of raising norms and productivity, these had made little or no progress among East Ger-man managers and workers who were unfamiliar with them and who were in any case less than enthusiastic about norm-raising ploys.[32] The movement clearly needed a new push. Above all, it needed a face, and Adolf Hennecke's fitted the bill. By mining 387 per cent of his normal coal quota in one shift (under specially prepared conditions), Hennecke and the movement named after him were supposed to inspire other workers to fulfil their potential by demonstrating how easy it was to overfulfil one's quota. Here the SED's economic and ideological goals *vis-à-vis* the German working-class intersected. This was simultaneously an organizational measure for increasing productivity as well as an *erzieherisch* attempt to raise the political consciousness of workers by presenting to them a model of sound socialist behaviour. Informed well in advance, party and union propagandists launched a massive campaign to popularize Hennecke and his 'heroic deeds'. Within days of his feat, Hennecke's face and name were seen everywhere. Newspapers were filled with astounding statistics and reports of local activists' feats. Workers in other industries supposedly emulated him, and telegrams poured in announcing new production records all across the SBZ. Activist posters were pasted everywhere, pins and medals were produced, even schools and streets were named after Hennecke. There was also a spate of embarrassingly puerile poems and songs about him, which arguably could only have hindered the movement more than helped it. One example offers a taste of their iconographic flavour:

Hennecke! Du bist der Mann, der uns begeistert!
Hennecke! Mit Dir wird unsere Not gemeistert!
Hennecke! Wir schwören Dir, wir wollen uns bemühen!
Hennecke! Durch Dich wird unsere Wirtschaft wieder blühen!
Hennecke! Du bist ein Held von unserer Klasse!
Hennecke! Du bist mit uns die starke Masse!
Hennecke! Wir wollen stets von Dir als Vorbild sprechen!
Hennecke! Du wirst der Brüder Knechtung auch im Westen
   brechen![33]

In spite of (or perhaps because of) such propagandistic efforts, reports from the factories offer little evidence that the movement worked, as most workers remained sceptical of production increases so long as problems of supply continued. In the words of a construction worker in Potsdam: 'Yes, if we all wanted to work like Hennecke and were in the position to do it . . . I often wait hours for sand because there is none, or the other way around for lime because I don't have any. It's the same with my colleagues as it is for me. See to it that we don't just stand around because there is no material, then Hennecke wouldn't even be necessary in the first place'.[34] Furthermore, the vast majority of workers correctly doubted the verity of Hennecke's heroic performance and knew good and well that a normal work day simply did not allow for such production increases. As one retired worker put it:

I've worked in factories and know what one can manage to do. But the idea that a worker nowadays triples his performance or even increases it sixfold seems impossible to me as long as everything happens in a normal way. In my opinion the Henneckes prepare everything hours in advance, pick out the best tools for themselves and get provided with the necessary materials. In short, it's actually just a big song and dance (*ein Theater*) that is being performed. I know what it's all about. We're supposed to produce more, the workers are supposed to work more, but one cannot do this like the Hennecke movement is doing it. That way you won't find any sympathy among the really honest workers.[35]

And indeed it did not. Despite their occasional successes, the Henneckists gained little influence over their fellow workers. In fact, their efforts won them more anger and hostility than admiration, as Hennecke himself had feared and quickly found out: 'When I came to the shaft the next day the mates (*Kumpel*) did not look at me anymore. That's anything but a nice feeling when you look them in the eyes and say "Glückauf" and they nod, yes, but you don't hear anything anymore. I used to be just Adolf, a miner like any other. But now there was a wall between us'.[36]

Opposition arose on a number of levels. The grim material circumstances led to an understandable aversion to working harder. A report from the Siemens-Plania works in Berlin-Lichtenberg described the scene thus: 'There were earnest and bitter faces, passionate discussions and vicious heckling. One worker pulled off his completely shredded shoe and placed his finger through the hole in the sole. "We're supposed to walk around like this! This is how we're supposed to stay healthy in order to work, to work even more?!" Turbulent heckling: "What did you actually have in mind?" – "At least give us shoes first!"'[37] The fact that the party cadre often participated in the first Hennecke-shifts hardly added to their attractiveness, and where Hennecke shifts were pushed through against the will of employees, would-be activists often found themselves supplied with the poorest material, sometimes even finding their machines damaged or tools missing.[38] There was also widespread resentment towards the lack of solidarity the activists were showing their colleagues. Not only were they separating themselves from the social framework of the work collectives and being singled out for special bonuses, they also ruined the energy-saving tricks of other workers; little surprise, then, that activists were often derided as 'norm breakers', 'slave drivers', 'wage cutters' and 'traitors to workers'. Hennecke recalled that even party and union functionaries at his mine reproached themselves 'for having produced a norm-breaker like me'.[39]

What seems to have repelled German workers from the Hennecke-Movement most, however, was again its 'Sovietness' – not in the sense of being modelled on the Stakhanov movement, but in its apparent display of acquiescence to Soviet rule and what many viewed as the Soviet exploitation of Germany. The numerous denunciatory letters and threats sent to Hennecke bear ample testimony to this: 'For a whole year now you've sold the sweat of your comrades to the Russians and taken your blood money (*Judaslohn*). You won't live another year, you scoundrel!'; 'You shabby rascal, you pimp of Soviet exploitation of German workers, you traitor to the German working people, you won't escape your well-deserved punishment!'; 'If you ever go to Russia again, take our advice and stay there, because someday you'll have to take to your heels anyway or else you'll hang from the nearest tree'.[40]

Under widespread scepticism and worker opposition, the Hennecke-movement and socialist competitions quickly degenerated to little more than empty rituals. Even the thin layer of activists they managed to produce was highly volatile and the activist-shifts generally no more than sporadic one-offs.[41] While Alf Lüdtke and Peter Hübner are clearly correct in asserting that the reaction in the factories towards the activist movement cannot be characterized as a solid front of opposition or simply be reduced to a question of willing participation or outright rejection,[42] either way the movement fell well short of its goal of inspiring East German workers to produce more and raising 'socialist consciousness' on the shopfloor.

From the shop councils to the FDGB

As the problems of implementing Order 234 show, during these early years the functionaries and managers in the factories were frequently unreliable in transmitting decisions made at the centre down to the shopfloor. This was especially true, of course, in the smaller and private firms, but also in the larger VEBs under state control. Again, purely technical difficulties were part of the problem. The only sure way for the 'top' of the party or FDGB hierarchy to communicate at all with the 'bottom' was to visit the factories, which was of course impossible for all of them given the shortage of automobiles and sporadic problems in train service. But another part of the problem was the new structures of authority in the factories as they developed during the crisis months after the war. Initially, power in the factories was divided between the new management and the employee-elected shop councils. The SED party organizations and FDGB factory union executives (*Betriebsgewerks-chaftsleitungen*, or BGLs) were usually either very weak or non-existent. In the bodies that mattered – the shop councils and management – there was remarkable personnel continuity from the period before 1945. Despite the thorough-going purge of previous owners and factory directors, many of the 'new' managers appointed by the Soviets were in fact mid-level technical and administrative employees who had worked in their respective factories for years and who possessed the necessary know-how to run them. According to SED statistics from summer 1947, while only 6.2 per cent of factory directors had previously worked in the same capacity, 31 per cent had been previously employed as white-collar workers, 24 per cent as 'business people' (*Kaufleute*), 18 per cent as engineers and only 22 per cent as 'workers'.[43] The social profile of factory managers in the Soviet Zone had not changed as radically as has often been assumed. Likewise, the shop councils were made up mostly of older, skilled veterans of their factories or of white-collar employees who enjoyed a certain degree of respect on the shopfloor. Since both the councils and the new management were mostly composed of long-term employees, there were often strong connections between the two, as well as to the employees – bonds which the Soviet practice of dismantling only strengthened.[44]

Because of the 'social democratic' tendencies of the shop councils and the rather dubious role they played in the implementation of Order 234, Soviet patience with them soon ran out. In 1947 and 1948, the BGLs were given a boost as a means of replacing them and putting more communist-loyal persons in positions of influence. This was not easy given the weakness of the BGLs up until then. Even in the large state-owned factories such as the Transformatorenwerk in Berlin-Köpenick, BGL members admitted in September 1947 that 'many workers do not even know that a union leadership exists here'.[45] At the Elektroapparatewerke in Berlin-Treptow, the BGL did little more than second the decisions of the shop council whenever it met, which was very seldomly.[46]

Although the shop councils were gradually replaced by the BGLs during the latter 1940s, in most factories the change was only one of name. Even in the large VEBs, there were strong personnel continuities. Not untypical was the situation at the Köpenick Transformatorenwerk, where both the BGL chairman and half of its regular members had held precisely the same positions in the shop council.[47] In most smaller and private factories the change was even less pronounced. In the privately-owned Kälterichter firm in East Berlin, union officials found as late as 1950 that the factory council and BGL were essentially the same. Half of the council belonged to the BGL, and half of the BGL belonged to the council; the two bodies even convened together fortnightly. 'There can therefore be no talk whatsoever of the BGL playing the leading role in the factory and functioning as an operative organ, because it simply does not exist . . . There is a list of the names of all the union functionaries, but that is it'.[48]

To be sure, this personnel continuity had its advantages for the FDGB.[49] The unions at the factory level were quite influential during these early years and enjoyed a certain recognition among the workers, who turned to them for all kinds of problems much as they previously turned to the factory councils. The problem, of course, was that the BGLs were hardly more controllable from the centre than the councils they had replaced, and as we have already seen often acted independently or in contradiction to orders from above. The loyalties of many factory functionaries still lay more on the side of their clientele than the union or party leadership. The triangle between management, BGL and employees was still fairly intact in many factories up until the early 1950s.

By contrast, the SED party organizations in the factories (*Betriebsparteiorganisationen*, or BPOs) were widely excluded from this. The party groups had little to offer in terms of technical expertise or influence, and in many cases existed merely on paper. It seems that the BPOs tended to attract the relatively inexperienced and unqualified rather than the highly skilled workers and old-established factory officials; their members thus found it difficult to penetrate the factory elite during these early years. As comrade Schulz from the BPO at the Klingenberg firm in Berlin-Lichtenberg explained: 'If one has not been working at Klingenberg for 10 years one does not have any influence or prestige. The comrades share this view. At the last shop-council elections not a single SED-comrade was elected . . . Of the 750 employees the BPO numbers 94 comrades. In spite of the strength of the group, it is impossible to fill the functionary positions'.[50] In many factories such personnel problems rendered the BPOs utterly unviable for months at a time, for instance at the large Siemens-Plania works in Lichtenberg: 'The first secretary has left in the meantime. He did not perform any collective work. Köllsch was expelled from the party for rabble-rousing against the Jews . . . The individual departmental groups could not work together, there lacked any kind of functionary body . . . The second secretary calls in 'sick' (*feiert krank*). He takes the protocol and the collected money home with him. All work within the group stopped, because no one was informed'.[51]

This general picture of weak, disorganized BPOs slowly began to change from around 1950 onwards, as the party groups began to gain influence over both the BGLs and factory management through replacing key members with younger party-trained cadre. There were two primary means of accomplishing this: dismissal on charges of illegal activity and careful control of union elections. Turnover rates for factory managers in the years after the war were extremely high due to both the flight of technical experts to the western zones as well as the search for scapegoats when production sank. At the Siemens-Plania works, for instance, the position of general director changed hands five times from 1947 to 1953, that of chief engineer six times.[52] Accusations of corruption and illegal activity often played a role in such dismissals; these charges were hard to define in the chaos and black-market society of the immediate post-war years and were broadly applicable for almost anyone in a position of authority. Many such accusations were thus motivated more out of personnel-political concerns than the desire to crack down on ubiquitous petty crime – a kind of low-level 'show trial' strategy mirroring, albeit in a much diluted form, the brutal 'cleansings' of Communist party leaders across Eastern Europe at the time. For example, at the Köpenick Transformatorenwerk, the popular BGL chairman (and former shop council chairman) Willich was expelled from the FDGB and repeatedly refused rehabilitation because of accusations of embezzling funds for the 1948 May Day celebration, despite being cleared of all charges for lack of concrete evidence. The fact that Willich not only enjoyed a certain respect among the employees, but was also described as 'close friends . . . with the former directorship which has left for the West' was clearly the underlying motive for getting rid of him.[53]

By 1950 at the latest – the year the FDGB officially acknowledged the leading role of the SED[54] – the party organizations in the factories also began to take direct control over union elections through the careful screening and selection of candidates, in the process excluding most of the original shop council members who had retained their positions in the BGLs. This process went at different speeds in different factories, with the larger state-owned enterprises again being the first affected. The result was that by around 1953 at the latest, the farce of an independent union was completely obvious to the average worker on the shopfloor. At the 1953 union elections in Berlin-Treptow, the general attitude was reportedly 'that it is pointless to have new elections, the union does not do anything anyway... The colleagues ridiculed the elections and said it all just exists on paper'.[55]

Broadly speaking, then, the party's attempt to gain control on the shopfloor was confronted by two primary obstacles. First, the more the unions in the factories were brought under central party control, the less respect and influence they possessed on the shopfloor. Improving the connection between 'centre' and factory officials came at the expense of the connection between the factory officials and the workers themselves. Second, even when the 'men of the first hour' were replaced by more reliable and better-schooled functionaries, this did nothing to solve the problem of raising productivity in a system with little incentive for either workers or managers to do so. Thus the need to raise productivity and discipline on the shopfloor remained a problem well after the turnover of factory cadre.

In 1951 the leadership tried yet another ploy: the so-called 'enterprise collective contracts' (*Betriebskollektivverträge*, or BKVs), which were essentially an attempt to integrate the production of individual factories into the overambitious first Five-Year Plan of 1951–55 and to decrease the overall wage expenditure in the state-run industries via a renewed attempt to introduce 'hard' norms and performance-related pay.[56] As one might expect, they soon ran up against many of the same problems that confronted Order 234 in 1947–48: widespread resentment among workers (especially towards those aspects of the contracts that anchored performance-related pay), coordination problems, unreliable local functionaries and factory managers, even isolated work stoppages. The problems of implementing Order 234 had set an important precedent in East German labour relations – or rather had in some ways marked the continuation of certain labour practices from the Third Reich, which were, as history would have it, reimported from the Soviet Union: namely, local functionaries and factory managers often distorted official wage policies for the benefit of workers in order to preserve the social peace on the shopfloor and retain a sufficient labour supply.[57] The campaign for the BKVs witnessed much the same phenomenon. In order to avoid any serious or potentially dangerous conflict between managers and employees, the disputes over the BKVs were often settled *en locale* via the kinds of informal mechanisms of conflict regulation that Peter Hübner has recently examined in detail.[58] From their previous experience with the introduction of performance-related pay, managers, low-level party and union functionaries as well as workers themselves had learned that it was easier to settle disputes over wages, norms and working conditions informally on the shopfloor without the interference of higher levels of the state, party or union apparatus that were unfamiliar with local conditions and less in tune with the everyday concerns of production.

In other words, the fault lines in the conflict-ridden effort to raise productivity and worker discipline on the shopfloor ran not so much between 'regime' and 'workers' as between the party and union leadership on the one hand and the logic and needs of the factories on the other. It was easiest for many factory officials and local functionaries simply to 'muddle through' and pay lip service to official wage policies without giving them too much attention. Thus by the time the SED officially announced the accelerated 'construction of socialism' in the GDR in July 1952, it was clear that neither workers nor factory managers were strictly adhering to the BKVs. Well after the creation of the GDR in 1949, the SED leadership still had not gained complete control of the shopfloor, much less the hearts and minds of East German workers.

Part 2
The Rush to Construct Socialism, 1952–53

With the rejection of the second Soviet 'Germany note' and West German signature to the European Defence Community, the Cold War took a new turn in 1952, and as a product of the Cold War, so, too, did the GDR. The announcement of the deliberate 'construction of socialism' at the fateful Second Party Conference in July not only marked a new era for the GDR in terms of its foreseeable longevity as a separate German state. It also marked a new departure on the domestic agenda, which the following four chapters will survey: a crackdown on the youth work of the churches, the establishment of armed forces, the start of agricultural collectivization and a general emphasis on investment in defence and heavy industry, all financed by cuts in social spending and tax hikes on the remaining private sector that marked a complete policy reversal away from the previous focus on improving living standards towards what was essentially a new austerity regime.

At base, the accelerated 'construction of socialism' consisted of pushing through a bundle of hardline measures that would supposedly overcome most of the setbacks and problems already encountered, and which in sum would constitute a major breakthrough in the realization of the communists' socio-political aims in East Germany. But in many ways it had precisely the opposite effect. In the short term, it led not only to the regime-threatening events of 17 June 1953, but also to a more general crippling of authority on the ground out of fear of a repeat performance. And in the longer term, it not only reinforced many of the problems that already existed (from the failure to control wages and productivity on the shopfloor to the resistance of farmers against collectivization), it also added a few new ones into the bargain.

4
The Origins and Effects of 17 June in the Factories

What was the initial reaction to the announcement of the accelerated 'construction of socialism' in the factories? While many workers were basically uninterested, their apathy producing little sediment in the archives, the picture painted by the internal reports is one of a wide array of responses ranging from excitement at the prospect of realizing what sounded like a decades-old goal of the workers' movement to a deep-seated scepticism of the type of 'socialism' the Soviet-style SED intended to construct.

Among some workers, especially older men who had been organized in the workers' movement before the Nazis took power and especially in the 'core' branches such as steel, coal and machinebuilding, the reports often (and probably somewhat optimistically) posit a 'positive attitude to the construction of socialism in general': 'We've been fighting for this for years. An old dream is finally becoming reality'.[1] But even among these veterans of working-class politics, there were still 'great unclarities' regarding precisely what the 'construction of socialism' meant. Many took this as an endorsement of greater self-regulation and worker-participation in the factory decision-making process – in direct contrast to the intention of increasing work discipline. Moreover, it was regarded as axiomatic among most workers, and not just the politically engaged, that the construction of socialism should mean the construction of a system of greater social equality. But this seemingly obvious notion seemed to stand in direct contradiction to recent government legislation, most notably the June 1952 Council of Ministers decree on the improvement of salaries for *Meister* and the intelligentsia. Reports from summer 1952 show that this caused widespread indignation among workers: 'One shouldn't hand everything to them on a plate. They get everything immediately and we have to wait for years'; 'we pay the state millions in taxes and don't get anything ourselves'; 'we just work so that the *Meister* and intelligentsia get their high salaries'; 'why are there special dining rooms for the intelligentsia?'[2] The fact that such egalitarian attitudes were deemed 'unclear' by the SED leadership also did not escape notice, least of all among the party rank-and-file. As one older comrade at the Volkswerft Stralsund succintly put it: 'If Karl Marx knew how his teachings are being interpreted, how an *asiatic* [my italics – CR] socialism is being made out of them, he'd roll over in his grave'.[3]

Whatever the initial response towards the announcement of the 'construction of socialism', it did not take long for most workers to feel the detrimental effects of this turnabout in the overall thrust of SED social and economic policy. Although the adverse effects of the new austerity regime were far worse for most other social groups (especially the lower-middle classes of farmers, artisans and small shopkeepers) this was little consolation, for the average East German industrial worker also saw his/her living standard deteriorate rapidly throughout the remainder of 1952 and the first half of 1953.[4] The problems associated with the agricultural collectivization, coupled with a poor harvest in 1952, led to a significant increase in food prices. Prices for textiles and shoes also rose with the end of rationing, as did the costs of travel after the hitherto generous state subsidies for commuters were cut. By spring 1953 many consumer goods began to disappear from store shelves. At the same time, factories were forced to clamp down on overtime, as the high wage bill was proving too expensive within the tightened budget. Thus while the cost of living was rising, the take-home pay of many workers who depended on overtime hours to make ends meet was shrinking. The resulting price-wage scissors represented the first clear downward trend in the living standard since the hunger crisis of 1947. A slogan painted on the door of the party office in the Pump and Compressor Works in Brandenburg asked a question that was on most workers' lips at the time: 'Why is the worker today still being bled white?'[5] By November 1952, sporadic food riots had broken out in a number of the major industrial centres in the south, including Leipzig, Dresden, Halle and Suhl, and throughout the following spring the internal reports show an unmistakable increase in signs of shopfloor discontent from all across the GDR ranging from 'rabble-rousing' to anti-SED graffiti to alleged sabotage.

To make matters worse, by May 1953 the government realized that it could no longer afford the accelerated 'construction of socialism' and had little choice but to attack the perpetual problem of wage inflation in the factories, announcing an across-the-board norm increase of 10 per cent in the factories. This had its own logic, in that norms were so low in many factories that they were commonly overfulfilled by 75–100 per cent. But because base wages were generally quite low in relation to the cost of living, overfulfilment was a crucial factor in many workers' wage calculations and for many was the only way to achieve a modestly comfortable living standard.[6] Taken together, these norm increases and the concurrent rise in prices amounted to roughly a 33 per cent drop in real wages for most workers, which – and this was important – was simply too much to be compensated for at the factory level. Meanwhile, the Soviets had been inundated with reports on the strain these measures were causing on East German society, and finally saw it necessary to intervene with a series of 'suggestions' for economic recovery – the so-called 'New Course' announced on 11 June. Although the SED immediately responded by steering a softer course *vis-à-vis* the middle classes and farmers, it curiously did not rescind the increased industrial work norms, which resulted in a wave of worker indignation as well as a number of isolated strikes.[7]

It was only on 16 and 17 June that the depth and extent of shopfloor anger were fully revealed. The tumultuous events of 17 June have been the subject of a plethora of studies,[8] so there is no need to offer more than a very brief recapitulation here. On the 16th, following conflicting signals in the official press about the retention of the increased work norms (which mirrored serious splits of opinion within the party leadership), workers at several construction sites in Berlin downed their tools and walked off the job, heading for the government quarter and demanding the reinstatement of the old norms. By the next day the protests and demonstrations – overwhelmingly comprised of industrial workers – spread to 272 cities and towns across the GDR. Demands for immediate improvements in wages, working conditions and the availability of consumer goods quickly mushroomed into more explicitly political demands for democratic elections and unification with the West. Shouts of 'we want more to eat' and 'where are all the swine?'[9] intermingled with cries for 'freedom' and workers chanting 'down with the Hunger-government!'[10] Demonstrators ransacked SED regional and district headquarters in several localities and in a few instances physically assaulted functionaries and soldiers. In a number of towns and cities, police and KVP units dispatched to quell the demonstrations gave up their weapons instead. In the end only the intervention of Soviet tanks could restore public order and SED rule.

Reports from factories all across the GDR speak of a diffuse dislike of the government (especially the 'goatie' Ulbricht), the SED, the Russians and the entire 'red riff-raff'. Indeed, the fact that most local functionaries and party members thought it better not to wear their party pins in the days preceding and following the uprising offers a telling gauge of the situation on the ground. So, too, does the fact that some union functionaries, especially the old pre-1933 union veterans still in the BGLs, were at the head of some demonstrations. As a report from Berlin-Treptow concluded a month after the disturbances, 'the behaviour of the members of party organizations, the FDJ members and the union functionaries during these days once again showed the insufficient connection of the members of our mass organizations with the party leadership. Around 50 per cent of our comrades did not step up at all. Some even agreed with the strike and joined the demonstrations, while the rest of this 50 per cent went home'.[11]

Of course not all of the thousands of demonstrators were necessarily convinced democrats opposing an authoritarian regime as a matter of principle. Comments such as that made by a Berlin worker to a DFD representative – 'Back then [in the Third Reich] we at least had something to eat and here we still can't get full after eight years'[12] – revealed a substratum of much more pragmatic concerns. The slogans of demonstrators in Stalinstadt, a city with a high proportion of expellees from the former eastern territories of the Reich, reveal a curious ideological mix: 'Down with the Government!'; 'We're supporting Berlin!'; 'We want free elections!'; 'Throw the polacks out of Germany!'; even fascist songs like '*Siehst Du im Osten das Morgenrot*' could reportedly be heard.[13] Nor should one assume that workers spoke with a single united voice on the issue of wages and norms. Calls for higher wages were especially loud among many lower-paid workers in relatively unskilled industries such as textiles, food preparation and paper, many of them women and former refugees, who also complained about what they saw as the unfair privileges enjoyed by workers in other key branches which received special deliveries of basic foodstuffs and other commodities.[14] Yet in the event it was workers in precisely these key industries who initiated most of the demonstrations, not the relative new-comers less familiar with the traditions of working-class solidarity and protest. And it should not be forgotten that the numerical majority of workers did not demonstrate at all. The massive up-heavals in Berlin, Bitterfeld, Halle, Magdeburg and Leipzig stood in marked contrast to the very minor disturbances in smaller indus-trial towns like Eberswalde and Calbe, where production never even halted.[15] In *Bezirk* Cottbus, most people were reported to have 'dis-tanced themselves' from the strikes, at least publicly, though few were prepared to make any overly pro-regime statements or con-demn them as the work of agents and provocateurs.[16] However much the majority privately sympathized with the aims of the demon-strations, most simply kept their heads down, wishing to be viewed as neither party stooges nor 'enemies of the state'.

But whatever the particular grievances expressed by different groups of workers, and whatever differences between responses in different localities, the fact of a large workers' uprising, its forceful suppres-sion and the lack of support from the West were key experiences for everyone involved and carried with them a number of conse-quences for the further 'construction of socialism' in the factories of the GDR. In the years that followed, the spectre of 17 June as-sumed downright mythical dimensions in both the factories as well as the halls of power. It immediately became a cultural icon syn-onymous with workers' discontent, a point of reference which could be invoked in order to give additional emphasis to expressions of anger and to make an implicit threat if the regime was seen to be failing to 'deliver the goods'. During the 1950s, reports around the anniversaries of the 17 June uprising commonly cite various 'provo-cations' from workers such as moments of silence on the factory floor, drinking bouts in the canteen, high rates of absenteeism, the increased distribution of hostile leaflets and the daubing of slogans such as 'Give us more to eat, or have you forgotten the 17th of June?'[17]

The party leadership learned two principal lessons from 17 June. First, it became more wary of shopfloor discontent and was deter-mined to keep it from mushrooming into any broader conflict. Surveillance in the factories was heightened as a means of keeping informed of the mood among the workforce, *Kampfgruppen der Arbeiterklasse* (workforce combat groups) were established as an on-the-spot force to preclude or quell any signs of unrest, and the state security service, the infamous *Stasi*, was expanded and improved to deal swiftly with any future signs of organized protest.[18] This wariness was illustrated no more vividly than on the anniversaries of 17 June: on 16 and 17 June 1955 the *Bezirksleitung* Berlin produced in its paranoid vigilance no fewer than 12 reports outlining the 'preventative measures' taken by the police against possible 'provocations'.[19] Secondly, on a more conciliatory note, the party leadership also learned that it could not risk such a heavy-handed venture again, and in fact moved swiftly to defuse the situation. None moved faster than Ulbricht, who, after all, almost lost his job because of the uprising and who was, according to the testimony of some of his colleagues in the *Politbüro*, haunted throughout the 1950s by the thought of a repetition of 17 June.[20] What makes this important for our purposes here is that this fear of its own industrial workforce effectively crippled the leadership on the shopfloor, where circumstances quickly returned to the *status quo ante*. The norm increases that triggered the uprising were rescinded, including the 'voluntary' increases that some workers were coerced into accepting from April 1953 onwards, and in contrast to the SED's original intentions, there was a general levelling of wages in industry. The overall living standard also improved as investment was diverted from heavy industry into consumer goods, housing and price and travel subventions, though none of this could bring about an immediate end to the discontent that had been building up over the previous year.[21]

Workers, for their part, also learned that there was little to be gained from open confrontation. This is not the same as saying that workers became more quiescent and 'resigned' in the face of the regime after 1953, as is sometimes implied in historical accounts. It is rather that their dissatisfaction and assertion of interests (broadly defined) thereafter tended to be channelled in different directions and expressed in different ways. The brutal crushing of the demonstrations by Soviet tanks left few illusions about the effectiveness of open protest – whether against specific government measures or against the regime as such – given the obvious reluctance of the West to get involved. Even as early as 18 June some workers were openly wondering why they even bothered to join the demonstrations. As one worker in a Prenzlauer Berg factory put it: 'It was senseless. I've spoken with my colleagues and they don't even know any longer why they went out into the streets'.[22] In the following years, open confrontation seemed even less promising. As one worker in Cottbus put it in 1961: 'We can't strike, no one supported us either on 17 June'.[23] But as we will see below, avoiding open conflict was by no means tantamount to submission on all fronts.

This points to what was probably the most important long-term consequence of 17 June on the East German shopfloor. The government never again attempted to introduce arbitrary blanket norm increases in such a way as it did in May and June 1953. In a sense, decisions over these issues had been displaced to lower levels of the regime apparatus in any event. By 1953 the kinds of local arrangements and informal 'deals' between factory managers and workers that developed in the latter 1940s and early 1950s were firmly established and due to expand further. After the shock of 17 June, even the most hard-nosed factory directors learned to bargain with workers, usually via the key figure of the brigadier or work-collective leader, in disputes over questions of pay, norms and working conditions.[24] Thus the established practice of 'grass-roots-negotiation', reinforced by the experiences of 1953, undermined the party leadership's ability to gain control over the shopfloor in the future. As we will see, by the time the government attempted to introduce a second general wage stop in the form of the *Produktionsaufgebot* in 1961–62, it found itself largely incapable of carrying it out at the grass-roots.

5
The 'Unforced' Collectivization, 1952–53

To the SED leadership in Berlin, agricultural collectivization represented a necessary escalation of the 'class struggle' in the East German countryside.[1] It was the central feature of the SED's agricultural policy throughout the remainder of the 1950s and early 1960s and was an essential component of the broader attempt to build a new socialist society. But what did the collectivization of agriculture look like in the villages and hamlets of the GDR? What was the role of local functionaries and officials in helping to carry it out? How did East German farmers respond to the foundation of LPGs and how did those who opposed them try to defend their farms against the claims of the state? As was also the case in the factories, many of the pre-existing problems of exerting control in the villages continued to plague the SED's efforts to transform the countryside. And what is more, the attempt to push through collectivization with force in 1952–53 only alienated most East German farmers even further.

Farmers and functionaries

The initial reactions to the foundation of LPGs clearly reflected the social and economic profile of the East German countryside, varying immensely between, on the one hand, new farmers who for years had been calling for moves towards collective farming as a means of more efficiently utilizing the scarce equipment and barns of divided *Junker* estates and, on the other, the predominately 'native' owners of larger, more productive farms who viewed collectivization as a threat. In July 1952 the Office for Information in *Bezirk* Potsdam conducted an opinion survey of 78 farmers in four

Kreise, 22 of whom were new farmers.[2] Only 18 of the 78 approved of the foundation of LPGs 'without reservation', seeing in them the opportunity to increase yields and improve their financial positions. Significantly, all 18 were new farmers. Of the 19 who said they approved of LPGs in principle, all demanded more information before considering joining one and most expressed unease about the possiblity of stronger farms having to 'carry' the weaker ones. Forty-one – over half – rejected LPGs out of hand, not least because of doubts about increased yields and the ability of the MAS to provide enough new equipment for 'mechanized production'. Twenty-five of these 41 farmers openly declared that LPGs would merely lead to Soviet-style kolkhozes and eventual expropriation of their farms regardless of whether or not they fulfilled their delivery quotas. That the 'positive' reception of LPGs was limited primarily to new farmers is broadly confirmed in other reports as well. As with the land reform, older orientations and frameworks of perception – in this case traditional habits of work and notions of private property – presented a stubborn obstacle to the collectivization campaign.

This is not to say, however, that the social and political fronts in the villages were so simple as pro-LPG/anti-LPG or that the decision to join was so straightforward. For one thing, there were naturally exceptions to the rule, such as the new farmer Ernst R. who was quoted as saying that he would rather slaughter all of his livestock than join an LPG.[3] Moreover, the decision to join involved a variety of different considerations. The problems of social stigmatization and injuring old friendships in the village undoubtedly kept some farmers from joining. According to one report from *Kreis* Seelow, although many farmers in the region were 'by no means opposed' to collective farming in principle, anyone expressing the wish to join an LPG was 'looked down on' by others.[4] Furthermore, joining an LPG was not an individual decision, but also involved other family members. One could hardly ignore the opinions of one's spouse or children, as they too had a stake in the management of a farm which they themselves might eventually inherit. There were even reports of parents refusing to bequeath their farms to their children for fear that the latter might enter them into an LPG and thereby forfeit the family property.[5]

Whatever the complexities of the decision to join an LPG, it is clear that collectivization was a hard sell to the vast bulk of independent farmers. There were myriad diffuse symptoms of protest throughout the autumn and winter of 1952–53. The painting of anti-collectivization slogans and the distribution of *'Hetzmaterial'* were widespread.[6] Somewhat less common were cases of apparent sabotage against LPGs, such as driving iron spikes into the ground in order to damage reaper-binders, infecting livestock and mixing glass or poison into feed. Arson against LPG members was also a growing problem in the eyes of the authorities, although it is difficult to know how many cases of alleged arson or sabotage were actually premeditated and how many were merely assumed to be crimes because they happened at LPGs. By contrast, there can be little doubt about the intentions behind most of the threats and cases of physical violence against functionaries and LPG members. VdgB functionaries campaigning for LPGs were frequently told that there was 'a tree waiting for them' in the village; some functionaries were even pelted with rocks.[7] The chairman of the local people's control committee (*Volkskontrollausschuß*) in Mechow, *Kreis* Kyritz, received a pair of menacing letters with threats to 'bash in his skull' and 'take revenge on his daughter' if he tried to 'introduce the kolkhoz'.[8] On the day before a LPG founding in Rodensleben, *Kreis* Neuruppin, threats were circulating throughout the village to the effect that whoever joined the LPG 'will have his bones broken'. On the following night 'kolkhoz-farmer' signs were hung on the doors of all the members of the LPG founding-committee.[9]

The *Volkspolizei* also reported numerous cases of recalcitrant farmers trying to hinder the founding of an LPG, sometimes successfully. One such incident in Garz, *Kreis* Pritzwalk, offers a taste of both the hostility between established farmers and newcomers as well as the divided loyalties of many less than reliable local officials. Seventy new farmers were invited to an assembly to discuss collective farming in the Soviet Union and to found a local LPG. In the event, around 120 farmers with enterprises of various sizes attended the meeting, some of whom the report describes as 'anti-democratic'. Once inside, the gate-crashers periodically interrupted the presentation with boisterous laughter about the putative performance of Soviet agriculture and comments to the effect that 'now they're taking away the land they handed out in the land reform'. Once this 'negative discussion' had reached a certain point, the mayor explained to the assembly that some of the new farmers had already agreed to found an LPG. As he read out their names they were assailed with threats from the others present: 'you should start building your casket soon', etc. Before he finished reading out the list someone switched off the lights in the meeting hall and a far less formal meeting reconvened on the street outside. There followed an impassioned discussion about the LPG between the village farmers, during the course of which the mayor himself began to waver on the issue, eventually concluding that if the village were to collectivize at all there would have to be two LPGs: one for the weak farms and one for the prosperous. As the report remarks, the events in Garz were by no means isolated occurrences, but rather 'give insight into the escalating class struggle in the villages'.[10]

Disapproval and scepticism extended well into the rural periphery of the party-state apparatus. The elite in many villages – mayors, members of village councils and VdgB committees – were often the same people or members of the same families who occupied such positions under the Nazis, and in some cases even farther back.[11] Many local officials, functionaries, *Bürgermeister* and police were also bound by ties of blood and friendship to the farmers whose enterprises they were supposed to be helping the state collectivize. More than in other milieux, this social proximity in the village and regular contact between representatives of the regime and 'ordinary' farmers time and again hindered the smooth and complete realization of the party leadership's political measures at the grass-roots. Moreover, the lower levels of the regime had to be built out of the wood that was available, and a sizeable minority of local officials were independent farmers themselves. In 1953, 18 of the 124 department managers on the district councils (*Kreisräte*) in *Bezirk* Potsdam were independent farmers or their offspring, nine of them 'small-farmers' (under 10 hectares), eight 'mid-sized' (10–20 hectares) and even one *Großbauer* – most of them in the agriculture departments of the councils. A further 15 were self-employed artisans unlikely to welcome the onset of collectivization. At the level of the local councils (*Gemeinderäte*), one step lower down the state apparatus, the personnel situation was even less auspicious. Even the social profile of those at the top of the local council hierarchy, the *Bürgermeister*, showed significant potential for conflict between one's personal interests and official duty to support the collectivization campaign. Of the 792 *Bürgermeister* in *Bezirk* Potsdam, 139 were independent farmers or their offspring (102 small, 25 mid-sized and 12 *Großbauern*), and a further 52 self-employed artisans.[12]

It is therefore not surprising that many local officials were unreliable representatives of the party line as far as agricultural collectivization was concerned. The leadership was well aware of this problem. As Ulbricht himself instructed the 'special plenipotentiaries' sent from the SED Central Committee into the countryside: 'Where *Bürgermeister* help *Großbauern*, they are to be removed from office immediately. The secretary is to take care of the work until another *Bürgermeister* is there'.[13] But the sheer scale of this problem meant that such measures were unworkable. As a state investigation of local authorities in *Bezirke* Potsdam and Rostock concluded: 'Generally speaking, the local councils and village aldermen support the founding and development of LPGs either insufficiently or not at all'.[14] *Bürgermeister* in particular were accused of not supporting the LPG campaign, which the report attributed not only to their 'ideological unclarity' and 'insufficient qualification', but also to their 'status' (*Stand*), social background and connections to *Großbauern*. Mayor H. of Peusin, *Kreis* Nauen, was 'rather disposed to help the wealthy farmers than to support the LPG', and indeed even went so far as to dissuade one struggling farmer from joining: 'Don't sacrifice yourself to that rubbish cooperative, you're lost in any case'. While mayor S. of Lützow was reportedly trying to convince local farmers that it was too early to found an LPG because the stronger farmers were against it, his assistant was busy pointing out to these stronger farmers that they would be worse-off financially if they joined one.[15]

Equally notorious for both their inactivity and their unorthodox views on LPGs were the village SED organizations. Of the 40 party members in Öhna, *Kreis* Jüterbog, only 15 to 20 were described as 'active at all', and even most of them openly disapproved of LPGs. Such inactivity and 'unclarities' at the party basis were hardly helped by the apparent heedlessness one level up the party hierarchy. The secretary of the party organization in Gussow, *Kreis* Königs-Wusterhausen, complained in the summer of 1952 that they had not even seen a *Kreisleitung* functionary since 1946. When one finally came to the village in the autumn and ordered an assembly, he himself failed to appear at it.[16]

In many villages the SED could hardly compete with the church in terms of either its organizational capacity or command of village loyalties. Although a 1953 analysis in *Bezirk* Potsdam found that only around 10 per cent of the rural populace regularly attended religious services, it emphasized that the churches influenced a far greater portion of the populace than attendance figures suggested.[17] Village pastors were reportedly most influential and respected whenever they spoke out against the injustices of the delivery quotas, the 'unfree elections', the arrested farmers and the coercion involved in the collectivization campaign.[18] The party and various mass organizations stood no chance of competing with the churches in terms of local festivals, celebrations and organizing free-time. It hardly helped matters that so many rural functionaries still had church ties. Even as late as 1958, 24.4 per cent of all local SED secretaries in *Bezirk* Frankfurt/Oder were still members of the church (whatever their actual beliefs), ranging from only 1.2 per cent in Stalinstadt (the model socialist city) to 42 per cent in *Kreis* Fürstenberg and an astounding 70 per cent in the very rural *Kreis* Angermünde.[19]

Given this backdrop of widespread popular disapproval, unreliable local functionaries and the continued influence of the church, it is scarcely surprising that the collectivization campaign proceeded sluggishly. By the end of 1952 there were only 1906 LPGs with 36 000 farmers in the whole of the GDR. Although the pace of collectivization accelerated somewhat during the winter, the number of LPGs had still risen to only 3789 by March 1953. But even these statistics exaggerate the support for the principle of collective agriculture at the grass-roots. Party ideologues were well aware of the purely economic motivations upon which many farmers' decisions to join LPGs were based, and piously hoped that the experience of working in a collective farm would go some way towards rectifying the 'ideological shortcomings' of many of the new collective farmers. But as they were to discover throughout the winter and spring of 1952–53, this 'economic thinking', as they called it, was not only a major factor in the decision to join an LPG, but also frequently determined their very functioning once they had been established.

A rather sobering report to the Ministry of Agriculture in April 1953 offers an insight into what it called the 'principal shortcomings in the consolidation of the agricultural production cooperatives' across the whole of the GDR.[20] The basic problem, it maintained, was that most LPG farmers were still bound by old-fashioned 'economic thinking' and were not working 'cooperatively enough' (*zu wenig genossenschaftlich*). Although most LPGs were indeed operating according to the letter of the LPG statutes, many were not observing their intended spirit. This was manifested in a number of different problems.

First of all was the admission of new members. The report cites numerous cases of LPGs intentionally admitting '*Großbauer* elements' and rejecting weaker applicants in order to strengthen themselves economically. As the report laments, 'this does not correspond with the principles of the [LPG] statute'. Secondly, in a fairly blatant attempt to use the LPG to their own advantage, some farmers tacitly established what the report called a 'cooperative within a cooperative'. According to the statutes of most LPGs, individual members were allowed to retain private plots of up to five hectares for their own use that were to be fertilized and worked by their owners. In a number of LPGs, the members combined their private plots and worked them at the expense of the LPG. In other words, the private plots were being illegally subsidized by the state through the cooperative.[21] Thirdly, many Type I LPGs, especially those with livestock, wanted to transform immediately into Type III cooperatives. Although this might at first glance appear to be a sign of a healthy 'socialist consciousness', the report complained that in most cases it came too soon, for the wrong reasons and without the 'necessary preconditions'; more specifically, that LPGs which found themselves in financial difficulties should not transform into Type III simply in order to acquire additional tax breaks and state entitlements. Members of the LPG Heldrungen in *Bezirk* Halle declared a Type III in spite of specific directives to the contrary from the SED *Kreisleitung* and local council, and on the very same day made an application for a special allocation of feed. Another group of financially strapped farmers in Suckow, *Bezirk* Schwerin, bypassed the Type I altogether and immediately founded a Type III. Only a few days later the LPG chairman sought help from the local council: 'We are now a cooperative Type III and all of us have an 8000 liter milk delivery debt as well as a sizeable grain arrears ... Help us now so that we will see joyful faces in the village again'.[22] Clearly, the decision to transform into a Type III was by no means a simple matter of overcoming 'ideological shortcomings' and 'economic thinking'. On the contrary, self-interested pragmatism was a primary motivation.

'New course', old problems

By the spring of 1953 it was apparent that the 'construction of socialism in the countryside' was causing a noticeable decrease in agricultural production and an alarming increase in the numbers of farmers leaving for the West. But instead of backing down from its confrontational course, the government systematically tightened the screws on the self-employed, including independent farmers, with a series of harsh austerity measures.[23] Independent farmers were effectively forced to choose between joining the LPGs or incurring drastic financial loss. Most opted for the latter, and many rapidly sank into debt, unable to keep up with the delivery quotas and increased taxes. To make matters even worse, East German courts were sentencing growing numbers of farmers to jail for failure to fulfil delivery quotas, even though in the vast majority of cases this was not intended as any kind of opposition.[24] The period from February to May 1953 also marked the peak in the number of indebted and 'devastated' farms confiscated by the state. By the end of May, 22 773 farms had fallen into state trusteeship – the majority of them large farms – 17 589 of which were confiscated during these four months alone. With mounting debts and the menacing threat of arrest, a swelling wave of farmers simply left the GDR. Both the absolute and relative numbers of farmers leaving for West Germany leapt in spring 1953; in March a disproportionately high 20 000 out of a total of 58 000 emigrants were farmers and their families.[25]

This heightened pressure on farmers during the spring of 1953 did produce some dividends for the collectivization drive: by June 1953 the number of LPGs had risen to 5074 with 146 900 members. But such success as was achieved on paper carried a terrible cost in terms of emigration and political credit for the SED. As events after the announcement of the 'New Course' on 9 June 1953 show, the SED had deeply alienated most independent farmers through its actions during the preceding eleven months. Although the New Course did redress the main grievances of farmers – rescinding the harsh tax and insurance measures, offering abandoned farms back to those who had fled and announcing a general moratorium on tax and produce-delivery debts[26] – the damage was already done and it was not so easily forgotten. There was naturally widespread relief that the government was climbing down: 'There is still a Lord God in heaven, thank God I managed to keep my livestock'; 'We can keep everything, we don't need to join the LPG, we're free!'[27] Indeed, the mood in many villages was one of celebration. In the days following the announcement of the 'New Course', village pubs were inundated by *Großbauern* toasting Adenauer, heaping abuse on the government and jeering at LPG farmers. One ecstatic *Großbauer* in Wredenhagen even rode his horse all the way up to the bar in the village pub, ordered a beer while still mounted and exclaimed, 'Now we're the bosses again!'[28] Rumours of the imminent collapse of the GDR were rife; one woman in Havelberg, for instance, reportedly walked about waving flowers and shouting 'Heim ins Reich'. There were even reports of independent farmers who had not yet plowed or fertilized their fields out of a fear of losing their investments in fuel and fertilizer suddenly beginning to work again after hearing the news of the government's turnabout. Yet this widespread relief was still accompanied by a certain scepticism and unease: 'Who will guarantee us that this communiqué will be kept?'; '. . . don't be fooled, it's all just peasant-baiting to find dim-wits to speak out against the West German elections. When these are over they will start back with what they've been doing even more sharply than before'.[29]

The news of the events of 16 and 17 June only heightened the political ferment in the villages. Although most rural areas in Brandenburg were reported as quiet, and though most farmers – however sympathetic with the striking workers – were not inclined to leave their work undone at their own expense (as one farmer in Briesensee responded to a group of striking industrial workers: 'I'm not crazy, I'm hardly going to strike against myself'),[30] there were isolated instances of considerable unrest. The most serious took place in Jessen, where on 17 June around 200 demonstrators gathered at the marketplace demanding the release of imprisoned farmers and an immediate 40 per cent reduction of delivery arrears. After talks between demonstrators and local authorities broke down, the crowd set off through the town and quickly swelled to around 1800 participants. The demonstration was eventually successful in freeing the imprisoned farmers, and the crowd could only be dispersed at around 3:30 p.m. with the help of a Soviet tank.[31]

Even in the relatively 'quiet' villages the SED's rapid about-face and rumours of an impending change of government emboldened many farmers to demand more thorough-going changes to the agricultural economy. The 'New Course' was, after all, only a partial corrective to the SED's previous agricultural policies, and simply was not 'new' enough to satisfy most farmers. A particular target of scorn was still the rigid and bureaucratic nature of the quota system. Although the government's reduction of the compulsory delivery quotas on 25 June was widely welcomed, it was often rendered meaningless by officials in the district and local councils who arbitrarily raised quotas for certain goods.[32] The reports clearly show a sharp rise in the number of petitions demanding an end to delivery quotas and a growing trend of refusals to deliver produce.[33] In some villages the pressure to refuse was great indeed; one woman even threatened to pull out the hair of a neighbour who wanted to deliver her milk anyway.[34] In *Bezirk* Cottbus there was even a number of party members and VdgB chairmen threatening not to deliver any milk if the authorities did not release imprisoned farmers.

Meanwhile, within the LPGs the announcement of the 'New Course' and the news of the events of 17 June also caused disquiet among the collective farmers. Many were afraid that the tax breaks, lower delivery quotas and other entitlements for the LPGs would be withdrawn and were angry that some of the land and buildings they had been using for storage, creches and club rooms would now be returned to their previous owners, effectively leaving many of the LPGs unviable.[35] By 1 July, 2097 confiscated farms were in fact demanded back and 1649 returned to their previous owners, many of whom refused to reimburse the LPGs that had taken them over for the costs of seed, fertilizer and other expenses incurred during their absence.[36] The result was a spate of work-stoppages in LPGs across the GDR.[37] In *Kreis* Seehausen, where the situation appears to have been particularly drastic, it was reported that in many villages 'the populace is referring to the collective farmers as rogues and rascals. It is impossible to get the [LPG] members to work. Comrade H., chairman of the LPG Kriden explained on the telephone that the members refuse to work because the *Großbauern* are returning to their farms. The chairman of the LPG Neukirchen explained . . . that he could no longer say anything to the collective farmers or else they would strike him dead. The collective farmers in Böhmertin likewise refuse to work. What is sketched here is visible in the entire *Kreis*'.[38]

As this report suggests, the government's retreat also exacerbated the pre-existing social tensions between members and opponents of the LPGs. As independent farmers regained a measure of confidence about their economic prospects, demands for 'equality for independent farmers *vis-à-vis* collective farmers' (especially regarding the distribution of seed and fertilizer) grew louder and the social stigmatization of LPG farmers swelled in many villages.[39] In Lindenau, *Kreis* Senftenberg, the derisive taunting ('your weeds are looking nice'; 'if one of you ever needs a piece of bread you can come to me') was so incessant that it reportedly drove the wife of the village LPG chairman to the brink of suicide. She pleaded with her husband to get out of the LPG 'in order to be left in peace'.[40] Thousands of other farmers left the LPGs as well, for a variety of reasons: the return of 'devastated' farms to their former owners, poor organization and morale and above all the argument that one had not joined voluntarily, but because of 'economic coercion'.[41] A wave of withdrawals and LPG dissolutions continued throughout the remainder of 1953, totalling some 564 LPGs and 33 000 farmers by February 1954.[42]

In sum, during the first big collectivization push of 1952–53, relatively few East German farmers had been coaxed into joining LPGs, and even fewer had actually been convinced of the virtues of collectivized agriculture. Part of the reason for this was the continued inability of the regime to overcome older habits of individual work and notions of private property. There was little that could change this, and the majority of independent farmers either opposed or at least remained indifferent to the formation of LPGs. The same was true of a significant proportion of local officials; hence the weaknesses of the LPG campaign also had to do with the incomplete control of the party leadership over its own apparatus at the grassroots. Contrary to widespread popular and even scholarly views, the choices facing East German farmers in 1952–53 were not as simple as joining an LPG, going to jail or fleeing to the West.[43] For one thing, there were numerous voices within the party leadership that urged moderation and argued against forcing such stark alternatives. More importantly, though, it is doubtful that the leadership's actual control in the villages was strong enough to force these alternatives had it even tried. The thicket of social contacts between rural functionaries and farmers acted as so many snares for the implementation of collectivization policies at the grass-roots. In many villages it was an 'unforced' collectivization. For in the event there was a fourth alternative which the majority of independent farmers, not to mention many local functionaries, pursued: namely 'muddling through', dragging one's feet and avoiding the step to collectivized farming where and how one could in the hope that the campaign would soon blow over. And it did blow over, for a while.

6
Mobilizing East German Youth

Of all the social groups the party leadership wanted to 'win over' for the socialist cause, the greatest expectations of all were placed on young people. Whatever misgivings there might have been about the political educability of the so-called 'sceptical generation'[1] of youths after the war, the generation growing into adulthood in the early 1950s carried many of the hopes of the ideologues and pedagogues in the SED. This age group was regarded as relatively untainted by the evils of Nazi socialization, and thus especially capable of becoming socialized in the values and goals of socialism. But in the bipolar Cold War universe of the early 1950s, the cultivation of young 'socialist citizens' also meant driving back other contemporary influences that were seen as threats: above all that of the churches, the western media and the widespread secular pacifism predominant in Germany at the time, which in the SED's view obscured the military threat from the 'imperialists' in the West. The younger generation was thus at the centre of efforts both to mobilize East German society against the West as well as to curtail the influence of the Christian churches. The main tool for accomplishing this was the 'Free German Youth' (*Freie Deutsche Jugend*, or FDJ), the official organization for youth which came firmly under SED control in 1948–49. But the problem faced by this organization, as well as by the SED itself, was that the twin goals of 'winning over' youths while at the same time indoctrinating and mobilizing them for the construction and defence of socialism were not very compatible.

'What about peace and bread?' Military recruitment and the contradictions of the armed forces

At the height of the Cold War, the most important aspect of mobilizing the East German youth concerned the build-up of armed forces, for which young men would naturally comprise the rank-and-file. The first major thrust of remilitarization in eastern Germany after the war came in 1952. Although the Soviets and SED had by this time already established a sizeable quasi-military 'police force' numbering around 20 000 men whose arms, uniforms and organization resembled those more of soldiers than policemen,[2] explicit plans for the establishment of 'national armed forces' for the GDR were first worked out in spring 1952 and publicly announced at the Second Party Conference in July 1952, in the context of the accelerated 'construction of socialism'. In connection with developments in the international situation in central Europe in early 1952 – the consolidation and strengthening of the western military alliance and the confusion wrought by the Stalin-note of March – the Soviets forced a mobilization of the various military forces in the eastern camp. As Wilhelm Pieck recalled from talks with Soviet leaders in Moscow on 1 April 1952, the object for the GDR was to 'create a People's Army without a big fuss' ('*Volksarmee schaffen ohne Geschrei*') by expanding its existing paramilitary forces.[3]

The nucleus of the incipient army was the 'Barracked People's Police' (*Kasernierte Volkspolizei*, or KVP) – so named in order to hide its decidedly military character before the establishment of a West German army – which comprised the bulk of the GDR's ground forces, including infantry, tank and artillery units. Complementing the KVP were the newly-founded *Volkspolizei-See* and -*Luft* units, which in every way apart from their names resembled naval and air defence forces, as well as the so-called *Betriebskampfgruppen* (*Kampfgruppen der Arbeiterklasse* after 1959) which were initially intended as a paramilitary force for the protection of factories but which eventually took on broader functions of civil defence.

The scale of the militarization programme was immense, and necessitated a correspondingly aggressive recruitment campaign. The planned overall strength of the KVP was approximately 160 000 troops, making a total of 200 000 including the marine and air units.[4] Although these perhaps unrealistically optimistic recruitment targets were not completely fulfilled in 1952–53, the armed forces did manage to gain around 60 000 new recruits in less than 12

months following the Second Party Conference of July 1952, totalling 113 000 troops by summer 1953.[5] The first prerequisite was to
coordinate the vast organizational machinery of the GDR for the
purpose of recruitment, including both the state and party apparatus
as well as the mass organizations. As an initial step, the government expanded its pre-existing registration capacity by establishing
225 local registration offices all across the GDR, in all of the larger
towns and principalities.[6] By summer 1952 all local *Volkspolizei* authorities with jurisdictions of up to 150 000 residents were instructed
to assign at least two officers to recruitment for the armed forces,
those with over 150 000 at least three, and the larger *Kreise* such as
Leipzig and Dresden up to eight officers.[7] Various bonuses were also
established as an incentive for winning recruits.[8] In October the
various regional registration offices were placed under the authority
of the central Recruitment Office (*Verwaltung für Rekrutierung*) of
the KVP within the Interior Ministry, which was responsible for
coordinating the entire recruitment campaign.

Among the mass organizations, the FDJ played the most important role by providing a forum for the recruitment of young people.
In May 1952, the SED leadership commissioned the FDJ to embark
on a systematic programme for educating the East German youth
about the 'great importance of the People's Police as the protector
of the people's interests'. Thenceforth one of its main tasks was
the recruitment and so-called '*Wehrerziehung*', or military education,
of all East German youths. The new emphasis on the virtues of
military vigilance was clearly expressed at the FDJ's Fourth Parliament in Leipzig at the end of May, when thousands of young people
carried rifles in strict military formation on their marches through
the city. Two new organizations were introduced in August 1952 to
aid the FDJ in mobilizing young people for armed defence. The so-
called 'Society for Sport and Technology' (*Gesellschaft für Sport und
Technik*, or GST) was officially founded on 7 August, and was, despite attempts to hide its paramilitary nature, clearly intended as a
kind of preparatory school for subsequent military training. The
other was the rather short-lived 'Service for Germany' programme
(*Dienst für Deutschland*, or DfD), which consisted of a six-month
period of construction work at KVP bases, but which in the event
resulted in more unwanted pregnancies than barracks.[9]

The organizational machinery enlisted for the campaign was thus
immense, and allowed for an almost total coverage of all recruitment opportunities in the GDR – a kind of saturation approach

only possible in what was at least formally a '*durchherrschte Gesellschaft*'[10] like the GDR and one which few young people, many of whom belonged to more than one 'mass organization', could possibly avoid. Not even those who did not belong to any of the mass organizations could easily escape the regime's recruitment overtures. If one missed the recruitment presentation at school or at work, one still might be visited at home by a police officer or representative of the local *Wohnparteiorganisation* (WPO). In short, the recruitment campaign came at young people from all sides – in the workplace, at school, in the FDJ – and in a number of different forms, ranging from the more common 'mass deployments' into factories to more personal (and less escapable) 'individual conversations'. But as we will see below, getting this sprawling network of state, party and affiliated agencies to recruit young people effectively at the grass-roots was not as easy as this makes it look.

From its previous experience in recruiting for the paramilitary 'police forces' after 1948, the SED leadership was well aware that raising the necessary numbers would not be an easy task in a society still feeling the effects of the last war and still by and large unconvinced of the necessity, let alone desirability, of East German armed forces.[11] While only a small minority of East Germans actively supported the project and a somewhat larger minority unenthusiastically accepted the argument that an East German military presence was necessary given developments in the West, what stands out most in the internal reports at the time are three interrelated strands of criticism: the high costs, the widespread fear of war, and the concern of deepening German division.

From an economic standpoint, the SED could hardly have chosen a less auspicious time to undertake a rearmament campaign of such vast proportions. Although the actual financial inter-connections involved in the broader 'accelerated construction of socialism' in 1952–53 were, of course, a matter of strict confidentiality, they were quite rapidly figured out by a populace still living under the constraints of rationing and still acutely sensitive to changes in wages and the price and availability of consumer goods. The expanding KVP was quickly perceived as an unnecessary and, more importantly, *unjust* economic burden. The sheer costs of weapons and equipment were not the only issue; the relatively high wages of soldiers and especially officers were also a source of resentment.[12] Given the repeated promises of improving living standards and the recent propaganda campaign against West German signature to the

European Defence Community, the SED's current attempt to drum up support for the KVP seemed blatantly hypocritical to most East Germans. During an assembly at the Houch factory in Berlin-Weißensee, workers even referred to Stalin to help prove this point: 'Stalin himself says it is impossible to strengthen armed forces and raise the living standard of the people simultaneously. Isn't then the strenthening of the KVP an attack on our living standard?'[13] Indeed, such sentiments appear to have been widespread even among the rank-and-file of the SED. At a party meeting in Prenzlauer Berg, for instance, the *Kreisleitung* was repeatedly confronted with angry comments from party members who were now essentially being asked to contradict their own previous argumentation: 'For weeks now the party press has reported that the signing of the Atlantic-pact and the re-militarization in the West means a squandering of the people's wealth, etc. We can hardly talk . . . Up to now we've preached "We shall not take up arms". It only costs money, pensions and wages . . .'[14]

The prospect of another war was also a constant source of concern throughout the 1950s, and any military build-up along the inner-German frontier was quite understandably viewed, as in the Federal Republic, with great trepidation. These fears were expressed in innumerable reports and myriad different ways: occasional runs on savings accounts, periodic outbreaks of *hamstern* (stocking up on food and other essentials), erecting bomb-proof shelters in gardens and the like. There was also more or less universal disapproval of any action that might serve to deepen German division. Whereas militarization campaigns are often occasions for nationalistic fanfare, this was a case – parallel to that in the FRG – of trying to excite people for a fighting force that ran against the grain of popular nationalist sentiments. Although with hindsight it seems unlikely that German unification was ever achievable in the 1950s, to most contemporaries it still seemed a viable prospect, and a highly desirable one at that. The expansion of the East German armed forces not only dampened these prospects, but also raised the spectre of German shooting on German in a future East-West conflict.[15] No one wanted war, and many still harboured hopes for German unification. The expansion of the armed forces seemed like a step in the wrong direction on both counts, even to many lower-level functionaries half-heartedly assisting with the recruitment drive.[16]

To a large extent, however, it did not really matter what the broader East German populace thought. A successful propaganda campaign was not absolutely necessary for the establishment of a sizeable fighting force; a successful recruitment campaign was. Although the sprawling network of SED-led organizations gave the regime unique advantages in this regard, it is important to recognize that persuading a young man or woman (primarily man) to enlist in the KVP, GST or DfD still depended on a face-to-face encounter. At some point the vast might of this organizational machinery had to confront young people as they were, with all their various interests and plans for the future. In the event, would-be recruits were often less well-disposed than the party leadership would have wished.

The internal reports exhibit a wide variety of responses from would-be recruits, ranging from a marked eagerness to join to a conditional willingness to defend the GDR if it is attacked all the way to outright refusal and illegal emigration to the West. Although they present certain interpretive problems both in terms of the sincerity of reported 'positive' reactions given the pressure to conform as well as the possibility of regime functionaries writing 'beautified' reports to their superiors, it nonetheless seems clear that the willingness to enlist – for whatever reason – was on balance far outweighed by refusals and by a general disapproval of rearmament, based on a range of different factors.

Given the deliberate cultivation of war-like values among youth and children under the Nazis, it is remarkable how much evidence of principled pacifism (by which I mean refusal to resort to violence under any circumstances) one finds in the reports. And considering the politically-charged, highly pressurized atmosphere in which the recruitment campaign often took place, it is also remarkable how forthright and unambiguous many of these pacifist refusals were. There are of course any number of possible reasons for this, and pacifist arguments might just as easily have been self-serving as principled. But it seems that one important reason was that, in their campaign to produce a peace-loving 'anti-fascist' youth, the SED and FDJ had to a certain extent been too successful for their own good. Many young people saw in the current idealization of the virtues of military vigilance and unquestioning discipline some of the very values they were taught to associate with the fascist past, not the socialist future. Consequently, many of those who refused to join the armed forces did so at least in part on the basis of the SED's own prior teachings. Indeed, the FDJ's new emphasis on '*Wehrerziehung*' and its decidedly militaristic displays at its Fourth Parliament in Leipzig drove many pacifist youths from

its ranks.[17] As one Berlin FDJ member who resigned his membership put it: 'it is unheard-of that Walter Ulbricht declares at the
Fourth Parliament that young people should attain the *Abzeichen
für gutes Wissen* and also become good sharpshooters. Shooting is
against the goals of the FDJ'.[18] In *Kreis* Loburg youths even founded
a clandestine group that called itself the 'FDJ Action Committee
against the National Armed Forces'.[19]

Of course not all unwilling would-be recruits responded in such
a courageous and forthright manner. Graffiti and defacement of
recruitment posters were rife throughout 1952–53. Fairly typical were
the slogans painted in *Kreis* Sangerhausen: 'We'll tear up our draft
papers, we don't want fratricide, not us (*ohne uns*)'.[20] Nor were all
expressions of refusal very pacifist. At the opposite end of the spectrum
from the principled peace-advocates, some young people met the
prospect of recruitment with violence. The reports posit an alarming increase in the number of anonymous attacks on FDJ functionaries
and *Volkspolizisten* during summer and autumn 1952, and explicitly
draw a causal connection between most of the attacks and the vic-
tims' recruitment activities. While many such attacks were simply
attributed to 'rowdies' who seemed to despise all figures of authority
regardless of their specific organizational affiliation, in some cases
the causal connection is unmistakable. Returning from a recruiting
trip to Patendorf, the loudspeaker-van from Leuna-Werk 'Walter
Ulbricht' had to stop because of what seemed to be a badly
imbalanced wheel. When the driver and passenger of the van got
out to inspect it, they discovered that the lugs on the wheel had
somehow worked themselves loose and bent the lug-bolts. Two cars
full of young men that had been following the van from Patendorf
soon pulled over to offer what initially appeared to be roadside
assistance. What they gave the recruiters instead was a rather grue-
some beating. Subsequent police inspection of the wheel confimed
that its lugs had been intentionally loosened in the village, and
that the attack had therefore been planned in advance.[21]

As one might expect, the majority of refusals to enlist lay some-
where between these two poles of violence and principled non-
violence. Probably the most common response, evident in more or
less all the reports on recruitment, was a Schwejkian reference to
the regime's own previous 'peace and bread' rhetoric: 'What about
the national hymn, that a mother will never again mourn her son?
What about the *Volkspolizei*? The national hymn has now become
obsolete'; 'Whatever happened to the slogan, "Peace is defended at

the work-bench"?'[22] There was also a certain social stigma attached to being in the KVP. Popular disregard for the KVP as suitable only for 'unemployed good-for-nothings' and 'the lowest kind of riff-raff' is evident in opinion reports from the shopfloor as well as interviews with East German refugees to the West in the 1950s.[23] Moreover, given the horrible memories of rape and plunder at the hands of Soviet soldiers in 1945, the KVP's Soviet-style uniforms, which replaced the previously modified *Wehrmacht* uniforms in autumn 1952, did nothing to diminish this social stigma. On the contrary, as one new recruit wrote to his girlfriend before holiday leave: 'We look like Russians in these uniforms . . . I don't dare come home at all'.[24] What the party leadership propagated as an 'honourable service' in the KVP seemed more like a disgrace to many East German youths.

The FDJ and the *Junge Gemeinden*

Besides the first mass recruitment push, the period from spring 1952 to summer 1953 also saw the first concerted attack of the atheist state on the influence of the churches among East German youth. While there had already been some minor disruptions of the Protestant churches' youth work in the latter 1940s, it was only with the broader 'Stalinization' of the SBZ from 1949 onwards that the struggle between church and state over the hearts and minds of the next generation took an openly confrontational course. Church events were occasionally hindered by tightened police regulations; religious instruction in schools was essentially abolished with the school reform of 1951, which explicitly based the educational curriculum in schools and universities on Marxism–Leninism; Christian students and even teachers were disadvantaged in their careers, some were even dismissed.[25] Yet the influence of the party and FDJ on young people was still deemed insufficient by the party leadership.

One reason for this was that the reform of the teaching profession was rather disappointing from the leadership's perspective, and failed to turn the schools into reliable conveyors of socialist ideology. There were huge problems at first in training new teachers to replace all those who were fired (which totalled around 50 per cent of all teachers in the SBZ at the end of the war), and it proved impossible to achieve the goal of creating a predominately 'working-class' teaching profession, which it was thought would guarantee its political reliability. For a number of reasons, former Nazi party members (who comprised 71.6 per cent of teachers in the SBZ) were not as rigorously dismissed as hoped for. This was due in part to the fact that some were allowed to stay in their positions by unreliable school councillors at the local level, and in part to the simple recognition by 1947 that it was necessary to re-hire former 'nominal Nazis' as a means of overcoming the desperate shortage of capable teachers in view of the extremely high rates of fluctuation among the poorly-trained new teachers.[26] Even though the new teachers as a group soon came to dominate schools across the SBZ (by 1949 comprising 45 244 of the total number of 65 207 teachers in the GDR), they did not turn out to be the committed socialist bulwark initially hoped for.[27]

Outside of the schools, the influence of the party via the FDJ was also rather tenuous at the grass-roots. In localities where the FDJ was strong, this was usually because it limited its activities largely to dances or other forms of entertainment. Although a small number of FDJ groups were very SED-oriented and politically active, politics did not play much of a role in most, and in the early years some groups were more dominated by the CDU or LDP than by the SED. When FDJ groups became more closely controlled by the SED and more politically oriented, they lost their appeal to many young people. As a dance-organizer the FDJ was quite successful; but if all it could offer was the message to 'work, learn and struggle', it had little attraction.

It was particularly in areas where the FDJ was weak that the churches were seen as a threat to its viability, and hence to the entire influence of the party among youth. Instead of recognizing that many young people were simply disinclined to such things as uniform clothing, flag drills and assemblies with rigid military discipline, the party leadership blamed the weakness of the FDJ on the 'negative' influence of the churches, especially the Protestant *Junge Gemeinden*. By 1950, there were clear tendencies to criminalize these groups as deliberate attempts to 'split' the East German youth and keep them out of the FDJ, not least because of the decidedly 'bourgeois' social make-up of the *Junge Gemeinden*.[28] The sharpening of laws permitting public events led to a number of church youth events being hindered. Yet most were still left unscathed, and 1951 was in fact marked by a fairly liberal atmosphere towards the *Junge Gemeinden* because the FDJ wanted to get as many Christian youths as possible to participate in the *Weltfestspiele* in Berlin in the summer of that year.

The harder line pursued from spring 1952 marked a new departure in church-state relations, and signalled the beginning of a
concerted campaign against the *Junge Gemeinden*. At the Fourth FDJ
parliament in Leipzig in May, where the new emphasis on military
vigilance was given public display in army-like marches around the
city, Ulbricht set the new tone by warning of the dangers of Anglo-
American 'agents and spies' infiltrating FDJ groups and trying to
bring the East German youth under the influence of the Christian
churches.[29] From the summer of 1952 the *Junge Gemeinden* were
officially regarded as a 'criminal organization', a kind of fifth-column
whose very existence undermined the organizational monopoly that
the FDJ was intended to enjoy. The mere wearing of the *'Kugelkreuz'*
pin as a designation of membership was treated as a symbol of
protest. Various administrative measures were tightened against the
Junge Gemeinden, including the hindering of church events, closing
church-run holiday camps, etc.[30] Although in July and August 1952
there were already open calls from some party leaders, especially
Willi Barth and Karl Maron, simply to forbid the *Junge Gemeinden*
outright, in the meantime the SED-leadership decided that the best
way to destroy their influence was to improve the attractiveness of
the FDJ.[31]

But the problem with this policy was that the FDJ groups barely
existed in many areas, and even where they were seen to be doing
'positive' work, they often maintained quite cordial relations with
the local *Junge Gemeinden*. Reports of cooperation and even co-
sponsored events at the local level were presumably the main reason
why Bruno Wolf, the director of the State Office for Church Matters,
was dismissed and arrested in January 1953.[32] There was also broad
overlap between the two groups in terms of membership; roughly
35 per cent of the *Junge Gemeinde* membership was also in the FDJ,
which the party leadership viewed as little less than a kind of fifth
columnism.

By early 1953 it was clear that significant improvements in the
effectiveness of the FDJ at the grass-roots level could not be achieved
quickly. There was little left to do but attack the *Junge Gemeinden*
outright, and in January 1953 the *Politbüro* passed a number of
measures which did just that: dismissal of all members from the
FDJ and sport organizations, further limitations on religious education, forbidding all public activities of the *Junge Gemeinden* and,
most importantly, hindering their members from advancing into
higher education. These new measures of course prompted vehement

protests from church officials throughout the GDR, who quite justifiedly saw them as a breach of earlier agreements as well as the GDR constitution itself, and who pleaded with government officials to take a more moderate course.[33] Although most of the measures were not strictly enforced at the grass-roots, students and pupils were nonetheless publicly enjoined to denounce the *Junge Gemeinden* and sever ties with them, which many did. By June a total of 712 young people were expelled from schools or universities for refusing to do so.[34]

Despite such 'successes', it seems that the attack on the *Junge Gemeinden* backfired as far as the military recruitment campaign was concerned. It was arguably a case of poor planning on the part of the SED that these two offensives coincided. With many of their members discriminated against at school, in some cases even expelled or blocked from entering higher education, the *Junge Gemeinden* not surprisingly proved to be a particularly impervious haven for young Christian pacifists. The extent to which they hindered the campaign in a given locality depended to a large degree on the views and personalities of particular pastors, their support or otherwise by the regional church and especially on the strength of the penumbra of church-affiliated organizations that they managed to build up and sustain in their local parishes. In the village of Schleife in *Bezirk* Cottbus, for instance, the unusually energetic local pastor not only presided over an active *Junge Gemeinde*, but also reportedly undermined the local FDJ group by persuading the young people in his church to resign. According to the SED *Kreisleitung*, the effects of his activities were manifested most conspicuously in KVP recruitment: 'We'd rather fly planes to West Germany' was reported as a typical response from youths in the village. Schools in which the *Junge Gemeinden* had a strong presence also feature in the reports as focal points for pacifist refusals to join the KVP: for example, the secondary school in Weida, where pupils unanimously and demonstratively expressed their refusal to carry weapons; and the agricultural-vocational school in Weimar, where pupils declared that they would rather be shot than enlist.[35]

With the advent of the 'New Course' in June 1953 and the subsequent meeting of party and church representatives in July, the government effectively climbed down from its confrontational position and no longer viewed the *Junge Gemeinden* as an illegal organization – indeed, not as an 'organization' at all. But the end of the open conflict merely masked the fundamental tension that still remained. The harsh measures of spring 1953 had managed to diminish the influence and popularity of the *Junge Gemeinden* only temporarily. Despite church officials' complaints of a weakening of the groups in 1953, the number of youths involved in them was greater in 1954 than in 1952 (119 855 compared to 108 417), and rose further to 125 025 in 1955.[36] It is thus little wonder that the *Junge Gemeinden* were still regarded as a threat to the FDJ. They continued to hamper its efforts to win members at the local level, they still cultivated and spread pacifist sentiments among young people, and worst of all from the perspective of the party leadership, they showed no signs of shrinking. The basic outlines of the conflict between church and state over the hearts and minds of East German youths had changed very little in 1952–53.

7
'Republikflucht': Fleeing the Construction of Socialism

Clearly, the year from summer 1952 to summer 1953 was a period of immense internal pressure in the GDR. It witnessed the first broadly-conceived attempt to reshape East German society by force and bring East Germans themselves into line with the expectations of the party leadership. Equally clearly, the bundle of policies that were pursued with such vigour during that year were exceedingly unpopular, and eventually led to widespread popular unrest. In the meantime they also led to record numbers of East Germans simply packing up and leaving for the West. The immense wave of some 225 174 emigrants during the first half of 1953 not only prompted the Soviet 'suggestion' of a change of course in the GDR, but also triggered a process of rethinking within the SED itself regarding the westward population movement.

Although the mass exodus of East Germans had clearly become a critical issue during the 'deliberate construction of socialism' of 1952–53, in the beginning it was not viewed as a serious problem, at least apart from desertions by police officers[1] and the flight of crucial technical experts. In fact, until the economy began to pick up in the early 1950s, it was actually perceived as a relief from the problems of overcoming unemployment and providing basic necessities. During the 1940s, a large portion of those who left for the West were expellees from the former eastern territories of the Reich whose arrival in the SBZ/GDR only aggravated the already grave shortages in consumer goods and adequate housing. Moreover, their irredentism vis-à-vis Poland, the Soviet Union and to a lesser extent Czechoslovakia constituted a potential political quagmire for the SED. For all these reasons the East German authorities were not unhappy to see as many of them as possible leave for the western zones. The same could be said of any other potential political opponents who would only make the construction of a Soviet-style socialist state more difficult.

The first visible signs of a nascent concern about mass emigration to the West emerged in 1950. Around this time the state began to compile statistics on both the numbers of emigrants to the West and the most common motives for leaving. The fact that Ulbricht himself was kept informed of these developments clearly shows that emigration was gradually becoming a matter of importance.[2] The 1951 'Order on the Return of German Identity Cards upon Emigration to West Germany or West Berlin' represents the first attempt at least to keep track of emigration, even if it was not yet deemed possible or necessary to control it.

It was only in 1952 that the East German government and (perhaps more importantly) the Soviets became concerned enough about the potential problems posed by mass emigration to take decisive measures against it. The first and most obvious attempt to limit the population movement across the inner-German border was the closure of the demarcation line with West Germany in May 1952 and the construction of a five-kilometer wide prohibited zone on the eastern side of the border, after which West Germany was only reachable for most East Germans via Berlin. The fact that the SED leadership was prepared to face the political costs of such heavy-handed tactics, which included forcibly transporting people out of their homes in the prohibited zone, demonstrates a determination to keep emigration to the West within certain limits. But given the continued existence of the Berlin loophole, such tactics alone could not solve the problem.

On 9 September 1952, only several weeks after the fateful Second Party Conference (and perhaps in anticipation of the wave of refugees during the upcoming winter of discontent?), the *Politbüro* created a special commission to deal specifically with the question of inter-German population movement. Franz Dahlem and Willi Barth were the key figures, and over the next several months they drafted a detailed proposal of 'Guidelines on Measures against *Republikflucht* and on Recruitment of Qualified Employees in West Germany' which the *Politbüro* passed on 6 January 1953,[3] and which set the tone for the entire campaign against the mass emigration up until the construction of the Wall in 1961.

The final version of the guidelines cobbled together by Dahlem and Barth contained a number of propagandistic and administrative measures. Official propaganda sought to frighten potential emigrants via wide publicity of the 'misery of flight' in western internment camps and of the difficulties experienced by refugees in finding suitable employment. It also vilified them as 'traitors' and even 'saboteurs' to the principles of socialism, portraying those who left illegally primarily as criminals or smugglers.[4] Attracting skilled labour from West Germany – especially members of the intelligentsia – via promises of accommodation and suitable employment was also made a priority. Most important were the administrative measures establishing a comprehensive system of information on the population movement. In every case of *Republikflucht* the motives for flight were to be carefully analyzed by the police. All information gathered was then to be collected into a central catalogue, which would include details about each refugee's background, possible criminal record, actions during the Nazi period and, of course, behaviour in the SBZ/GDR. Such information would, it was hoped, aid in the accurate diagnosis of the reasons for *Republikflucht*, which would in turn allow for the formulation of appropriate policies to combat it.

Clearly, the party leadership was not short of ideas about what the various state and party organs should do to combat *Republikflucht*. The crucial question was whether or not any of their ideas would have much effect, or indeed be carried out on the ground in the first place. The signs were rather unpromising from the very beginning. As early as 5 January 1953, just a day before the *Politbüro* passed the draft of guidelines against *Republikflucht*, Dahlem wrote to Barth expressing his concern about forgetting to include precise details as to who was responsible for controlling the execution of the guidelines: 'If this does not happen, little will be done in practice'.[5] Although the Interior Ministry expanded the mandate of the *Abteilung Bevölkerungspolitik* for this purpose on 30 January,[6] not even this clear delineation of responsibility could overcome the difficulties of mobilizing a vast and not yet very well-oiled regime apparatus at the grass-roots.

Dahlem's worst fears soon came true. As the number of refugees soared to record heights during the spring of 1953, little was done to curb the flow. It did not take long for the Central Committee, which was fed a constant stream of reports on emigration from the *Volkspolizei*, to recognize the complete failure of the East German state to deal with the mounting refugee crisis. In March 1953, the month with the greatest efflux of East Germans in the history of the GDR, the Department of State Administration reacted by harshly criticizing the 'monotonous and ineffective' propaganda in the press, the 'very weak' efforts of the mass organizations and the failure of the police to complete the cataloguing system or to give serious attention to the underlying reasons for *Republikflucht*, most cases of which were still nonchalantly attributed to 'unknown causes'. Not a single agency involved was left unscathed. As the letter concluded: 'as of the beginning of March 1953, those comrades made responsible by the [*Politbüro*] resolution have hardly done a thing worth mentioning'.[7] SED internal reports in 1953 confirm this overall picture of inertia. According to an April report, 'some of the *Bezirk* secretaries and a large portion of the *Kreis* secretaries handled the *Politbüro* resolution as only informational ... Only in few cases was the implementation of the resolutions begun quickly'.[8]

One of the main difficulties in motivating lower-level functionaries to do something about the wave of emigrants was the widespread view that the problem would go away once the sharpened regulations of spring 1953 were rescinded, a view that was initially confirmed by the rapid drop in emigration after the announcement of the 'New Course' in June (see Figure 11.1, p. 152). But as the numbers rose again steeply from September onwards, the continuing lack of action made it clear that the inertia had deeper roots. This was, in any event, the conclusion drawn by the Central Committee, which once more vehemently criticized the mass organizations for 'completely neglecting' the problem, the police for failing to 'deal with *Republikflucht* seriously' and the party apparatus for 'hardly observing' the *Politbüro* guidelines.[9]

Clearly, the political volte-face in the early 1950s on the question of mass emigration at the central level was not mirrored by an equally rapid change in the attitudes and activities of lower-level functionaries, many of whom simply did not view it as a pressing problem. Moreover, the problem lingered on during the following years. In the words of a SED Central Committee report of May 1954: 'The regional and district councils and the *Bürgermeister* still act extremely passively towards *Republikflucht*. They often do not know what methods could be used to combat it effectively. Only in the rarest cases are the reasons for flight carefully analyzed. Many functionaries still view this task as the jurisdiction of our security organs'.[10] The 1954 year-end report on illegal emigration describes the state apparatus as 'generally apathetic towards *Republikflucht*'; even the state secretaries were merely keeping informed of the problem but undertaking no efforts to combat it. 'Many comrades' within the party, it complains, were also still 'unclear about the effects of *Republikflucht*'.[11] At the Graphic-Design Studios in Leipzig, there was even a send-off party for one worker leaving for the West in which the BPO members themselves participated.

A 1954 Central Committee investigation at the BFG Mining Equipment Works in Lauchhammer offers a particularly vivid illustration of the widespread apathy among *Kreis*-level and grass-roots functionaries concerning the emigration problem. Prompted by a report about alleged indifference on the part of the BGL and the complete lack of knowledge about the reasons for the 21 cases of *Republikflucht* since June 1953, three Central Committee instructors were dispatched to Lauchhammer on 21 May. Their first stop was the party *Kreisleitung* in Senftenberg, where they discovered that the director of the Department of State Organs, comrade F., was not in the least informed about *Republikflucht* in the district and undertook absolutely nothing against it, mistakenly assuming that it 'was a matter for the Economics Department'. But the director of the Economics Department was no more informed than comrade F., and explained to the instructors that, 'Up to now I have only concerned myself with the plan fulfillment of the People's Own factories'. Another comrade in the Department of State Organs thought it was the business of a 'special instructor' directly seconded to the SED First Secretary, as he thought was spelled out by a recent Central Committee resolution (which prompted the reader of the report at Central Committee headquarters to scribble an indignant question mark in the margin). The second stop for the instructors was the Senftenberg District Council (*Rat des Kreises*), where the 'overview and comments on the questions of *Republikflucht* [were] similar to those of the *Kreisleitung*'. By the time they arrived at the BFG Lauchhammer, what they discovered could hardly have come as a surprise. As comrade D., the BPO secretary for agitation and propaganda, explained, the party organization in the factory had not yet bothered with the issue because they thought the numbers of illegal emigrants were relatively low.[12]

This dissociation of the activities of grass-roots officials from resolutions at the central level was only slowly and partially overcome during the course of the 1950s with improvements in the information system and the gradual professionalization of the party-state apparatus. But even so, such improvements as were made could be of only little help. For even if all the anti-*Republikflucht* measures devised by the leadership were seamlessly implemented at the grass-roots, this still left the main problem unsolved. Millions of East Germans preferred their prospects in the West to what they saw in the GDR.

Part 3

From Setback to New Offensives, 1953–61

In terms of its authority at the grass-roots, the party leadership was in many ways in a worse position in the wake of June 1953 than in the chaos years after the war. By trying rapidly to push through a number of major policy objectives, it had managed not only to undermine most of the limited popular support that it had, but also to alienate the majority of Christians through its attacks on the church and to irritate a raw nerve of pacifist and German nationalist sentiments through its remilitarization campaign. Worse still, many of its own functionaries had proven unreliable at the moment of truth, and the record wave of emigrants to the West caused incalculable economic and political damage. Yet the embarrassing setback of summer 1953 was nonetheless only temporary, and had taught the leadership an important lesson: any attempt to push through its aims with force on numerous fronts at once was too risky to try again.

The new offensives of the 1950s, though pursued with similar vigor, were thus carried out in a more selective and piecemeal fashion. They were also carried out by a grass-roots apparatus that was slowly becoming more dependable and against an overall backdrop of gradual improvements in the material living standard. All of these factors contributed to the relative success of the various collectivization, recruitment and productivity campaigns of the 1950s in comparison to the simultaneous push of 1952–53. Yet these campaigns were still only *relatively* successful, as the following chapters will show. While they occasioned no mass protests, which was an obvious improvement from the regime's point of view, they were still broadly characterized by popular apathy and opposition, as well as by local functionaries who frequently proved unable or even unwilling to carry them out. And in the end the new offensives of the 1950s and early 1960s contributed to a mounting refugee crisis that could only be solved by locking people into a state which still only a small minority actively supported.

8
The Factories from 17 June to the Socialist Brigades

The events of June 1953 were not only extremely frightening for the party leadership, they were also very illuminating. They revealed a situation in the factories far worse than most officials at party headquarters had imagined. Not only was the SED regime broadly rejected by the industrial workforce, the very group that now theoretically exercised control under the 'dictatorship of the proletariat', but also many of its functionaries at the factory level had proven unreliable to the point of turning against it in its moment of weakness. The response in the Central Committee was not just to rescind the unpopular norm increases that had driven workers on to the streets, but also to redouble efforts aimed at 'cleansing' the functionary apparatus in the factories as well as 'educating' and mobilizing the industrial workforce for its allotted role as carrier of the socialist system. All of these efforts faced significant difficulties. The problem with purging the apparatus was that it needed to be balanced by the twin imperatives of retaining sufficient expertise in the management and maintaining an anchor on the shopfloor. The problem with mobilizing workers was that most bore little resemblance to their image in Marxist–Leninist theory, showing little inclination to leave the representation of their material interests to the official unions, much less transform themselves into 'socialist personalities'.

Management, union and party

As we have seen, the triangle between management, BGL and workforce was still intact in many factories at the beginning of the 1950s despite party efforts to pry its way in. The SED leadership had not yet managed to excise all remnants of '*Sozialdemokratismus*' and '*Nurgewerkschaftertum*' from positions of influence, whether in the management, unions or even some party groups. In many factories the union leadership still included a few older veterans of working-class politics, still remained somewhat anchored on the shopfloor and still enjoyed a degree of respect among the workers. It was symptomatic of the personnel situation that union functionaries tended either to be at the head of the demonstrations in June 1953 or not participate at all. Although the process of breaking this triangle and bringing it all under party control was given an added impetus by the events of 17 June, and although a 'new guard' of young party-trained functionaries was appointed in the factories throughout the 1950s, it still proved difficult to bring either management or the union apparatus at this level under strict central control.

Much of the problem in the mid-1950s still consisted of finding enough interested and qualified persons. The situation at the VEB Herrenbekleidung Fortschritt in Berlin-Lichtenberg, where at the January 1953 union elections 'forty-five functionaries were elected, without some of them wanting to be or anyone telling them what tasks they were to perform', was by no means exceptional.[1] Even in the large VEBs it was often impossible to make do without re-hiring some of the officials who had lost their positions for acting 'negatively' on 17 June.[2] As one might expect, the situation of the functionary apparatus in smaller factories was significantly worse, and was frequently characterized by complete disinterest and inactivity. At the VEB Akkurat in Berlin-Lichtenberg, a laundry employing 120 women and 49 men working under rather primitive conditions, *Kreisleitung* instructors succinctly concluded that 'the BGL has not managed to win any influence in the enterprise'. The BPO was essentially non-existent, and 'only formally carried out' its infrequent assemblies. The relatively new factory director, comrade Meyer, 'has no contact with the colleagues in the factory and the workforce no trust in him'. By contrast, the technical director Wilms, a long-standing manager in the factory with no party affiliation, 'has been able to win over the colleagues'. It was precisely persons like this, old-established factory elites who enjoyed the respect of workers on the shopfloor and who kept their distance from the party and FDGB, whom the leadership tolerated the least. As was so often the case, the long tenure of Wilms in the factory – the source of much of his authority – turned out to be his undoing in the end. As the instructors' report revealingly recommended: 'because of the suspicion that the technical director Wilms has connections with the former proprietor Krause, he is . . . to be dismissed'.[3] Summary dismissals such as this made the BGLs and BPOs anything but more popular among most workers, and the result was that few took the new authorities in the factories seriously. There was widespread indifference towards union elections, assemblies and meetings, which quickly degenerated into meaningless rituals for everyone involved. At the VEB Herrenbekleidung Fortschritt the BGL elections had to be repeated several times in 1955 in order to get even the statutory minimum turnout: 'The union functionaries in the section branches must be told time and again to explain to the colleagues the importance of carrying out union elections'.[4] As this report also suggests, the gradual takeover of the leading union positions resulted in a cleft within the union apparatus itself at the factory level, between the more closely-controlled BGLs and the subordinate '*Abteilungsgewerkschaftsleitungen*', or AGLs, which represented individual sections of workers in large VEBs and which were largely staffed by honourary functionaries. In the rather typical words of a 1959 brigade report from the VEB Elektroprojekt in Lichtenberg: 'as always, a serious weakness is still the insufficient connection between the BGL and AGL'.[5]

Needless to say, there was even less connection between the BGLs and the workers themselves. During the course of the 1950s the unions all but disappeared from the shopfloor. Many became caught up in their own internal squabbles and personal intrigues, and few played any role in workers' eyes beyond that of glorified travel agent and, after 1956, administrator for social insurance. The FDGB was more firmly in the party's hand, but as a result had lost much of its intended 'transmission' effect in the factories. As a transport worker in Lichtenberg put it: 'the BGL is never to be seen, they never come out of their meetings, sometimes they don't even return a greeting'.[6]

As for the party organizations at the factory level, despite bringing some limited technical expertise under their roof during the course of the 1950s, they were nonetheless by and large unable to capitalize on the weakening of the unions, and still found it difficult to expand their influence beyond the realms of upper management and union leadership. Like the BGLs, they, too, enjoyed little respect among most workers or technical personnel, and in some cases still found it difficult to occupy positions of influence. Even in large factories such as the VEB Elektrokohle, party secretaries still complained in 1958 that 'comrades are not considered for new positions in the factory; rather, the only ones who get into the commanding heights are those who have already worked there for twenty years and are well acquainted with the management'.[7] This is hardly surprising given the constant complaints in the Central Committee of the lack of technical competence among political functionaries. Although most of the factory directors had themselves donned the party pin by the mid-1950s, many saw the party groups and their pretenses to co-determination in the factories – the so-called 'principle of collectivity' – as little more than a nuisance.[8] Even when party members took up new functions in the factories, it seems that many wanted little to do with the unpopular BPOs once in their new positions. As party secretaries from factories in Berlin-Köpenick complained at a 1956 meeting:

> The fact is that the comrades in the union and management no longer feel like comrades from the moment they take over these functions, but rather say that we are now the union or management. One could cite dozens of examples of this. We have to achieve a change here, and make sure that these comrades also stand up as members of the party.[9]

Against this backdrop, the difficulties in getting the party rank-and-file in the factories to take an interest in party life are anything but surprising. Even in the large VEBs it was difficult to get many of them even to attend regular meetings, much less carry out any other functions. In the VEB Elektrokohle it was reported that 'the comrades only come to assemblies when there is pressure "from above" and when one "begs on one's knees"'. Attendance rates at party meetings usually hovered around 45 per cent, sometimes dropping to as low as 32 per cent. Most of the BPO members were reported to be 'party-tired', and many hoped for a more 'mild' party life. It was revealing of their priorities that a large proportion attended a birthday party for their comrade Prahl instead of a party assembly when the two coincided.[10]

As for the majority of non-politically-organized workers, the SED groups in the factories were widely regarded with disdain. For one thing, the workers who joined the BPOs frequently did not number among the more 'respectable' workers – the highly-skilled and better-paid veterans – and consequently enjoyed little respect. As a party investigation at the VEB Wälzlager in Berlin-Lichtenberg concluded:

'Generally speaking, in the past the comrades were not always models in terms of their moral behaviour or with respect to work. This still affects the entire argumentation'.[11] Moreover, the BPOs' perceived role as the 'long arm' of the party leadership tended to isolate them and make their presence on the shopfloor unwanted. In the VEG Baumschule in Johannisthal, for instance, comrade Fritsch 'was dug at several times and called a SED-spy' by one of his colleagues. When asked by another party member why he did not 'smash in the colleague's face' for slandering him, Fritsch answered 'that then a mob of ten men would surely go after him until there was nothing left of him'.[12] Faced with this mixture of indifference and latent hostility, many party secretaries in the factories were at a loss as to what to do. One secretary's summary of the situation in a Köpenick factory was symptomatic of the situation in factories all across the GDR: 'We have to do something to make the BPO into a fighting organ. The hard thing, though, is that we don't know how we can mobilize the workforce'.[13] The SED-leadership was consolidating its hold in the factories, but the more it did so, the less appeal it had to workers themselves.

'Erziehung', protest and indifference on the shopfloor

This situation clearly did not tally with the SED's ideological expectations. In the party's official world-view, industrial workers, especially those in the 'core' branches of energy, heavy-industry and machine-building, were the nucleus of the 'progressive' forces in history. Having suffered most from the exploitation of the capitalist system, they of all people should understand the merits of socialism and be prepared to make sacrifices to help it come to fruition. But throughout the period covered here, and indeed throughout the entire history of the GDR, the difficulties of mobilizing the majority of rather indifferent and *'eigensinnig'* industrial workers to play the leading economic and political role assigned to them remained one of the greatest disappointments among party officials from the *Politbüro* to the factory level.

As we have already seen, low productivity and poor work discipline were perennial problems which the party tried to solve via various forms of wage tinkering and production competitions. But given the lack of a clear and consistent connection between wages and productivity, the shortage of skilled labour, frequent problems in the supply of raw materials, extremely generous sickness compensation and the crucial elimination of independent unions for representing workers' interests, there was little disciplining incentive on the shopfloor. Reports throughout the 1950s are full of complaints of 'loafing' (*Arbeitsbummelei*), 'work restraint' (*Arbeitszurückhaltung*), and various other forms of 'insufficient work discipline' such as feigning illness, arriving to work late, going home early, drinking on the job, taking unscheduled breaks, refusing to carry out certain tasks, etc., all of which was based on a variety of motives ranging from a desire to maintain low norms to procuring scarce consumer goods or cultivating one's small plot of land at home during working hours. This was by no means unique to the GDR; labour historians have long interpreted such behaviour as subtle ways of asserting interests, expressing discontent or opposing unpopular measures on the shopfloor. And this is not to say that shopfloor politics in the GDR was merely a story of workers' opposition to the ever-increasing regimentation in the factories. Rather, this story is for the most part one of a tacit arrangement of political passivity in exchange for social concessions, of a small measure of social autonomy in the factories whose ambivalent effects were to lend the regime a degree of stability it otherwise would not have had, but at the same time also to undermine its economic viability in the long-term.

From the perspective of the party leadership, the social concessions granted in the wake of 17 June 1953 represented more a setback in the campaign to raise work norms and productivity than a long-term political settlement. There were still periodic attempts to raise norms and reassert control over wages in the 1950s, albeit in a piecemeal fashion and without direct involvement of the party leadership. But workers still adopted a variety of strategies for opposing or escaping them. Most drastic among these were the periodic strikes and work stoppages throughout the decade, though most remained purely local affairs and were usually quite quickly, effectively and quietly dealt with at the local level – not least because factory functionaries themselves were in a highly precarious situation if superior levels of the party or union, or worse still the 'state organs' (read: police and/or *Stasi*), became involved. It is impossible to say with any certainty whether the number of strikes rose or fell over this period since many minor work stoppages undoubtedly were not reported in the first place. For what it is worth, the FDGB registered 166 work stoppages or strikes in 1960 (which Herbert Warnke himself conceded was 'not nearly all of them') the vast majority triggered by a sudden decrease in wages resulting from arbitrary, unnegotiated norm changes or poor organization of supply and production.[14] As such, they were far less politically motivated expressions of discontent than merely attempts to push through demands that up until then had been rejected by the factory BGL. Even during the politically explosive autumn of 1956, most strikes appear to have been motivated by proximal material concerns. A strike at the BKW 'Freundschaft' in *Bezirk* Cottbus, for instance, was triggered by a simple case of underpayment for unloading a truck. Another strike at the VEB Preßwerk revolved around the common issue of norm levels, as did the threat of a work stoppage at the steel works in Brandenburg.[15] The overwhelming bulk of such strikes were small, spontaneous and basically unorganized, involving on average only slightly over ten participants.[16] As Peter Hübner has shown, their result was often a compromise solution: for example, returning to work in exchange for mitigation of the cause of grievance, usually either with remuneration for the period of the work stoppage or the opportunity to make up for lost wages with extra overtime.[17]

But given their politicization by the regime and the threat of punishment or arrest for participating (again, the 'state organs' were often called in if an agreement could not be reached quickly), strikes were the exception and not the rule, and workers often did not need to strike in the first place. Because of the threat of sanctions or, in extreme cases, even imprisonment, most strategies of asserting interests and opposing changes to the material status-quo were more subtle and indirect. Given the shortage of labour, one of the most common and effective means of avoiding a cut in one's wages or working conditions short of downing one's tools was simply to switch jobs, or at least threaten to do so. Systematic statistics on fluctuation in the GDR are apparently unavailable for the 1950s, but a report on the third quarter of 1958 gives an idea of its scope. During these three months alone the rate of fluctuation was 5.1 per cent in state-run industry as a whole, ranging from 3.6 per cent in the relatively well-paid coal and energy branches to 14.7 per cent in construction.[18]

Many, though by no means all, such cases of job-switching represent a kind of hidden conflict between workers and employers in which one simply sought a different position that more closely met one's expectations instead of protesting or negotiating with managers – a practice not all that uncommon in the West.[19] The problem was most acute at the large construction sites for the GDR's huge heavy industrial projects, which had to draw labour from a large radius and where a sizeable proportion of workers only commuted home on weekends. At the Schwarze Pumpe coal and energy site, for example, rates of fluctuation were approximately 10 per cent monthly, and disaffected workers frequently used the threat of leaving as a means of improving pay, working or living conditions, thus forcing enterprise directors into a 'social-political defensive'[20]: that is, to build flats and improve consumer provision in order to keep enough workers there. To use the terms of Albert Hirschman's classic study, this awareness of the possibility of 'exit' (opting out) and willingness to exercise it in the knowledge that one could obtain work elsewhere gave added backbone and force to workers' 'voice' (interest articulation).[21]

For these reasons, factory managers and functionaries were wary of disrupting the material status-quo. As several BPO secretaries explained at a party meeting in 1953: 'In our factory this issue seemed for us a hot potato that we did not want to touch'.[22] Indeed, there was a general tendency for functionaries to talk with workers only when things were going well; no one wanted to be the bearer of bad tidings. As a *Kreisleitung* functionary at Schwarze Pumpe put it: 'When there's something in the pay-packet one can talk with the miners, otherwise one has to stay away from them'.[23]

The combined result of this 'hidden bargaining' at the factory level was a continually worsening distortion of official wage and norm structures. Whereas the average norm fulfillment in the VEBs in 1956 stood at 136 per cent, with around 3 per cent of workers overfulfulling by 200 per cent, by 1961 these figures had climbed to 160 per cent and 15 per cent, respectively. The tendency towards wage-drift was also clear in the decreasing proportion of tarif wages to overall wages (Table 8.1).

As Table 8.1 suggests, there were significant variations in different branches of industry. The preconditions for 'norm deals' were more favourable in machine-building and metal-working, which involved countless different work processes, than in, for example, coal-mining, where quantification of individuals' performance was relatively straightforward. This was the main reason why coal miners' earnings gradually sank below that of workers in the metal and chemical industries during the 1950s, not surprisingly prompting demands in the pits for 'wage corrections' by the latter half of the decade.[24] There were also significant differences within individual

Table 8.1 Percentage of tarif wages as part of overall wages, 1952 and 1958

Year	1952 (%)	1958 (%)
Mining and metallurgy	83	66.80
Heavy machine-building	77	58.90
General machine-building	77	58.30
Electrical engineering	77	63.20

Source: BAB SPK E-1, Nr. 13480, bl. 4, in P. Hübner (1995), *Konsens*, p. 66.

enterprises. The possibilities of informal wage bargaining depended on a number of factors, not least the personal relations between management, *Meister*, and brigadiers, who quite often acted as spokespersons for groups of workers. Hence it was not at all uncommon for brigades doing the same work to be paid differently.[25]

These were the kinds of problems facing the SED's practical attempts during the 1950s to raise productivity and discipline in the factories. But diligence and productivity at work was not the only expectation placed on East German workers, and sources of friction were by no means limited to material issues. The related ideological attempt to transform them into 'socialist personalities' and 'win them over' to the SED's cause also demanded active 'sociopolitical' participation. These efforts fared little better, and workers' indifference towards the regime's various overtures for participation remained a constant source of frustration for party officials.

As we have seen, this disinterest was clearly manifested in the consistently low turnout at factory assemblies, party and union meetings. It was also reflected in the level of discussion even among those who attended. More often than not, such meetings became completely bogged down in everyday complaints. Even during the turbulent autumn of 1956, one local party secretary in Berlin-Köpenick summed up his impression of the 'political discussions' in the factories as follows (and probably not without some opening beautification):

Our press is eagerly read and people are paying attention to our argumentation. The positive discussions are prevailing. However, time and again they end with our own circumstances, whereby questions of production, difficulties regarding raw materials, problems with the provision of goods, the bonus system, the abolition of ration cards, the pension question and sectarian attitudes towards the intelligentsia take up the majority of the discussion.[26]

Workers' disinclination towards the regime's efforts at mobilization and 'education' was also manifested in a number of other ways, including switching off political broadcasts at one's workplace, demonstrative coughing during political presentations, refusals to sign resolutions endorsing specific domestic or foreign policies, to participate in the various competitions or 'movements', to join the East German armed forces, to volunteer for a stint of work in the countryside or to make contributions in support of striking workers in capitalist countries.[27]

Of course most workers were not completely indifferent to 'politics', and there were innumerable minor acts of more explicitly political protest in the factories. But it is symptomatic of popular protest in general in the GDR that criticism at factory assemblies and other public gatherings was generally limited to economic grievances, whereas most, though not all, expressions of specifically political dissent were anonymous. The most common forms of the latter were the daubing of 'enemy slogans', swastikas or other critical graffiti on factory walls, bathroom stalls or in public places, defacing political posters or inventing clever witticisms, neologisms and even subversive secret greetings such as 'SALEM' (*Soldaten Aller Länder Erstürmen Moskau*) or 'KONSUM' (*Keine Oder-Neisse, Sondern Unsere Memel*).[28] Popular graffiti themes included demands for democratic elections, the dissolution of the government, the ousting of the Soviets and unification with the West. However open and incessant were material complaints, there was little willingness for explicit political protest on the shopfloor.

Refusals to discuss political issues in a public forum did not, therefore, necessarily reflect a lack of interest. Silence or reservation was often more a manifestation of caution than apathy, of the desire to avoid making comments that might lead to trouble. Although the *Stasi* was not yet as present in the factories during the 1950s as in later decades, the fear of exposing oneself to the possibility of arrest should not be underestimated. And although workers generally showed more willingness to speak openly in assemblies dedicated specifically to production issues, even this was limited by the widespread impression that making suggestions did not change things anyway. As one worker in Potsdam complained: 'Once again there is a little Heine up there at the controls and everyone has to dance to his flute. But no one listens to the opinions of workers...'[29]

One of the most vivid illustrations of the array of material and political obstacles facing the SED's efforts to mobilize industrial workers was the highly-publicized campaign for 'brigades of social-ist work' in 1958–60.[30] As a 'higher form' of collective organization, the 'brigades of socialist work' were supposed to offer a more suit-able framework for the development of the 'new *Mensch*' than the production brigades introduced in 1950. What made the 'brigades of socialist work' qualitatively different from their forerunners were their educational functions outside the realm of work – not just '*sozialistisch zu arbeiten*', but also '*sozialistisch zu leben und zu lernen*'. Even the families of members were to be involved in the life of the brigade, which might include weekend trips, recreational activities, sporting events, and the like.

By far the greatest hindrance to the movement was this new emphasis on one's behaviour and activities away from the factory. It was one thing to declare oneself willing to be more efficient or diligent at work, but it was quite another to play the role of up-standing 'socialist worker' at home as well. Even among groups of workers favourably inclined to joining a 'brigade of socialist work', few had any idea what 'socialist living' would entail. As one report put it: 'It appears that the call "*sozialistisch lernen und leben*" (es-pecially *leben*) presents greater problems than the call "*sozialistisch arbeiten*"'.[31] Among younger workers in particular, comments such as 'do we have to become a socialist brigade? We can fulfil our economic tasks and arrange our private lives however we like!' were reported time and again. Women workers in Berlin often asked about shopping in the West: 'They say that if one forbids them to do this, they would not work in a socialist brigade'.[32] Some religious workers refused to join because they feared that their religious ac-tivities would be curtailed, above all that their children would have to undergo the secular *Jugendweihe*; a number went so far as to declare that 'joining a brigade of socialist work is a profession of atheism'. Even SED members by and large refused to join because 'there would be too many stipulations for one's personal life and they therefore feel hindered in their personal matters'.[33]

It did not take long, however, to overcome these knee-jerk reac-tions and find workers willing to join. By the end of 1959 there were officially 59 324 'brigades of socialist work' with 706 657 mem-bers; by the end of 1960 the number had risen to 130 024 brigades with 1 669 208 members (though, it should be noted, only a small minority made concrete obligations to increase production).[34] But once they were founded, the 'brigades of socialist work' hardly func-tioned as the models of politically-conscious behaviour they were intended to be. The prescribed sociability embodied in the phrase *'sozialistisch leben'* indeed became a source of fun and an important social network for many East German workers, but this was because brigade members by and large 'privatized' it for themselves. The 'brigade evenings', though popular, were in practice little more than traditional *Stammtische*, and attempts to instrumentalize such social gatherings were often utterly futile. In other words, the price for this 'success' of the brigade movement was its degeneration quite literally into a kind of *'Biertischsozialismus'*. As one brigadier in the Brandenburg steel works exclaimed: 'If there is going to be a political talk and I have to pay for my own beer, I'm not coming!'[35]

This understandable disinterest of most workers for the ideological aspects of the socialist brigades did not, however, keep them from trying to use the brigades to their own advantage. There was a variety of motives for joining or founding such a brigade, above all the opportunities they presented for the collective articulation of material interests to factory managers and weakening the power of the *Meister* on the shopfloor. Another important motive that has generally been overlooked was the prospect of improving work organization, of being able to 'work properly' for once. As we will see below, the constant disorganization and problems with supply was a major factor behind the flight of skilled labourers to the West. Many of the socialist brigades, at least the more 'engaged' ones, agreed with the party leadership's arguments about the necessity of improving productivity in relation to pay, but at the same time realized that much of the problem lay in poor organization and supply, which workers tended to blame on managers instead of the planned economy as a whole. The attempts of the socialist brigades to take on various competences in the factories such as establishing their own plan figures, determining their own norms, calculating and administering the payment of bonuses, procuring supplies, even making their own decisions regarding vacation, hiring, firing and transferring workers[36] reflected not just a desire to squeeze out more factory resources for themselves, but also to create the necessary preconditions for 'working properly'. Thus the degree to which the brigades succeeded in pushing through these demands for greater autonomy and participation in the factory decision-making process can in some ways be interpreted as the *success* of the campaign at mobilizing workers to improve productivity and work discipline,[37] though even here there was little 'active' political support for the regime.

The problem, of course, was that from the perspective of the union and party leadership this degree of autonomy went too far, and threatened to hollow-out the hegemony in the factories that had so arduously been constructed over the previous decade or so. The anti-'syndicalism' campaign of 1960 (as the tendency towards self-regulation by the brigades was incriminatingly called) was clearly a reaction to what the leadership viewed as a threat to its power in the factories, a breach of the principle of democratic centralism.[38] The result of the crackdown was widespread disappointment and anger on the shopfloor, quite literally the 'demobilization' of industrial workers into the defensive position of refusing incursions 'from above' that characterized the atmosphere in the factores for most of the 1950s and indeed for most of the rest of the GDR's history.[39] Though a considerable portion of the industrial workforce was, for a short while, nominally engaged out of the sullen apathy that characterized the atmosphere after the experience of June 1953, the party leadership forced workers back into it again.

As the case of the socialist brigades makes particularly clear, to characterize the behaviour of most industrial workers as *'Eigen-Sinn'* is insufficient as an explanation. While this concept neatly captures the dynamics of 'passive loyalty' on the shopfloor in exchange for social concessions, it overlooks the important connections between the micro-milieu and the system as a whole, in particular the crucial absence of collective action beyond small groups. After all, *'Eigen-Sinn'* and 'interest' exist in every society. The problem in the GDR was that workers were deprived of any large-scale independent institutional framework for interest representation, and were thus effectively excluded from formal negotiating. The only weapons left to them were small acts of non-conformity and informal mechanisms of asserting interest, the 'weapons of the weak'.[40] Much the same can be said of other social groups ranging from farmers to self-employed artisans and shopkeepers.

It is crucial to recognize that this attenuated brand of local social autonomy, though problematic, was not an immediate threat to the regime. On the contrary, if anything it contributed to its stability by channeling material frictions in the factories into less politically explosive directions. Yet it is also important to recognize that these countless small acts of self-interest on the shopfloor – the sick days, slow-downs, refusals to participate in production competitions, etc. – were nonetheless both politically and economically important. For their sum total was not only a discrediting of the SED's self-stylization as a party that represented workers' interests, but also an ever-inflating wage-bill and insufficient productivity gains, a gradual 'chipping away at the state'[41] that the regime was unable or unwilling to change at the factory level, at least as long as the border was open.

9

The Villages from Stalemate to Collectivization

Although few farmers participated in the demonstrations of 17 June, the mood in the villages was in many ways more agitated and the signs of discontent more long-lasting than in the factories. The party leadership had deeply alienated most peasants in 1952–53 with its harshly punitive taxes, increased delivery quotas and arrests of struggling farmers, and was well-advised to soften its course. Though collectivization remained the central feature of agricultural policy during the following years, it was pursued after 1953 in a milder manner via various tax and price incentives along with certain disadvantages in terms of access to machinery, all designed to make individual farming less attractive. Even so, this softer course still won the SED few friends in the countryside throughout the 1950s, and the LPGs by and large remained a kind of 'Notgemeinschaft' of weak farmers whose poor economic performance rendered them unattractive to most independent peasants. Over the years it became increasingly clear that a fully collectivized agricultural economy could only be achieved through an all-out assault on individual farming. But as it turned out, even the fully collectivized 'socialist village' was still only a hybrid of the SED's aims, farmers' interests and the older 'village milieu'.

The 'coercive economy': material discontent and popular opinion in the countryside

It seems fairly safe to say that East German farmers were even more dissatisfied with life in the GDR than industrial workers. While angry and grumbling farmers were neither anything new in German history nor confined to the eastern side of the inner-German border, the discontent in the East German countryside of the 1950s was widespread and deep-seated indeed. Much of it was economically based. East German farmers in the 1950s had long been accustomed to a tightly regulated agricultural economy. Under the Nazis they had been forced to render fixed surpluses to the state, and during the Soviet occupation they were forced to turn over fixed quotas of specific goods. But even after decades of chafing against the 'coercive' German agricultural economy, many independent East German farmers in the 1950s still found the SED's punitive policies towards uncollectivized farms intolerable, above all the despised delivery quotas. A police report summed it up thus: '. . . all of the laws and measures of our government run up against a complete lack of understanding among the farmers. Again and again they talk effusively about the free market economy in West Germany. The reports also show that our state organs have almost no connection to the farmers and completely neglect their educational work (*Aufklärungsarbeit*)'.[1]

Clearly, the notion that the GDR system of compulsory delivery was 'accepted by most farmers' because it 'guaranteed purchases of produce, privileged small and mid-sized enterprises and thereby entailed elements of social security'[2] is overstretched, at least apart from a minority of weak small-scale farmers. Rather, in the words of a farmer from Walchow, *Kreis* Neuruppin, the problem in a nutshell was that 'it simply is not good here agriculturally . . . The most capable farmers leave because the compulsory delivery quota is too high and the prices too low. Anyone who cannot sell *freie Spitzen* cannot make ends meet'.[3] Farmers adopted different strategies of trying to have their delivery quotas and arrears reduced. One strategy was simply to refuse to pay them, which was not altogether uncommon when quotas or debts were arbitrarily reduced in neighbouring *Kreise*.[4] Another was to hide a portion of one's produce and sell it privately on the black market, often in collusion with state buyers in the VEABs (*Volkseigene Erfassungs- und Aufkaufsbetriebe*, or state registration and buying agencies).[5] There is of course no way of ascertaining how many farmers did this, as only an unknown percentage were ever caught. Certainly the practice was extremely widespread during the black-market years immediately following the war, and judging from the reports during the 1950s it seems safe to assume that the practice was still fairly common.

There were numerous other focal points of economic complaint, including soil classification (according to which delivery quotas were set), problems with the supply of feed, seed and fertilizer (which one police report admitted sometimes made farmers' work 'downright impossible') as well as the very designation of farmers with over 20 hectares of land as *'Großbauern'*.[6] But apart from the quotas, the greatest source of complaint was the dire labour shortage in agriculture. This was particularly burdensome for mid-sized and large-scale independent farmers with younger children, many of whom simply could not fulfil their delivery quotas – much less produce any lucrative *freie Spitzen* – without additional help, which was often unavailable. Enterprises under 10 hectares had certain advantages in the context of the labour shortage and the SED's discriminatory policies against larger farms. Their smaller size not only had the advantage of lower taxes and delivery quotas, but also of allowing one or two members of the family to work outside of the family farm and thereby receive ration cards as dependent providers. Owners of mid-sized farms without sufficient help could neither find the time to work elsewhere nor easily keep up with the high taxes and delivery quotas. This was precisely the problem for Lieselotte F., who, like hundreds of other farmers in a similar position, wrote a formal petition to President Pieck in the hope of mitigating her plight. As she explained in her letter, those farms 'with the bad fortune of being larger' than 10 hectares were 'poorer than ever before'.[7] Working alone, she and her husband eventually had to consider joining an LPG to keep the farm solvent, but found that it was nearly impossible to get accepted without a sufficient contribution of labour to accompany the land. Her petition, like so many others, represented a last-ditch effort to keep the farm viable.

The SED did try to mitigate the labour shortage by recruiting industrial workers for agricultural service. The campaign 'industrial workers into the countryside' (*Industriearbeiter aufs Land*) began in earnest in 1954, and by 1955 had managed to bring some 16 000 workers into the agricultural sector, at least for a short while. It was hard enough getting volunteers to go: most workers argued that they were too old, knew nothing about agriculture or could not be separated from their families. But even when workers were deployed in the villages, problems with inadequate accommodation, poor food and low pay prompted many to return home as soon as possible. In many cases they were also rejected by villagers as intruders, especially party enthusiasts who also went around the villages as political agitators. And in any event, these additional labourers were of no help at all to independent farmers, since they were deployed only on collective farms, state-owned estates and MTS.[8]

Farmers were well aware that the SED's policies of militarization and concentrated investment in heavy industry only exacerbated the agricultural labour shortage. For one thing, the opportunity to escape the boredom of the village and see something new drew a disproportionately large number of rural youth into the KVP and NVA. This prompted widespread peasant resentment. As under the Nazis, the armed forces were widely viewed as a waste of state resources more profitably invested in agricultural machinery and a waste of young men's energies more usefully deployed on undermanned farms. There were numerous cases of farmers, even SED members, refusing to allow their sons to enlist.[9] Moreover, the better pay and shorter working hours in industry that attracted increasing numbers of rural youths and farmworkers into the cities were also broadly resented. Here the interests of East German industrial workers and farmers were at odds, and the latter overwhelmingly felt that they were losing out.[10] The introduction of the 45-hour week in several branches of industry in 1956 triggered widespread demands for increased wages and reduced working-hours for farmers as well: 'No one thinks of us farmworkers. The industrial workers who already have it easier anyway now only need to work 45 hours per week to get the same pay they used to get for 48 hours. We, on the other hand, have to work 60 hours and more and under more difficult conditions than in industry'.[11]

Instead of strengthening the heralded 'alliance of workers and farmers', the SED's own economic policies were rather serving to undermine it. Decades-old peasant feelings of having to 'shoulder the burden', of being exploited for the benefit of the urban masses, continued throughout the 1950s, sustained not only by memories of the hoardes of hungry urban pilferers roaming the countryside during the latter 1940s, but also by a deep-seated dislike towards the 'coercive' planned economy that kept down prices for their produce.

This economic discontent could not help but have a bearing on more specifically political attitudes. As was also the case with the complaints and grumbling among industrial workers, it is difficult to separate the two. The broad definition of political dissent adopted by the SED, which included such time-honoured farming practices as venting spleen on whatever government was in place, makes distinguishing them on the basis of internal reports rather problematic. Yet at the same time, it seems unnecessary to do so since the vast majority of East German farmers did not separate economic grumbling from political dissent themselves. A party report of September 1954 cited the remark of one farmer in Brandenburg as typical of the mood in the countryside at the time: 'I shit on the entire government. We farmers used to live better. Today they take everything away from us and we are forced to shop in the HO . . .'[12]

Fortunately for the SED, such hostility did not form the basis of any organized rural opposition during the 1950s. Although the reports give the impression that farmers were generally more forthcoming than industrial workers in *expressing* their discontent with the regime as such, the general rule that protest of all kinds tended to be fragmented and basically ineffective applies to them as well. If anything, given the deep divisions in the villages, rural protest was even more fragmented, which partially explains why the internal reports seem less concerned about its possible ramifications than about the prospect of industrial protest. After the collectivization push of 1952–53, most farmers simply contented themselves with heaping verbal abuse on the government and party leadership while trying – generally as individuals – to get their delivery quotas reduced however they could. The idea that the SED leadership had to find measures to counter a 'rebellion of the Green Front' during the 1950s would therefore appear to be a gross exaggeration.[13]

Yet the problems confronting the SED's attempt to 'win over' farmers to the socialist cause and mobilize them via 'socio-political' participation were, if anything, even more daunting than in the industrial sphere. This was most clearly visible at election time. Internal reports during the 1954 and 1958 elections complain that most farmers felt ignored, like second-class citizens, and for this reason saw no reason to participate in political life. In the reported words of one despairing farmer from Königs Wusterhausen, 'what use is it to go to the elections? They don't change the question of the delivery quotas!'[14] The result of such feelings of powerlessness was a profound political apathy that was manifested in the extremely poor attendance figures at election assemblies in most rural areas. Many farmers refused to vote because it would be tantamount to a statement of support for the LPGs. As one group of farmers succinctly put it in 1954: 'One cannot vote for one's own dispossession.'[15] What the bulk of independent farmers still feared and hated most was the prospect of expropriation of their farms. Although there were occasional signs of principled political criticism from farming circles such as demands for separate election lists, a government that represented farmers' interests and the introduction of a free-market economy, the political attitudes of independent farmers were characterized for the most part by a self-defensive hostility towards the SED and a stubbornly conservative, phlegmatic indifference to most other issues not directly related to their farming interests. There was remarkably little change in this regard over the previous several decades. The comments of a group of farmers near Potsdam in 1954, which can serve here as an illustration of a broad swathe of peasant opinion across the GDR during the 1950s, could just as easily have originated from reports under the Weimar or Nazi governments: 'We shit on the elections. We don't care who governs here – it can just as well be the Kaiser – the main thing is that things go well for us'.[16]

The coercive state: forced collectivization, 1958–60

Against the backdrop of such stubborn self-interest, it is perhaps somewhat surprising that the more subtle pressure for collectivization after June 1953 managed to achieve what it did. By the end of 1954 the number of LPGs in the GDR had already surpassed that of summer 1953, rising slowly and steadily throughout the 1950s and accounting for 37 per cent of all arable land by 1958. But this did not satisfy the SED leadership, and by the end of the 1950s patience was running out. It seemed that the combination of discriminatory economic pressure against independent farmers and privileges for collective farms had reached the limits of its effectiveness. So long as farmers were left to join LPGs 'voluntarily', further substantial growth in the collective sector seemed unlikely. The poor economic performance of most LPGs only confirmed this general aversion to collective farming. As late as 1959, 14 per cent of the LPGs in *Bezirk* Neubrandenburg still produced no profits of their own, surviving instead solely on state subventions. Moreover, even when LPGs managed to achieve profits, the incomes of their members rarely exceeded DM 5000 per annum. Under these circumstances it was impossible to attract economically strong farmers, some of whom earned over DM 20 000.[17] Despite assurances of differentiated remuneration within the LPGs according to the amount and quality of land contributed, wealthier farmers still had to reckon with a substantial decrease in income that the vacation provision and child-care facilities of the LPG system could not fully offset. The prospect was simply not alluring. If 'socialist relations of production' were to prevail in the countryside, only one solution remained: the exertion of greater pressure. The switch to a harder line began in 1957, after the supporters of a softer agricultural policy – most notably the Director of the Academy for Agriculture Kurt Vieweg and *Politbüro* member Fred Oelßner – had been purged in the wake of the Hungarian upheavals. The change of tack was confirmed at the Fifth Party Convention in July 1958, where the newly sanitized SED leadership publicly declared its aim of completing the socialist transformation of agriculture. These announcements, along with the dispatching of hundreds of agitation troops into the East German countryside, managed to persuade a significant wave of farmers to join LPGs in the summer of 1958, largely because of rumours of an impending forced collectivization and fears of having to join later under less attractive terms.[18]

Although the 'principle of voluntarism' was still putatively adhered to, there were numerous abuses by local officials eager to impress their superiors. In the coal areas of *Bezirk* Cottbus, for instance, there were attempts to get miners possessing small plots of land to join LPGs by making their jobs contingent upon a 'positive' response.[19] In other areas local officials refused to sell even the simplest of equipment and supplies such as plowshares or seed to independent farmers. The use of agricultural equipment in particular became an increasingly powerful weapon. The MTS had long received all new machinery and spare parts, thus making independent farmers, who were not able to buy their own equipment, increasingly dependent on them. The June 1958 Council of Ministers decree on the expansion of the MTS effectively sharpened the already discriminatory policies against independent farmers regarding access to machinery, spare parts and the level of rental fees. Whereas 64 per cent of the total deployment of MTS machinery in 1955 was on LPGs, in 1958–59 this figure quickly rose to between 80–90 per cent. At the same time, farmers were also required in 1958 to have their own equipment inspected by the police, which in many cases resulted in arbitrary confiscation. The rather predictable consequence was a wave of organized smuggling rings stealing parts from MTS or from scrap heaps and selling them to independent farmers.[20] As Erich Mückenberger complained to the regional party secretaries, 'Such measures achieve precisely the opposite of what is intended. The independent farmers feel pressured and stir up the entire village against the collective movement and against the local party leadership'.[21]

The thought of even greater difficulties in procuring equipment was itself enough to drive some farmers, such as Herr S. of Steinbach, *Kreis* Seelow, into a LPG in the summer of 1958: 'I entered the LPG because the Fifth Party Conference will probably decide that the MTS can no longer work with independent farmers'.[22] But most were still unmoved. Fairly typical of the attitude among self-employed farmers was that of Herr F. of Dobberzin, *Kreis* Angermünde: 'They should come around here once, my cudgel is constantly at the ready. I'd rather cut my grain with a scythe than join an LPG'.[23] Which is precisely what some did. In a number of villages farmers tried to solve the equipment problem by establishing what one report called 'certain forms of mutual assistance', which generally entailed coordinating the use of privately-owned machinery among a group of independent farmers, sometimes on a village-wide basis. In cases where privately-owned machinery was still insufficient, determined LPG opponents even organized brigades to cut grass and grain with hand-held scythes. In Glienecke, *Kreis* Beeskow, even the village pastor was enlisted in the local scything operation.[24]

Yet such instances of solidarity remained local. There was no organizational framework for broader collective action against the sharpened regulations, and the increased pressure in 1958 was producing dividends for the SED. By the end of the year the total number of LPGs in East Germany had risen from 6691 to 9637, an increase of over 40 per cent, with most of the new foundings occurring in the second half of the year.[25] But this second push in the drive to full collectivization soon reached the limits of its effectiveness as well, as the number of LPGs once again levelled off during 1959. By the end of that year the collective sector could boast only just over 800 new LPGs, with a total number of only 10 465 – a meagre rate of increase compared to 1958. What is more, it seems that some of the 'success' of 1958 was the result of fudged figures: functionaries in *Bezirk* Frankfurt/Oder were even putting VEG land into LPGs in order to pad out their statistics.[26] The slower pace of LPG formation also had to do with widespread, albeit vain, hopes that the agitation for collective farming in summer and autumn 1959 was merely window dressing for the upcoming tenth anniversary of the GDR in October. Official celebrations in East Germany were always preceded by the deployment of agitation troops seeking 'positive' statements, declarations of loyalty and other forms of approval as grist for the propaganda mill. According to some reports, this was a central focus of 'many discussions' with independent farmers: 'resist the temptation to give in to the SED offensive, the tenth anniversary will soon be over and then we will be left in peace'.[27]

The only solution for the SED was to increase the pressure on the remaining independent farmers yet again. In autumn 1959 swarms of agitators were dispatched into the countryside, armed with a new, more uncompromising message. Joining an LPG had always been presented as a contribution to the strengthening of the peace-loving GDR. Now the emphasis was placed on the logical correlate of this assertion: namely, that refusal to join was tantamount to an act of sabotage against the East German state. This new, more aggressive line of argumentation was given teeth by the Council of Ministers decree of 29 October 1959, which authorized the arrest and detention of farmers for precisely such forms of 'sabotage'. Any illusions about a softer course after the tenth anniversary quickly dissipated. In the first three months of 1960, the villages were literally overwhelmed by the sheer numbers of agitation brigades and the *Stasi* arrested scores of farmers on the basis of the Council of Ministers decree.

What did this agitation and pressure in the villages look like more concretely? What role did the local officials and functionaries play and why was the campaign more successful than in 1952–53? While there were still plenty of passive and unreliable representatives of the regime at the grass-roots, the establishment of party-controlled agricultural training colleges throughout the mid-1950s and the constant replacement of older officials by new cadre meant this was somewhat less of a problem than during the first collectivization push. Party members from the towns and cities were also deployed – like the Soviet '25 000ers' of the early 1930s – in far greater number to assist in this second collectivization drive should the rural apparatus prove untrustworthy to carry out the new measures. Moreover, the kind of pressure that was exerted was more economically severe, more individualized and more threatening than before. Despite official claims that joining an LPG was still voluntary, it is clear from internal reports that some overzealous local officials made use of the threat of arrest and punishment as a means of 'persuading' farmers to join. In most such cases it was not so much a matter of threatening to haul someone in on trumped-up charges as it was to convict them on some previous offence: usually tax debts, failure to fulfil a quota, or other forms of so-called 'sabotage'. As the state attorney's office in Cottbus explained to the SED *Bezirksleitung*: 'in the *Kreise* we visited, Forst, Luckau, Lübben and Herzberg, there was a tendency among the local councils to use the cooperation of the local state attorney in order to achieve a stronger effect in discussions with farmers with delivery debts ... With this method the farmers must have been under the impression that they either had to join a LPG or reckon with criminal proceedings'.[28]

Such was the case of Herr Winzer, for instance, who was summoned to appear at the state attorney's office in Forst to discuss his delivery debts. Upon arrival, Winzer was told he was punishable by law for his debts and should reckon with prosecution. Not surprisingly, when urged by the local council to join a LPG he immediately did so because, as the report put it, 'there was nothing left for him to do'. Initial proceedings against him were stopped the day after he officially became a LPG member.

Such incidents of coercion were by no means rare, though in some *Kreise* it was clearly more common than in others. Whereas the local state attorney and party leadership in *Kreis* Finsterwalde had early on decided against such tactics, there were reports of similar cases in other *Kreise*. In fact, the state attorney's report goes on to complain that instances of criminal proceedings being quashed upon joining a LPG were so well known in the villages that many farmers were actually under the impression that punishable offences were simply not pursued if they did so. In Spremberg, one farmer who had illegally withheld 50 kilograms of butter took the bargaining initiative himself by informing the local state's attorney that he would join a LPG if the proceedings against him were stopped.[29] While it is true that such overt threats were unnecessary in most cases and that a mere 'discussion' with a farmer often sufficed to convince him/her to join, this does not mean that pressure by the state authorities was not being exerted. The vast majority of those who had not been personally threatened knew or had at least heard of others who had been, and many deduced that there was little point in resisting. Indeed, the repeated appearance of a *Volkspolizei* car in the village – or even worse, a black Soviet-made sedan from the local MfS office – was itself enough to persuade some farmers to join an LPG.[30] For most others, the loudspeaker-vans that occasionally drove through the villages verbally pillorying recalcitrant individuals and 'reminding them of their delivery debts' was more than enough to drive the message home.[31]

As village after village was reported as *'vollgenossenschaftlich'*, or completely collectivized, agitation troops increasingly turned their attention to the remaining problem spots (*Schwerpunkte*) within their jurisdictions (often those villages that had witnessed little change as a result of the land reform), sometimes having to go to extraordinary lengths to 'persuade' these most steadfast LPG opponents. The agitation campaign in *Kreis* Senftenberg, which stood at the bottom of the table in *Bezirk* Cottbus, may serve as an example of the massive scale of the operation in these more problematic areas. After 'severe criticism' from the *Bezirksleitung*, the local party secretary self-critically conceded that the 'older methods' of dispatching brigades comprising three to five agitators were clearly no longer appropriate for the task at hand.[32] The 'great deployment' had failed to achieve a correspondingly 'great success', not least because it was almost impossible to persuade the many *'Kumpelbauern'* in the area (village miners who maintained small plots on the side) to swap their well-paid mining jobs for poorly-paid farming ones despite occasional threats of dismissal if they refused to join.[33] In reviewing their collectivization strategy, the *Kreisleitung* therefore decided to use the proven methods of the 'comrades in *Kreis* Eilenburg'.[34] This entailed no great revision to the overall approach of pressure and threats, but consisted rather of expanding the operation beyond the small three- to five-member brigades into ten brigades each comprising 40 to 50 agitators recruited from the ranks of the police, state institutions, factory managers and representatives of mass organizations. According to a follow-up report the number of brigades in *Kreis* Senftenberg eventually reached 11, with 'a few more' in the making by the beginning of March.[35] It was deemed important that these inflated brigades thenceforth be led by 'experienced comrades'. Indeed, the entire *Kreisleitung*, with the single exception of the secretary for economic matters, were 'out in the villages' during February and March; the first secretary himself led a brigade in Bühlen. In order to hinder the growth of any form of solidarity among aggrieved farmers, the brigades also began spending the night in villages in order to have 'constant contact and uninterrupted influence' on the local inhabitants. In response to reports from other areas about the 'consolidation of enemy forces' after the departure of the agitation brigades, they eventually began leaving two or three agitators behind in newly collectivized villages for the purpose of 'consolidating' the fledgling LPGs.[36]

The immense deployment in *Kreis* Senftenberg of some 500 of the 'best and most experienced comrades' in the agitation brigades quickly paid off. By 25 March the *Kreis* was proudly declared '*vollgenossenschaftlich*' apart from a few isolated farms. But besides making a mockery of the putative 'principle of voluntarism', the massive scale of the agitation campaign also clearly reveals the stubborn opposition of many independent farmers against collectivization. According to official census statistics, there were a total of 3531 farmers in *Kreis* Senftenberg in 1964.[37] Even if we assume that this figure had dropped slightly since 1960, this means that there was a ratio of one agitator for every seven or eight farmers in the entire *Kreis* during February and March 1960. However, as around one-half of all farmers had already joined LPGs by the beginning of 1960, the ratio between agitators and the remaining independent farmers during these two months was actually closer to one for every four. Given the duration of this most acute phase of the collectivization campaign – around seven weeks – it is clear that the agitation brigades were able to visit recalcitrant farmers for considerable amounts of time and on many occasions. And given the looming threat of arrest for failure to comply, it only seems surprising that there was still a handful of independent farmers left as of 25 March. Granted, such a huge operation was not necessary in all *Kreise*. But the example of Senftenberg clearly illustrates the excessive pressure that the SED was prepared to exert, and did exert, in order to achieve the 'complete socialist transformation of agriculture'.

How did independent farmers react to this unprecedented onslaught? As in 1952–53, there were many different symptoms of protest and opposition. Most noticeable was the wave of emigration to the West (see Figure 9.1). In the first quarter of 1960, 1682 farmers (not including their families) left the GDR; in April alone the number was 1304.[38] There were various jokes and slogans pertaining to the flight of farmers westwards: 'We're founding an LPG Type IV, the farmers over there and the land here' (the slogan rhymes in German: 'Wir gründen eine LPG Typ IV, die Bauern drüben, der Boden hier').[39]

Throughout 1960 the *Volkspolizei* also regularly reported on what appears to have been an epidemic of 'criminal activity' in agriculture, although it is, again, difficult to determine how many of these supposed 'crimes' were intentional, let alone expressions of pro-

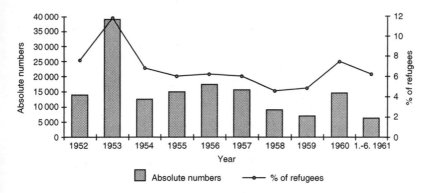

Figure 9.1 Emigration from the agricultural sector

Source: Bundesministerium für gesamtdeutsche Fragen (1961), *Die Flucht aus der Sowjetzone*, p. 17.

test. A *Volkspolizei* analysis of criminality during the first half of 1960 posits a marked increase in serious crimes in the countryside including arson, poisoning and neglecting livestock, sabotage against LPGs, 'diversion' of machinery and equipment, slandering the state, and rabble-rousing (*Staatsverleumdung, Hetze*).[40] Other signs of an 'increase in enemy activity' similarly recalled those of 1952–53: the spreading of rumours, physical attacks against agitators, anonymous threats, destroying propaganda posters and disrupting LPG founding assemblies. In the first half of March alone there were 41 cases of 'anti-democratic crimes' in the GDR directly connected to agricultural collectivization, and no fewer than 8 cases of suspected arson against LPGs totalling hundreds of thousands of Marks in damage.[41] Yet opposition on the whole tended to be passive, and despite the many parallels one might draw with the collectivization drive in the Soviet Union, there was nothing like the scale of violence, insurrection and destruction of property as in the desperate circumstances of 1930s rural Russia.[42]

Indeed, the unrelenting pressure and threat of sanctions or imprisonment resigned most farmers to their fate. In the words of one despondent farmer in *Kreis* Zerbst: 'one cannot swim against the current forever'.[43] By March there were even cases of farmers cheerlessly forming LPGs themselves without the 'assistance' of the dreaded agitation brigades. But in most cases, it should be noted, this was an angry resignation born out of frustration at one's own powerlessness. As one farmer in *Kreis* Weißwasser put it, 'don't think that things will remain like this. One day you [agitators] will pay for this'.[44]

The official view that joining an LPG was still voluntary was understandably a source of widespread righteous anger. At the LPG 'Einigkeit' in Reitwein, *Kreis* Seelow, the vast majority of farmers who had recently joined angrily insisted that they had been forced to do so and were under the impression that they 'would have been picked up by the police if they refused'. Like many other farmers across the GDR they demanded that the word 'voluntary' be stricken from the LPG statute and replaced with the words 'on the orders of the local council'. The attempt to win subscriptions for the VdgB magazine *'Der freie Bauer'* (the free farmer) only added insult to injury. In *Bezirk* Potsdam a 'large number' of farmers – in the village of Zootzen all but two – refused to buy it or cancelled their subscriptions with the argument that 'there are no free farmers anymore'.[45] Even local party functionaries voiced similar complaints. As comrade Pfeiffer from the village party executive in Stradow put it: 'I was forced into the LPG and they even hounded me with the *Volkspolizei'*.[46]

Though the right to withdraw one's membership was still formally upheld after the 'socialist spring' of 1960, the requisite 'march through the institutions' and unwillingness on the part of officials to accept resignations made it all but impossible in practice, as illustrated by the case of a group of farmers in Groß-Lubolz, *Kreis* Lübben, which was followed closely by farmers in neighbouring villages hoping to dissolve their LPGs. This village had long been considered a *'Schwerpunkt'* – many former NSDAP members; problems during June 1953, autumn 1956, and especially spring 1960.[47] By October 1960 nine LPG members had tendered their resignations with reference to point 27 of the LPG statute which maintained that 'withdrawal from the cooperative can only be effected through written declaration and after the end of the harvest'. The SED *Kreisleitung* immediately deployed a brigade to discuss the matter with them, but without any success. Since the farmers subsequently heard nothing from either the *Kreisleitung* or local council, four of them went on 3 December to discuss the issue at the Ministry for Agriculture and Forestry, where officials told them that it was a matter for the local council. Still nothing happened, so the four farmers went to the Agriculture Ministry again on 3 March 1961, where a different official told them that their resignation was in effect as of March since it had been handed in the previous August.[48] The resulting confusion finally prompted a larger meeting on 20 March including an official from the Agriculture Ministry, the local *Bürgermeister*, the chairman of the local council and the *Kreisleitung* secretary for agriculture. After reportedly 'hard' discussions, several of the farmers agreed at least to try working in the LPG before resigning. Three still refused to withdraw their resignations, and were eventually summoned for another discussion with the local council chairman, the first secretary of the party *Kreisleitung*, the local state's attorney, the local *Stasi* commander and several other officials. As the presence of the *Stasi* and state's attorney suggests, the aim of this last meeting was intimidation. The discussion with Herr Altkuhkalz reportedly began with the words: 'The highest offices of the district are represented here; you won't get out of here until you have signed an agreement that you will participate in the LPG'. After being 'worked over' from 8:00 until 11:30 a.m., Altkuhkalz refused to say any more 'for fear of making a slip of the tongue', whereupon the local council chairman Hofmann threatened him that 'if you do not want to talk any more, we can still get you to speak'. Similar 'discussions' were held with the farmer Kuschke and then Lindemann, who was simply told that the LPG would use his fields regardless of what he did.[49] Understandably, the local lawyer Rasmus who had supported the three farmers fled to the West soon afterwards.[50]

In view of both the responses of farmers as well as the heavy-handed tactics on the part of the regime, there seems precious little to recommend Siegfried Prokop's recent argument that 'from the Baltic to the Fichtelberg the vast majority of independent farmers declared themselves willing to join an LPG. The majority did this voluntarily. Others felt coerced and for a long time could not get over the fact that from now on they had to work on an equal footing with the former maid or farmhand'.[51] While many pre-viously self-employed farmers no doubt resented their loss of status, it is simply impossible to believe that the majority of the 450 000 farmers and their families who had withstood the pressure to col-lectivize for eight long years suddenly changed their minds in the spring of 1960. Moreover, despite Prokop's careful attempt to dis-cern those farmers who were not coerced in the sense of 'feeling' coerced,[52] there can be little doubt that the vast majority not only *were* coerced, at least indirectly, but also *felt* that way. There also seems little to recommend the idea that the party leadership was in some way absolved from responsibility for the many 'administrative excesses' on the ground because of its constant calls for moderation and admonishments to respect the principle of voluntarism.[53] As was also clearly the case in the Soviet Union, where Stalin mendaciously washed his hands of the activities of local party officials in his infamous 'Dizzy with Success' article, the reports streaming into the Central Committee unambiguously showed that collectivization simply could not be accomplished at the grass-roots without coercion, regardless of what the 'top' preached. At best such calls for moderation were a case of self-deception on the part of the party leadership, at worst a case of sheer hypocrisy.

'From paper into practice': continuity and change in the 'socialist village'

There is no doubt that coercion was necessary to transform the patterns of ownership in the villages of the GDR, and it was both the willingness as well as improved ability of the party leadership to exert it that produced the results. By the time the last East German village officially declared itself *vollgenossenschaftlich* on 14 April, only around 7 per cent of agricultural land in the GDR remained in private ownership. But the 'socialist transformation of agriculture' still existed for the most part on paper. As one report put it, proclaiming a village to be *vollgenossenschaftlich* was relatively easy; the hard part was to convert the LPGs 'from paper into practice'.[54] This process was by no means completed during the 'socialist spring' of 1960. Actual collectivization at the grass-roots entailed more than coercing farmers into signing LPG statutes. Furthermore, the SED had used so much force in reshaping East German rural society into its new mould of collective ownership that in the process the mould itself got bent out of shape. The rather distorted result was not precisely what the party leadership had envisioned.

Certainly the greatest problem was getting the new LPG farmers actually to farm collectively. Joining an LPG was, as we have just seen, often more a matter of resignation than a sign of willingness to adopt new farming practices. As one brigade report from *Bezirk* Cottbus succinctly put it, 'Among the farmers there is a great reluctance to begin working collectively'. The agitation brigades left behind in the villages for the purpose of 'consolidation' could do little to change this, plagued as they were by high rates of fluctuation, agitators being intimidated and too scared to discuss the LPGs with farmers, and more generally what one report described as an 'extremely low level of political-ideological education'.[55] As a party instructor deployed in *Bezirk* Cottbus lamented: 'The constant exchange of responsible comrades leads to no one being held responsible, not even leading functionaries... The authority of the [SED] *Kreisleitung* is insufficient. This is shown by the fact that out of the 90 comrades from the factories, mass organizations, etc. who were deployed in order to strengthen the brigades in the villages, only one-third appeared'.[56]

The weaknesses of the 'consolidation brigades' were further compounded by the continuing unreliability of local party and state organs in the villages, which the reports commonly castigated for 'passivity' towards the LPGs. Although the political education and selection of local officials had improved considerably since the first collectivization push of 1952–53, there was still significant potential for conflict between one's personal interests and professional duties in early 1960. In *Bezirk* Potsdam 17 of the 221 section directors in the district councils were still farmers, most of them directors of the agricultural sections involved in collectivizing.[57] As for the *Bürgermeister*, 90 of 776 were still farmers or their offspring, many not yet in LPGs by the end of 1959.[58] But this was only a small part of the problem, for many local officials, regardless of their social background, simply did not support the principle of collectivized agriculture, at least not wholeheartedly, and were especially repelled by the coercion that was involved. In many villages they made little effort towards formulating statutes or organizing collective methods of work after the initial agitation brigades had left. In the neighbouring villages of Cammer, Damelang and Freienthal, *Kreis* Belzig, ten days elapsed between the founding-assembly of the local LPG and the introduction of 'further measures'. This 'breathing space', according to party instructors deployed from Berlin, allowed an 'increase of enemy influence' in the villages, which was expressed in a growing number of complaints of coercion, demands for lower delivery quotas as well as 'various types of passive resistance' to the actual organization of the LPGs.[59]

Such 'passive resistance' continued for a remarkably long time. There are numerous reports throughout 1960 and 1961 of farmers continuing to work 'individually' (i.e. like they always had) under the guise of the LPGs and essentially refusing to abandon their old ways of work: 'We have not yet taken up collective work, and if one wants to push it through it will be with force and with poor results because there would be no personal interest . . .' It was widely hoped that the LPGs would soon be dissolved again, as they had been in Poland. In the village of Hohenleibisch, *Kreis* Liebenwerda, newly collectivized farmers were even laying stone border markers in the evenings in order 'to know immediately where things stand when the times change'.[60] In a number of villages in *Bezirk* Cottbus it was proving difficult merely to elect an executive board for the new LPG even months after officially becoming *'vollgenossenschaftlich'*. In Freiwalde, for instance, persistent threats against anyone who would attend an election assembly had made it impossible up until July 1960 for the local LPG to produce a member turnout of over 10 per cent despite trying five times since March. In Byhlen, where farmers were reportedly trying to bring in their first harvest as soon as possible so that the next harvest could also be done individually, the local LPG chairman's pressure for the organization of collective methods in the village resulted in little more than his barn being burned.[61] At the end of September 1960, it was estimated that some 290 LPGs in *Bezirk* Potsdam were working 'individually' (a figure which the regional council itself deemed too low); an investigation in *Kreis* Belzig found that only 20 of the 107 LPGs there were operating according to statutes.[62] This problem did not go away quickly; in summer 1961 there were still entire villages that had not even begun to work collectively.[63] Despite the formal 'completion of socialist relations of production' in the countryside, 'muddling through' and doing things like they were always done was still a viable alternative for many farmers, at least for a while.

The 'socialist spring' of 1960 did not, therefore, put an immediate end to individual farming practices. Even less did it signal an immediate end to the older social mentalities and values in the countryside that had plagued the land reform and first collectivization push. The social hierarchies in the countryside as they had emerged in the later 1940s proved remarkably tenacious, and in many villages *Großbauern* continued to dominate village life and advance their own interests under the changed circumstances. No longer in control of the VdgBs, but duly elected to the executive boards of many LPGs, it was from these new positions of authority that they commonly hindered the development of collective methods of farming and in some cases managed to maintain the traditional social and economic distinctions in the village. There were, for instance, numerous cases of new LPGs functioning essentially as exclusive *Großbauer* clubs denying membership to weaker farms. But even in villages where all the farmers belonged to a single LPG, the division between rich and poor, between bosses and farmhands, often remained intact. In the village of Wendemark, the traditional social hierarchy passed all but unscathed into the new collective structures. One LPG in the village was composed of only one 'reactionary' *Großbauer* and two small farmers, and in the words of a party report was run essentially as an 'estate' (*Gutsbetrieb*) under the big farmer's supervision. There were similar threads of social continuity reported at the LPG in Neulingen, where the wealthier and more influential members even set up a 'wage-fund' for day-labourers.[64]

To be fair, this continuity of village hierarchies was not merely attributable to the *Großbauern*. The reports clearly show that the social mentality of many small farmers and farmhands had also changed very little over the years. Some small farmers who performed seasonal work for their wealthier neighbours in exchange for using their machinery failed to see what the SED called the 'hidden exploitation' in this relationship, tending instead to perceive an advantage that they would lose upon joining an LPG. In fact, many had actually made their own entry into an LPG contingent upon that of the farmers for whom they occasionally worked. As one party official in Cottbus remarked, such attitudes of paternalism and village solidarity hindered the entry of some of the wealthier farmers who, because they were thus able to retain a sufficient supply of labour, had no pressing reason to join.[65] Simply put, the 'class struggle in the village' failed to materialize in many quarters.

In other quarters, however, the class struggle ran out of the SED's control. Only against this background of a continuing cleft between the 'haves' and 'have-nots' in the countryside does the resentment – 'sectarianism' in SED parlance – among many collective farmers towards the forced entry of the powerful *Großbauern* make sense. Although the wealthier farmers represented on the one hand a desirable economic boost to the struggling LPGs, on the other they also entailed a loss of influence for their long-standing members. Especially among LPG farmers who had contributed only small parcels of land there was a growing fear that 'we will now have to work more than before – we do not want to work for the *Großbauern*'.[66] In some villages this 'sectarianism' was based merely on practical considerations such as the filling of adminstrative positions by newcomers or the distribution of reserve funds among the old members.[67] In other villages, though, it took on more antagonistic forms. In Neukirchen, *Kreis* Seehausen, long-standing LPG members actually created a separate herd for the cows of newcomers to be kept on more sparsely grown meadows. Relations between the long-standing LPG Type III and the newly-formed Type I in Petershagen, *Kreis* Angermünde, were so poor that the Type I members had to cut their grain with hand-mowers and scythes because the Type III refused to loan them any machinery.[68]

Whether such hostility was simply a matter of economic self-interest, revenge for earlier poor treatment at the hands of established farmers or perhaps, ironically, due in part to the very success of the SED's propagandistic vilification of *Großbauern* no doubt varied from village to village, and can hardly be answered conclusively. But it is in any event clear that many collective farmers were no more enamoured with the consequences of forced collectivization than were their recently self-employed colleagues. And as for the latter, whose nagging fears of expropriation had now become reality, the experience of being coerced into a dreaded 'kolkhoz' engendered anything but a desire to help build socialism in the countryside. In summer 1961, over a year after the forced collectivization, the anger was still almost palpable at an assembly at the LPG Krachsheide, *Kreis* Beeskow: 'We don't want to hear the word socialism any more, leave us alone. Enough people have already cleared out (for the West), and there's still room for us'.[69] Though there may still have been room in the Federal Republic, by then there was precious little time left to get there.

10
Youth and the Threats to Socialism

As we have seen, 1953 was hardly a banner year in the history of the SED's campaign to win the support of the younger generation. The KVP recruitment campaign and the persecution of the *Junge Gemeinden* alienated tens of thousands of youths and led to an alarming loss of members from the FDJ. Although the party leadership acknowledged that its own zealous policies were themselves partly to blame for this sad state of affairs, and temporarily eased the pressure on the church youth groups and would-be recruits after summer 1953, it rather typically placed the lion's share of responsibility on the medium rather than the message – that is, on the failures of the FDJ to mobilize young people effectively. Granted, these failures were clear enough. The leadership's withering criticism of the FDJ in October 1953 offers an insight into the state of the organization at the time: unattractive to young people, its structures 'undemocratic' and many of its functionaries untenable.[1] Although such blunt criticism of the youth organization's work was rare after the shake-up of summer and autumn 1953, subsequent developments showed that it could in many ways just as easily pertain to 1955, 1958 or even 1961. For however the party leaders might try to improve the medium, its effectiveness could not but be constrained by the more or less unchanged message.

Despite the FDJ's overhaul after the setback of 1953, its actual effectiveness as 'transmission belt' between party and young people remained rather limited. Throughout the 1950s, the FDJ groups were still weak in many localities, the numbers involved in the *Junge Gemeinden* were holding steady (at least until the closing years of the decade), and it was still proving extremely difficult to persuade sufficient numbers of young men to join the armed forces, let alone convince them that West Germany was an enemy and military threat. In fact, the problems of mobilizing and gaining influence over the East German youth appeared to be growing only worse by the mid-1950s. The difficulties associated with recruiting 'volunteers' for the armed forces were, if anything, on the increase, and at the same time there was a growing fascination among East German youth for Western culture and fashion. Besides the pre-existing obstacles presented by the church, the widespread pacifist sentiments and the broad aversion to the strict discipline of military life, the Western youth subculture thus emerged in the mid- to latter-1950s as another perceived threat to the effectiveness of the FDJ at the grassroots, one more hindrance towards efforts to 'win over' and mobilize the next generation for the socialist cause.

Coercion, aversion and evasion: recruiting for the NVA

As in 1952, much of the party's concern revolved around the issue of armed defence. As the Cold War deepened and the opposing military alliances of East and West crystallized in the mid-1950s, the Soviets and SED leadership soon agreed that it was necessary to upgrade the GDR's military defences once again. Recruitment was the key area that needed improvement. After the curtailment of recruitment efforts in the wake of the events of June 1953, enlistment results had proven 'completely unsatisfactory'.[2] So in spring 1955, against the backdrop of an escalating arms race between the superpowers and West German entry into NATO, the SED Central Committee initiated a second recruitment push that lasted through to the official deployment of the *Nationale Volksarmee* (NVA) in December 1956.

In terms of its popular reception, the establishment of the NVA on 18 January 1956 was little different from that of the KVP in summer 1952. Despite the switch from Soviet-style to more traditional German uniforms, which one Western news report erroneously claimed had 'broken the ice' in relations between the NVA and East German populace,[3] it is clear that there was still widespread disapproval of an East German army. And despite occasional reports of support for the armed forces among older people who 'emphasize that it is high time that young people finally get some polishing up',[4] supporters of the armed forces were clearly in the minority. It would seem impossible to arrive at any reliable numerical figures on the level of popular support. For what it is worth, the Berlin regional union executive for local trade was prepared to hazard a guess that only around one-third of those in his constituency spoke out in favour of the NVA (some of whom were probably telling functionaries what they wanted to hear) whereas two-thirds were either 'unclear' or expressed 'arguments of the class enemy'.[5]

Insofar as there was any discernable change from previous years, it seems that concerns about German division and the threat of an inter-German war were significantly *more* prevalent during the 1955–56 recruitment push than in 1952–53. Although the KVP's official title as 'garrisoned police force' offered only the smallest fig-leaf for its army-like nature, and although most East Germans seemed well aware that this could only serve to deepen German division, the official establishment of the NVA as a competing army to the West German *Bundeswehr* nonetheless seems to have dispelled whatever residual illusions there still were about the consequences of opposing armed forces on chances for German unification. The result was a new sense of urgency to pacifist sentiments on both sides of the Cold War divide. 'We'll never shoot at our brothers in West Germany' was a common response in reports during 1955–56.[6]

In terms of recruitment techniques, the campaign of 1955–56 showed both certain continuities and significant changes from 1952–53. Although the mixture of promises and pressure was essentially retained, the balance tipped visibly towards the latter in 1955. Despite certain changes that had been made to the recruiting system at the end of 1953, the KVP was still unable to retain a sufficient supply of new troops. Because the cohort of soldiers who had joined during the 1952–53 campaign were coming to the end of their three-year period of service in 1955, it was estimated that the KVP/NVA faced a 50 per cent shortage in the number of troops in the mid-1950s.[7] The only solution was to increase the pressure. Recruitment targets were raised dramatically in some *Kreise*; one official who fled to the Federal Republic from Bad Doberan told West German interviewers that the local recruitment target was arbitrarily raised overnight from 20 to 200 'volunteers'.[8] Such rapid increases inevitably led to excesses on the part of recruiters, who sometimes resorted to such coercive techniques as threatening someone with the loss of his job, ordering young men to a recruitment office 'for a discussion' followed by delivering them directly to a NVA unit, or even, in a few cases, getting a group of young men drunk in order to deliver them to the NVA.[9]

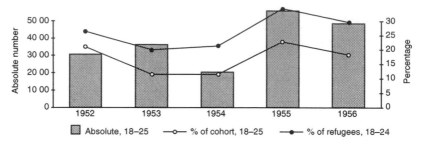

Figure 10.1 Emigration out of the GDR, males, aged 18–24/25

Sources: R. Wenzke (1994), 'Auf dem Weg', p. 265; H. Heidemeyer (1994), *Flucht und Zuwanderung*, p. 49.

As far as responses from would-be NVA soldiers were concerned, such crude tactics hardly won the armed forces many sympathetic supporters, as was reflected in part by the rising numbers of young male refugees to the West (see Figure 10.1). The party leadership was well aware of this, and sent admonitions to the *Bezirks-* and *Kreisleitungen* warning that the 'methods of pressure, of commandeering and administering . . . are not only unsuccessful, but on the contrary can cause serious damage'.[10] Indeed, complaints about the repulsiveness of the 'sledgehammer method', as many young men called it, led to the gradual adoption of more subtle 'nerve deadening' and 'attrition tactics', whereby recruiters would systematically pester young men, sometimes for weeks on end, in the hope that they would give in and enlist simply in order to be left alone.[11]

Of course none of these methods were very attractive to anyone subjected to them. A report from the Synthesewerk Schwarzheide illustrates how even the comparatively subtle 'nerve-deadening' tactics were often more repulsive than persuasive. As recruiters (to use their own words) 'systematically led discussions and exhausted all possibilities to win the youth for honourable duty' in the NVA, young workers openly declared to the NVA major in charge of the forum that it was not right that recruiters 'never leave them in peace at all' and constantly exert such 'full-blown pressure' to join. One youth was so exasperated that he swore he would join the *Bundeswehr* if not left in peace immediately.[12]

In many cases the exertion of such pressure merely resulted in insincere agreements to enlist. At the end of the 1950s there was a rising trend of young men not honouring their resolutions to join;

in 1960 this came to 15 per cent of all resolutions made.[13] As a report from Frankfurt/Oder explained, many youths made a resolution simply 'in order to escape the bothersome recruiters, then they rescind their resolution, change jobs, sometimes even move to another area in order to avoid further conversations with recruiters'.[14] There were even reports of youths temporarily leaving for the West with the intention to return simply in order to be considered unfit for NVA service 'for cadre-political reasons'.[15]

What happened when someone rescinded his resolution? While there was no legal obligation to honour them, recruitment commissions could threaten youths with any number of sanctions. The menacing letter sent by the local recruitment board in Cottbus to Wolfgang B. gives an idea of the kind of scare tactics that were sometimes used in order to pressure youths to abide by their agreements:

> After a number of discussions at your factory, you have refused to perform your honourable duty in the ranks of the NVA. Every citizen of our state must be a conscious fighter for peace and for the defence of our homeland ... Many citizens are organized, are comrades-in-arms for peace, unity and socialism. But you set yourself in a stubborn and reactionary manner against our state ... We hope that you will still become a socialist citizen and that you will want to defend our homeland. If you do not follow our advice, we will then take other steps. We will investigate your place of work, whether or not you are influenced by reactionary circles there. We will arrange for your factory to transfer you to Cottbus (with your consent). Perhaps you are influenced by your sport friends. We remind you once again that you declared yourself willing to perform your duty of honour in the ranks of the NVA.[16]

Whether or not Wolfgang B. changed his mind upon receiving this letter, simply ignored it or became one of the 33 116 males between the ages of 15 and 25 who fled the GDR in 1960,[17] it seems clear that many young men in the GDR were repelled more by these coercive recruitment methods than by the idea of enlisting itself. The argument that 'I'll join the NVA if conscripted, but not voluntarily' was an increasingly common response to the high-pressure recruiting tactics of the latter half of the 1950s. If coercion was necessary to maintain a sufficient supply of recruits, why not be forthright and introduce conscription? Although such a response might be interpreted as merely a way of getting oneself off the hook without appearing too *'staatsfeindlich'*, the fact that such attitudes were commonly observed by Infratest interviewers among young male refugees to the West strongly suggests that it was not merely evasive rhetoric. The worst thing about recruitment in many young men's minds was the unpleasant methods combined with the idea that it was voluntary: 'Conscription is much better than the kinds of methods they have over there'; 'If universal conscription were introduced, then participation by everyone would simply be a matter of course *(Selbstverständlichkeit)'.*[18] As much as the party leadership and NVA generals would have liked to introduce conscription, it was still a while before it came to that.

Divided loyalties: motives for enlisting and the problem of local functionaries

Conventional wisdom has maintained that, whatever parallels one might draw between the responses of would-be recruits in the GDR and the *'ohne mich'* movement in West Germany in the 1950s, the crucial difference was that in the GDR 'unwilling' youths faced far more pressure to join, sometimes in the form of being branded 'hostile to the state', sometimes various occupational or personal sanctions. Although the evidence in the East German archives supports this view in general, it also enhances and qualifies it in a number of ways. What stands out most in the internal reports is the frankness and direct manner of many refusals, which suggests that young men were not terrified of opening their mouths on this issue. Throughout the entire period before the introduction of conscription in 1962, instances of refusal, even if expressed very explicitly, were by no means universally punished. In fact, even the young emigrants attempting to gain refugee status in West Germany on the basis of being coerced into joining the East German armed forces often divulged during their interview proceedings *(Anerkennungsverfahren)* that friends, family and other acquaintances had continually refused to enlist and remained unmolested apart from repeated attempts to recruit them.[19] Yet cooperation was declared a question of loyalty to socialism and the GDR, so it was hard to refuse membership in the KVP, NVA or GST without exposing oneself to accusations of being hostile to the state, which might carry with it any number of undesirable consequences. Why then did the KVP and NVA experience such difficulty in winning young recruits? And how did so many would-be soldiers in the GDR refuse military service without incurring any meaningful sanctions?

In the event, joining the armed forces was not necessarily a question of loyalty or a matter of *'Farbe Bekennen'* to either the would-be recruit or the 'regime' itself. As was so often the case, what the SED-leadership propagated in abstract black-and-white terms of 'positive' versus 'negative' attitudes, of 'loyal' versus *'staatsfeindlich'* behaviour, looked far more complex at the grass-roots. Two points are important here. First, a refusal to enlist was not necessarily a clear rejection of the GDR or socialism or, for that matter, armed forces in principle, just as willingness to enlist was not necessarily a sign of approval or support. Lower-level functionaries were well aware of this and often acted accordingly. Secondly, and more importantly, conflicts and contradictions between different elements of 'the regime' at the grass-roots offered significant opportunities to avoid recruitment.

Young people's reasons for joining or refusing to join were manifold, and could not automatically be construed as 'political' reasons, however hard the party leadership may have tried to define them as such. Many of the refusals described above reflect very basic human desires that cannot be reduced to a simple question of loyalty: not wanting to be separated from friends, family or colleagues; a reluctance to leave a job which one enjoys or to put off one's studies; not wanting to give up such cherished moments as Saturday night at the films, sleeping late on Sunday morning and going 'boogy-woogy' dancing in West Berlin. In any event, insofar as enlisting was perceived by young people as a 'question of loyalty', this generally gravitated *against* the recruitment campaign. As one politically wary youth in Pritzwalk explained: 'If the times should change again, then people would say, "Look there, he's also one of the ones who went voluntarily"'.[20]

By the same token, an agreement to enlist was by no means tantamount to a declaration of loyalty to the GDR. Whereas military service represented to some people the annoying interruption of a satisfying career, to others it represented a way out of a poorly paid, dead-end job or perhaps a temporary stopover before moving into another line of work. Of the dozens of KVP deserters questioned by West Berlin authorities during the second half of 1954, 63 per cent admitted that they had enlisted voluntarily because they saw in the armed forces an alternative occupation that they could take up without any prior training once further advancement in their current occupation was no longer possible. Among the other desirable attractions of the KVP mentioned by deserters were the relatively high wages, the opportunity to acquire a driving license free of charge and the opportunity of getting special training as an airplane mechanic, marine engineer or radar technician which was unavailable elsewhere. Though it is difficult to quantify, it seems that, as one might expect, factories with a high proportion of skilled and relatively well-paid workers were less fertile recruiting ground than agricultural areas or factories employing predominately unskilled labourers.[21] The promise of occupational training was especially attractive to young men from rural areas, who saw in the KVP a chance to 'see a few things' outside of their sleepy villages or to 'finally escape the boredom of farming.'[22] Judging from the opinion and morale reports, it would also seem that, on the whole, there was precious little difference in political outlook between rank-and-file soldiers and the general populace.[23] As Willi Stoph complained to the Central Committee Convention in April 1955: 'the pacifist attitudes that are common among a certain portion of the working-class have a negative effect on members of the KVP . . . and we have determined that when on vacation, young soldiers spread the widest range of hostile opinions'.[24]

As for the second point, 'the system' was more self-contradictory, had more conflicts of interest and loyalty and offered more room for manoeuvre for those disinclined to enlist than the simplistic notion of '*Farbe Bekennen*' allows. Despite the inbuilt advantages for military recruitment in a formally '*durchherrschte Gesellschaft*' like the GDR, there were nonetheless significant disjunctures between the various components of the East German apparatus of power involved in or at least affected by the recruitment campaign, not to mention numerous organizational problems. For one thing, the ambitious, and sometimes unattainable, recruitment targets were a perpetual source of headaches, and success at fulfilling them varied dramatically from place to place. The October 1952 success rates of the various *Kreise* in *Bezirk* Halle, for example, ranged from 32 to 75 per cent. Faced with reprimands from their superiors, functionaries in poorly performing districts often tried to show that the discrepancy lay in the erroneous calculation of the target figures, and not in any shortcomings in their own work. Figures were therefore occasionally reviewed and revised, much to the confusion of everyone involved.[25] Moreover, lower-level functionaries often found it impossible to juggle their regular tasks with additional recruiting duties. As the SED secretary for *Kreis* Jena complained to the local FDJ secretary, 'it doesn't matter what you do. If you fulfil the recruitment target other tasks get neglected and you get it in the neck; if you solve your other problems and neglect recruitment you also get it in the neck . . .'[26] Given the pressure involved, many simply did not like recruiting and wanted to get back to their old jobs as soon as possible. Among the SED *Kreisleitungen* in *Bezirk* Potsdam there was 'moaning' about the extra work, as well as reports that the 'discipline and eagerness [to recruit] is none too strong'.[27]

Little wonder, since recruiters encountered all kinds of problems in their dealings with other functionaries. Reports often complained of a lack of technical or organizational support from either the party or mass organizations, which, as we have just seen, were often more concerned with their own regular duties.[28] Even less helpful were local state officials and *Bürgermeister*. The mayor of Schnolde, *Kreis* Pritzwalk, even took it upon himself to advise youths that 'whoever does not want to join the People's Army should leave the republic, then when he returns he won't be called up'.[29] Least helpful of all were the managers and BPO secretaries in the factories. Given the unceasing pressure to increase production and efficiency, many were quite understandably reluctant to forfeit their young, productive employees for military service which many of them deemed unnecessary. Like thousands of comrades across the GDR, the party secretary at the Ziegelei Rädel near Brandenburg openly told recruiters to 'leave our workers in the factory, we already have so few'.[39] The *Bürgermeister* and local party-secretary in Stendal even organized a local counter-campaign against the recruitment of young farmers and farmhands. Most forthright of all was the director of the Zeiss optic works in Jena, who not only ordered that all recruiters be banned from the factory premises, but even got police support to enforce the order.[31] As a Ministry of National Defence report of 1957 put it, 'Serious discussions with factory directors, cadre directors, progressive *Meister* and brigadiers . . . must be organized in the factories'.[32]

One way of circumventing such problems was to instruct local officials to send young men directly to the local recruitment authorities. But even this method had its problems. For instance, one particularly uncooperative BPO secretary at the Ifa tin foundry sent nine workers of suitable age to the police authorities in Leipzig, all of whom had to be rejected because of various physical handicaps

or chronic diseases. When the police discussed this uncanny coincidence with the nine men, they all admitted to informing the
party secretary about their health conditions beforehand as well as
pointing out to him that their disabilities would surely preclude
any service in the armed forces. 'That's not so important', the secretary reportedly answered, 'the main thing is that you appear at
the local recruitment commission . . .'[33] Yet the recruitment authorities
were themselves sometimes part of the problem, at least in the
early years. In Berlin-Treptow, the director of the local registration
office reportedly showed 'no initiative at all in recruitment', but
was rather inclined to 'play cards in the registration office with the
civilian employees', and occasionally even failed to appear for presentations scheduled in the factories. Dismissing him made little
difference, since his successor showed similar tendencies. The main
difference according to a local party instructor was a preference for
table tennis over cards.[34]

Towards the end of the 1950s, the worsening labour shortage made
factory functionaries even less inclined to cooperate with recruiters.
The practice of giving the most lucrative jobs only to those who
would not interrupt their employment by joining the armed forces
appears to have become increasingly common,[35] and some economic
functionaries even tried to change the minds of workers who had
already enlisted by offering them more money. As exasperated military
recruiters in *Bezirk* Cottbus complained in early 1961: 'The economic functionaries are a serious weakness. On repeated occasions
and in a number of enterprises, youths who have pre-enlisted suddenly
receive a considerable pay increase and then rescind their enlistment agreement'.[36] The situation in Berlin-Treptow was concisely
summed up as follows by a *Volkspolizei* officer at a 1958 recruitment commission meeting:

> It is all well and good, but how do things look in reality? We
> are not welcomed by the party secretaries at all anymore. At the
> Motor Works we were nearly thrown out. When comrade Pabst
> started talking about recruitment, one of the others got away
> and went back to the shopfloor. All in all we can say that we are
> regarded as a fifth or even sixth wheel on the cart.[37]

The result of the increasingly uncooperative stance of many factory functionaries were signs of growing resignation among recruiters.
One manifestation of this was the high turnover rates on recruitment

commissions. By the end of 1961, 27 of the 49 officials appointed to the Cottbus regional recruitment board in 1958 had quit; in *Bezirk* Potsdam eight directors of the *Kreis* commissions had quit in 1960 alone. How did officials in the Ministry for National Defence account for the turnover? As a report to the SED Central Committee explained: 'The motivations that cause colleagues to take this step are above all the high intensity of the work and the great nervous strain *vis-à-vis* the slim successes in recruitment. For these reasons many officers and officials prefer to take up work in the economy'.[38]

In turn, the growing sense of resignation led to widespread 'formalism' on the part of both recruitment commissions as well as party and FDJ functionaries who were supposed to be helping them. The unceasing pressure to get enlistments meant that recruitment sometimes followed the *'Tonnenideologie'* of quantity over quality. In the Ministry for National Defence there were frequent complaints about commissions carelessly enlisting youths under the age limit of 18 or individuals with criminal records, cases which frequently ended in desertion.[39] As for the FDJ functionaries, the Ministry for National Defence complained in 1960 that: 'In general it can be said that the regional and district executives of the FDJ compose good resolutions for the patriotic education of the youth . . . Because of the insufficient control on their actual implementation, the resolutions have only a slight influence on the recruitment results'. Honecker's admonitions to support the recruitment drive reportedly had 'no effects worth mentioning'. Rather, the comments of the FDJ secretary in *Kreis* Wanzleben were quoted as typical: 'The main thing is that we have a lot of signatures, what comes after that is another matter'.[40]

It would thus seem that the internal study on 'the problem of personnel acquisition for the NVA on the basis of the volunteer system' commissioned in 1972 by the Ministry for National Defence was only partially correct in its conclusion that, despite the 'untiring efforts of all members of the regional and district commandos under the leadership of the party organizations', the reason why so many were 'not in a position to realize the tasks put to them' and why 'the personnel quotas of many troop formations were only 55–65 per cent fulfilled for junior officers and 75–80 per cent for soldiers' was first of all the 'principle of voluntarism' itself, and secondly the 'underdeveloped consciousness' of many youths regarding the necessity of service in the armed forces.[41] Another major factor that this ignores was that many recruitment commissions were not working very 'untiringly' at all, but were plagued by high turnover rates, 'formalism' as well as the uncooperative stance of other local officials.

In sum, what the party leadership propagated as a coherent plan to raise a 'volunteer' army at the same time as raising productivity looked very different at the grass-roots. It was in this overlap between 'regime' and 'society', the articulation point where official policies were actually put into practice, that the contradictions of these two policy imperatives became unmistakably visible to both local representatives of the regime and would-be soldiers alike. In turn, these contradictions caused cracks to open up between the central authorities that dictated 'official' policy and local functionaries confronted with realities on the ground. And it was in these narrow rifts, under the shelter of a sympathetic local functionary willing to ignore or at least dilute central directives, that young men could often find temporary or lasting refuge from having to perform their 'patriotic duty' in the armed forces.

'Negative influences': the Church and the West

In the meantime, the problems of unreliable local functionaries and unpliable youths also plagued efforts to 'protect' the younger generation from the influence of the church and western popular culture, both of which were regarded as a serious threat to the political and moral health of the next generation of socialist citizens.

As we have seen, the Protestant youth organizations emerged from the conflict of 1952–53 only temporarily weakened, and in fact recovered significantly over the following year or so. But the detente between church and state was only short-lived, and came to an end in late 1954 with the introduction of the *Jugendweihe*, a secular alternative to church confirmation which the SED tried to use as a means of diminishing the church's influence among young people. The party leadership had long recognized that the confirmation ceremony was little more than a cultural or family tradition for most people, that the secular celebration afterwards was more important than the church event. But because church leaders knew that many parents wanted their children to undergo confirmation, they used it as a means of Christian education by insisting that candidates first attend courses on Christian doctrine. The *Jugendweihe* followed much the same idea. Although presented as no more than a ritual marking the transition into maturity of young people who were to play active roles in socialist society, the celebration was to be preceded by a series of lessons in what was essentially a materialist, atheist world-view. A network of nominally independent local and regional committees, which in reality were quite closely controlled by the SED, were established to popularize the celebration in schools and neighbourhoods.[42]

Despite insisting that there was no intention for the *Jugendweihe* to act as a substitute for Christian confirmation, the SED had to reckon with a strong response from the church, which understandably took the position that the two were in principle incompatible, that one must choose between them. The actual introduction of the *Jugendweihe* unleashed a storm of protest from church officials and concerned parents in 1955, growing louder and louder over the following years as it became increasingly viewed as a prerequisite for entry into the *Oberschule*. Besides writing petitions and complaints to the authorities, local pastors also undertook house visits, led meetings and sent letters to parents.[43] While a majority of parents and youths (indeed, even many with strong religious convictions) were apparently willing to undergo both ceremonies, most chose confirmation over the *Jugendweihe* when faced with exclusive alternatives. In the words of a housewife near Potsdam: 'We'd be happy to send our children to the *Jugendweihe*; but if the children can't be confirmed, it will come to nothing'.[44]

Here the SED leadership had slightly miscalculated. Although it was quite correct to assume that, for most people at least, the secular celebration was the most important aspect of confirmation, party leaders underestimated the indirect influence of the church and religious traditions on the broader populace, including many SED members and functionaries. In 1956–57, around 12 000 party members insisted that their children undergo Christian confirmation; many, especially in rural areas, were clearly opposed to the *Jugendweihe* and were unwilling to popularize it in their communities.[45] Little wonder, therefore, that there were continual complaints in the Central Committee, even as late as 1957, about the weakness or non-existence of the local committees overseeing the *Jugendweihe*. Agitation was basically left to the party instructors and full-time secretaries in the *Kreisleitungen*, who got little help from other organizations at the local level, not even the FDJ.[46] Given this backdrop, it is hardly surprising that the *Jugendweihe* was no immediate sensation. The breakthrough came in 1958, after talks between church leaders and more conciliatory state officials failed to make headway. By spring 1958, the *Jugendweihe* unambiguously became a state-sanctioned substitute for confirmation, replete with its own education course, an oath to support socialism and, most importantly, significant drawbacks for those who did not 'voluntarily' participate. This affected parents where they were most vulnerable: their children's future. Whereas only 17.7 per cent of the age cohort took part in the *Jugendweihe* in 1954–5, by 1958 this figure had leapt to 44.1 per cent and in 1959 reached 80.4 per cent. Church leaders, fearing that their adamant stance on the incompatability of the *Jugendweihe* and Christian confirmation might lead to the extinction of the latter, eventually backed down, and in practice did not refuse confirmation to those who participated in the state-sanctioned ceremony.[47] In contrast to the conflict over the *Junge Gemeinden*, the SED emerged from this second battle with the church over the East German youth as the clear victor, at least in terms of organizational capability. But whether this actually diminished young people's religious sensibilities or the influence of the church in a more diffuse sense is less clear.

Indeed, as far as 'winning over' East German youth was concerned, the regime still had its work cut out. The introduction of the *Jugendweihe* was more a struggle with the church than with young people themselves, many of whom could quite easily reconcile the desire for church confirmation with the need to undergo the state-sanctioned ceremony as a necessary compromise with the prevailing political conditions. However much this might be viewed as a victory over the church, it was all but meaningless in terms of winning the active support of youths. Far more problematic than the attempt to eliminate the church as an 'internal' disruptive factor was that of minimizing the diffuse, yet seemingly universal 'external' influence of 1950s western youth culture. Significantly, this problem presented no clear institutional opponent like the church whose activities could easily be hindered by 'administrative measures'. Since the institutional cause was out of reach, the only course of action was to attack the symptoms themselves, which lay in the free-time activities and cultural preferences of young people. As such, this campaign was far more intrusive into the everyday lives of individuals. And it was above all this intrusive aspect that ultimately made it rather counterproductive in terms of either detracting from the popularity of western popular culture or winning much support for the regime.

The purpose of the FDJ was to *organize* free-time, to steer it in directions compatible with the values the regime officially espoused: that is, the remarkably traditional and decidedly petit-bourgeois 'socialist morality' of 1950s–60s East Germany. This principle of organization, combined with the normative models of respectability and disciplined behaviour that young people were supposed to emulate, rendered the FDJ and the entire 'socialist culture' that it embodied unattractive to many young people. It seems a fair generalization that youths in most societies want to individualize themselves, to set themselves apart from their parents; there is little desire to be 'organized' or 'mobilized'. Under the circumstances, the FDJ could not compete with the mildly rebellious attraction of western popular culture.

Even western novels were widely considered superior to their socialist counterparts. An examination of book-borrowing patterns at the clubhouses for young workers in the Leuna-Werke, Dürrenberg and Lützen found that youths not only read less overall than the party hoped, but also that East German books were viewed as more predictable and schematic. The popular '30-Pfennig' novels from the West – mostly romances, 'wild West' adventures and spy stories – were not only more interesting in their own right, but also had the added attraction of being circulated secretly.[48]

The preference for western films was even stronger, as local party and FDJ officials were well aware. Cultural officials at the Leuna-Werke, for instance, could not help noticing that western films tended to draw large crowds, whereas Soviet and East German films usually lost money. Hence most of the films they showed were from the West, much to the surprise and displeasure of party leaders. Although the comrades in charge of cultural events at Leuna, when questioned by Central Committee officials, blamed this imbalance in part on the supply of films 'from above', the fact that the Western origin of films was emphasized in their advertisements – 'Tonight another marvelous West-film!', 'Marvelous western comedy that no one should miss!' – suggests that they, like many local culture officials across the GDR, were more interested in filling seats than in Cold-War cultural battles.[49]

As popular as western films were, the greatest threat in the eyes of the SED and FDJ leadership was American 'beat music', derided as a prime example of 'western decadence' and 'American lack of culture' (*Unkultur*). Transmitted across most of the GDR by Radio Luxemburg, RIAS and 'Freies Berlin', 'rock and roll' music quickly became as popular among East German youths as among their western counterparts. Elvis Presley was particularly idolized; fan-clubs sprouted up in numerous towns and cities.[50] Much of the apprehension felt by functionaries and parents towards this particular aspect of the 1950s youth subculture was similar to that in the West: the hip-shaking was seen as immoral and degrading to young women, and also contradicted the normative ideal of a strictly disciplined and controlled masculinity. But what made it so dangerous in the eyes of the East German authorities were two other concerns. First, like the influence of the church, its very existence was viewed as a threat to the monopoly position of the FDJ and thus to the political mobilization and education of youth more generally. Two young men in Potsdam stated the problem succinctly: 'We don't concern ourselves much with politics, we like to listen to RIAS, Luxemburg and "Freies Berlin" where there is hot music'.[51] Second, western beat-music was regarded as nothing less than a form of 'psychological warfare' and 'moral and spiritual poisoning of our youth',[52] designations which not only labelled it a political problem along the lines of 'agitation hostile to the state', but also aided its conflation with various other forms of youth delinquency and criminality.

Many of the youth gangs and 'rowdies' of the 1950s indeed followed western cultural fashions and models as part of their non-conformist repertoire. Gang names such as 'Rock 'n' Roll Bande', 'Broadway Bande' and 'Texas Bande' were gleaned from western films, as were the commonly adopted nicknames like 'Jimmy' or 'Mack'.[53] In condemning such behaviour not only as deliquent, but also 'west-oriented', the SED and FDJ mistook the symptoms for the causes. Instead of recognizing this fascination with western culture and frequent trips to West Berlin as an *expression* of youthful rebelliousness or an iconoclastic disaffection with the constant calls to 'work, learn and struggle' for the glory of socialism, officials rather regarded it as the *source* of these problems. And instead of viewing the many minor instances of delinquency and non-conformity such as vandalism, petty theft and disturbing the peace as an expression of high spirits or a reflection of the problems of youth socialization within the GDR, they instead tended to externalize them and blame them on the 'influence of the West'.

The fact that such youth 'criminality' was highest in the border areas around West Berlin – that is, in the metropolitan area of large city where one might expect it to be highest – reinforced this one-sided view. Interestingly enough, so, too, did the fact that many youths who were caught committing such pranks and petty crimes adopted this official language of 'western influence' in an attempt to displace the blame from themselves and thus mitigate their punishment. For instance, when the youth gang 'Amorbande' in Brandenburg was broken up in 1958 after a series of petty thefts, police emphasized in their report that its members 'unanimously expressed that their actions were prompted by their visits to West-Berlin cinemas and other events'. Likewise, when two young men in Kleinmachnow were arrested after getting drunk and bashing a few streetlamps on their way home from the cinema in West Berlin, they 'admitted' to succumbing to 'high spirits' as a result of their sojourn across the border.[54]

The conclusion drawn from such cases of supposedly nefarious western influence was, predictably, more organization, above all improving the attractiveness of the FDJ. But for a number of reasons, the FDJ was in little better position to compete with western popular culture in the latter half of the 1950s than it was with the *Junge Gemeinden* in the earlier part of decade. For one thing, its functionaries at the local level still left much to be desired in terms of enthusiasm and ideological schooling. Turnover rates were extremely high; for example, at the RAW Revaler Straße in East Berlin, 51 of the 72 FDJ secretaries elected in 1960 were new. An investigation of 52 local FDJ secretaries found that only four had any political schooling at all (and even that was very meagre), no more than half ever read the FDJ publications *Junge Welt* or *Junge Generation*, and only eight ever read the party organ *Neues Deutschland*. As a result, so the report concluded, most were not addressing the issues the Central Committee thought they should be: '... there was almost no discussion at all over such issues as the fact that many youths listen to the NATO-station Luxemburg, change money in West-Berlin and go to the cinema there'.[55]

Moreover, it still proved impossible to attract most youths and at the same time proselytize for socialism and convince them of the evils of the West. Many youngsters felt that the only time the FDJ took an interest in them was when it wanted something from them such as a signature on a resolution or participation in a demostration. As two young men in East Berlin put it: 'There's nothing going on in the FDJ'; 'The FDJ seems to me like a political prayer meeting after work'.[56] In fact, where the FDJ was most popular was where it was playing American beat-music, for instance at the FDJ clubhouse in Mühlhausen, which local youths dubbed the 'Rock 'n' Roll Palace', or at the clubhouse in Erfurt, the main hang-out of the local 'Presley-Bande'.[57]

In itself, none of this diffuse and unorganized interest in things Western constituted much of a threat to the regime or its plans for the 'socialist education' of young people, especially when one considers the relatively positive ratings it received from younger refugees to the West.[58] What made it so dangerous in the eyes of the party leadership was that it expressed the growth of a collective sub-culture among youths that escaped FDJ control, indeed that often sprouted up precisely as an alternative to it in the first place. Thus the continual efforts to increase organization and control as a solution to the problems of youth socialization in the GDR – insofar as they were manifested at the grass-roots, which was patchy to say the least – in effect only added to the political significance and iconoclastic attraction of Western popular culture, and in the process set an unpromising precedent for efforts to steer young people's interests and free-time activities in the decades to come.

11
The Problems and Possibilities of the Open Border

By offering a relatively easy way out for those who had had enough of the GDR, the open border to the West placed certain constraints on the entire process of constructing East German socialism. Until the erection of the Berlin Wall in August 1961, an unceasing haemorrhage of citizens – some three million between 1945 and 1961 – served to characterize and caricature the problems of social and political transformation in East Germany. The problem of *Republikflucht* was clearly a crucial factor to both the political and economic stabilization of the fledgling regime. But beneath the rather abstract questions of 'regime stabilization', *Republikflucht* was also a defining characteristic of everyday life in the early GDR, and moreover typified many of the problems the SED leadership had in controlling it. The open border placed significant limits on the SED dictatorship, and not just in terms of economic damage and undermining claims to political legitimacy. As the previous chapters have shown, it also placed limits on the regime's control over 'local politics' in the factories, villages and neighbourhoods of the GDR, from industrial relations to military recruitment and agricultural collectivization. The open border gave 'ordinary' East Germans a power they otherwise would not have had – a kind of 'trump card' should the claims of the state go too far – which even those who stayed in the GDR were occasionally able to use to their own advantage.

Official discourse and unofficial realities

The problem of *Republikflucht* was an extremely difficult one for the party leadership to counter, and in a number of ways the official rhetoric surrounding it made the task even harder than it was in the first place. As was already mentioned, throughout the 1950s there were constant complaints of insufficient attention being paid to the issue in the lower levels of the regime. Much of the reason for this inertia was the simple overburdening of grass-roots officials who had other priorities and other tasks to fulfil. But it also had to do with the narrow official understanding of the roots of the problem. From the very beginning, the reasons for *Republikflucht* were largely externalized and explained away by a kind of conspiracy theory of 'organized *Abwerbung*' (wooing-away) by capitalist businessmen or by the West German Federal Ministry for All-German Affairs (*Bundesministerium für gesamtdeutsche Fragen*). According to countless newspaper articles and internal reports, such *Abwerbung* was occasionally done via letters or illicit flyers, sometimes through discussions with western agents in the GDR or while the 'victim' was in the West, and on a broader basis via West German press and radio.[1] These methods were perceived to be so devious and effective that they became an object of study in themselves.[2] By the end of 1953 at the latest, such notions and vocabulary had become the ritual centrepiece of official discourse on *Republikflucht* in the GDR, not only in official propaganda, where one might expect it, but also in internal classified correspondence.[3] The narrow ideological parameters of interpreting *Republikflucht* not only affected the type of research conducted on the problem, but also hindered the regime's very ability to communicate about it internally. In other words, the establishment of a centrally-dictated and heavily ideologized vocabulary within the East German party-state apparatus was a pyrrhic victory in terms of its effects.

Though there were critical voices within the upper levels of party and state that argued for a more impartial understanding of the reasons for the mass emigration, some even arguing against the very notion of 'flight' itself in favour of the less loaded term 'emigration',[4] these remained exceptions and were in any event largely purged or removed from positions of influence in the crackdown following the Hungarian troubles of 1956. Moreover, even when the party/state apparatus acknowledged its own shortcomings and mistakes – usually in terms of 'heartless bureaucratic behaviour' towards the intelligentsia on the part of local officials – its 'self-criticism' never extended beyond the formal methods of the exertion of its power. This not only nourished the comforting illusion that the problem was solvable within the parameters of the GDR as it existed, it also meant that the elusive solution was viewed not in the reduction of the presence of the state in people's lives (which was undoubtedly one of the primary underlying causes of flight), but rather in its further extension. In the words of a 1961 *Volkspolizei* analysis: 'The main link in the chain is the improvement of work with the people and their integration into the leadership and steering of the state'.[5] The 'real causes' lay not in a surplus, but rather a deficit of the state. Thus a major element of the SED's anti-*Republikflucht* policy was to correct this deficit through 'increased vigilance', heightened 'ideological struggle' and strengthening the 'educational and mass cultural work' within the populace.

Viewed from below, however, the problem appeared very different. Many local officials and lower-level functionaries knew from daily experience that the very 'vigilance' and 'ideological struggle' that the party leadership was calling for was a large part of the problem in the first place – hence their merely 'formal' handling of the problem of *Republikflucht*, as numerous Central Committee reports complained. These different perspectives between centre and periphery prompted frequent reproaches from the party leadership, for example at a 1954 meeting between Central Committee officials and the regional directors of the SED population policy (*Bevölkerungspolitik*) departments, where the latter were upbraided for failing to see the work of the ubiquitous enemy:

> In the reports that we receive from you there is not one single example of how, on the basis of uncovering the causes of *Republikflucht*, the party organizations then turned to leading the struggle, above all the ideological struggle, against *Republikflucht*, mobilizing the working people in the factories in order to expose the *Abwerber* and shatter the enemy rumours. Above all there must be an end to the fairy tale of *Republikflucht* 'for family reasons'. In almost all cases the true reason is entirely different: incitement by the RIAS, promises of western *Abwerber*, enemy rumours. A worker in the GDR who is ideologically steadfast [*gefestigt*] does not move to his aunt or mother-in-law in West Germany for so-called 'family reasons', giving up his livelihood here and possibly even leaving the furniture standing. The functionary who believes in 'family reasons' is politically blind.[6]

This dogmatic view at the 'centre' not only obscured many of the reasons for flight and hindered the ability of local functionaries to deal with the problem practically, in many ways it also made the problem worse. To offer an illustration, in summer 1955 a group of SED instructors was deployed to investigate the alarming rate of illegal emigration among university personnel. The investigation was anything but impartial, and the question of enemy *Abwerbung* was again a foregone conclusion. The instructors complained that although party functionaries and staff at the universities agreed that enemy *Abwerbung* was organized and carried out 'in a certain way', there were never any clues that could lead to uncovering it. In any open-ended investigation the most obvious interpretation would be that 'enemy activity' did not play a significant role, which would also explain why party functionaries within the universities did not devote much attention to it. But the instructors nevertheless blamed it on 'extremely insufficient political-ideological work' and on insufficient research that was 'not carried out in the awareness that the class enemy is behind it'. In its conclusions the report punctuates this profoundly blinkered analysis by recommending intensified 'political-ideological work' at the universities, which in all likelihood would prove counterproductive.[7] Thus began the curious vicious circle that repeated itself time and again in schools, factories and scholarly institutes all across the GDR. Every case of flight of an important individual prompted an inquisitorial investigation and tightening of political control which was in many cases one of the main reasons for leaving the GDR in the first place.[8]

Such recommendations were of little use to functionaries on the ground, and not surprisingly had little impact on their activities. Central Committee reports on the situation in the universities in 1959 still found precisely the same problems as in 1955: 'The political evaluation of *Republikflucht*, the uncovering of deeper causes as well as the formulation and implementation of appropriate measures for the effective containment (*Eindämmung*) of flight and winning back scholars are criminally neglected'.[9] Cases of flight were merely 'registered', too often with hopelessly vacuous conclusions such as 'presumed cause: political unclarity'. As usual, the report recommended intensified 'political-ideological work'. But apart from those officials who were explicitly responsible for investigating motives and hindering further incidents of emigration (the local police forces and internal affairs officials in the district councils) most local functionaries gave the problem little attention. As a 1956 party investigation in the factories of Treptow concluded: 'In all investigations carried out by the commission, it is clear that the BPOs do not concern themselves at all with the causes that led or still could lead to *Republikflucht*.[10] Even the few who took an active interest in the problem recognized that there was little they could do to solve it. As the party chairman at the VEB VTA in Leipzig explained to Central Committee instructors: 'We've carried out assemblies, held lectures against *Republikflucht*, even carried out differentiated discussions, but have not had any great success with it'.[11]

In an attempt to get grass-roots functionaries to play a more active role, special commissions were established in the late 1950s in most towns and large VEBs for the purpose of hindering *Republikflucht* and trying to convince former refugees to return. Most met only sporadically, were plagued by poor attendance and did little more than discuss recent incidents of flight.[12] Fairly typical of the factory commissions was the one in the VEB Transformatorenwerk 'Karl Liebknecht' in Köpenick. Not only did it have perpetual problems getting all eight members to appear at meetings, it degenerated to a mere virtual existence within about a year of its founding in early 1959. By the time the chairman comrade Horn had quit in July 1960, the commission had essentially fallen apart because of disinterest and lack of time on the part of the functionaries involved. After that it took six months to find a new chairman, and even then the appointee immediately tried to be released from his new function. As a report from May 1961 succinctly put it: 'one cannot speak of any activity on the part of the factory *Republikflucht*-commission'.[13]

While the problems associated with getting grass-roots officials to help stem the tide of people to the West was by and large limited to mere inactivity or at least 'insufficient attention', the complementary practice of attracting immigrants and returnees with promises of work and prioritized accommodation faced even greater difficulties. Because of the severe shortage of housing, the problem was serious in sheer numerical terms. Roughly ten per cent of those who left the GDR returned, at least for a while before many went West yet again. It was calculated that, between 1954 and 1961, 1.27 per cent of the total GDR population were returnees, with another 0.39 per cent first-time immigrants.[14] *Bürgermeister* and local council officials responsible for housing in their districts (*Referate Wohnungswesen*) were constantly swamped by irate letters from desperate families and individuals who had already waited years for adequate housing. From their perspective, official policy on *Republikflucht* was simply not consistent with the SED's promises of improved living conditions for workers. In trying to redress the continuing housing shortage, they had no interest in either 'winning back' former refugees to the GDR or, for that matter, in keeping people from leaving. For them, every emigrant to the West represented not so much a political embarrassment for the SED or a drain of skilled labour as it did another available flat. By contrast, every returning refugee or immigrant from the West was viewed less as a vote of confidence in the GDR than a 'burdensome applicant' for scarce housing. As a 1957 report from *Bezirk* Halle put it, a large proportion of *Bürgermeister* were of little help in attracting Germans eastwards 'because then they have to concern themselves with finding accommodation'.[15]

There were similar problems in finding suitable employment for immigrants, who were often rejected or given the worst jobs available so as not to anger other workers or because of previous bad experiences with returnees from the West, who not infrequently showed poor work morale, committed petty thefts of materials and left again after a short period of time.[16] This reticence to hire returnees hardly made them feel welcome, for example the truck-driver Gerhard Klammt from Rehbrücke, who complained at the district council in Potsdam that the local FDGB office was going to hire him, but gave the position to someone else the day after they heard he was a returnee.[17] Such problems were common enough for the Interior Ministry even to propose in 1956 that the Labour Ministry create a central office responsible for finding appropriate work for returnees and immigrants, and that the office have the power to order factories and offices to hire them.[18] Ironically, such 'sectarian' behaviour among local functionaries towards returnees and first-time immigrants was only bolstered by the stigmatization of those who illegally crossed the border as smugglers and criminals. As one *Volkspolizei* report explained in 1958: 'The comrades . . . are in part of the opinion that the only kind of people who return or come from West Germany to the GDR have done something illegal (*etwas auf dem Kerbholz haben*) and are of no valuable help to the construction of socialism in the GDR'.[19]

The myriad reasons and motives for flight

Yet whatever difficulties the attitudes and interests of local functionaries presented, the main reason why the regime had so little success in controlling the population movement was that it was based on such a broad range of factors and motives. Debates as to why so many East Germans left the GDR are as old as the problem itself. Unfortunately, the evidence at hand cannot offer a definitive answer. There are, to be sure, thousands of previously inaccessible analyses of the motives of SED-members who left the GDR produced by the various regional and district party control commissions,[20] as well as numerous surveys conducted in West Germany on refugees from the GDR. But the results of both are of limited value due to the impossibility of formulating categories of questioning capable of capturing the amalgamation of reasons for fleeing, the problem of self-selection in the SED expulsion proceedings, as well as the fact that the interviewees in West Germany had a built-in interest to portray their flight as primarily politically motivated in order to receive the status of political refugees and thus be entitled to special compensation under the Federal Law on Expellees (*Bundesvertriebenengesetz*).

Further complicating the picture is the fact that the analysis of motives for *Republikflucht* has always had a number of political implications. Given the overall context of competing systems between East and West Germany, it is not surprising that official portrayals of *Republikflucht* in the West tended to place political repression in the foreground, despite the fact that only 20 per cent of the immigrants from the GDR were granted the identification-card 'C' for political refugees.[21] The same was true of portrayals by refugee organizations, which stressed political motives not least in order to elicit understanding and acceptance from their fellow citizens in the Federal Republic. By contrast, scholarly accounts have tended overwhelmingly to emphasize the importance of economic factors in the decision to leave the GDR.[22] Not without justification did Ernst Richert describe the mass emigration from the GDR as an 'internal migration to more favourable living conditions'.[23]

Yet both views are inadequate, for the motives behind *Republikflucht* were extremely complex and cannot neatly be separated into a political versus economic schema. For one thing, economic and political factors were often inseparable. Career prospects for individuals in the GDR were to a large extent tied to political factors such as involvement in various socialist organizations or to one's social background, and many left for the sake of their children's careers. Moreover, the GDR had a thoroughly politicized economy, and many people, especially engineers and managers, fled out of fear of being held responsible for problems in the factories over which they had little or no control – for instance faulty planning, receiving plans too late or numerous changes to the production plans – or out of frustration with the bureaucratic nature of the East German economy.[24] The reuniting of families also remained an important factor until at least the mid-1950s, and many of those classified as refugees were merely children or dependents of those who had decided to leave. There were also significant differences in terms of age and occupation. Young people were on the whole more likely to be motivated by a desire for adventure or individual fulfillment than those with established careers and families. People possessing significant amounts of immobile property – farmers, for instance – were on the whole less likely to leave than others. Even among farmers there were significant differences between 'natives' loath to sever ties with land that had been in their families for generations and 'new farmers' who were not as well-off economically and had less emotional attachment to their farms.

The thousands of police and party investigations of individual cases of flight give an idea of the wide variety of motives for leaving, though any kind of quantification on the basis of these reports would be impossible since they were not carried out in a systematic fashion and generally offer only one or two reasons which themselves were mostly impressionistic. The reports produced by the western refugee camps are also too problematic to serve as the basis for any quantification, given that their analyses were so closely connected to changes in refugee-policy, conceptions of the situation in the GDR and changing definitions of 'political' versus 'unpolitical' refugees.[25]

One thing on which all the various sources agree is that the range of reasons for leaving the GDR was broad indeed. Despite all the talk of *Abwerbung*, even internal SED and state correspondence occasionally recognized this. In one of the more differentiated and conscientious attempts to grasp the complexities of the situation, the deputy chairman of the State Planning Commission Duscheck listed above all the 'numerous shortcomings in the organization of our factories', which prompted many skilled workers to leave simply in order to be able to 'work properly'; the widely held opinion that the economic problems in the GDR were 'insurmountable'; problems integrating youths into the work sphere; the shortage of accommodation, which meant that families often had to live apart for long periods of time; various material concerns such as the lack of consumer goods; and a range of 'bureaucratic and heartless measures, exaggerated regulations, etc., that anger people'.[26]

This focus on broad societal problems in the GDR was typical of the few differentiated overviews elaborated at 'the top'. By contrast, the reports of individual cases written by local police or party officials generally emphasized more proximal and personal reasons for leaving. A list of fairly typical motives reported (in characteristic staccato form) for the flight of employees at the Köpenick VEB Transformatorenwerk in 1959 gives an idea of the scope: 'Trip to West Germany rejected, fiancée left Republic shortly beforehand'; 'Father left Republic and took entire family'; 'Had pro-West attitude, which meant he could not be delegated to study. All relatives in West Berlin and West Germany'; 'Strongly religious (Catholic)'; 'She was in factory only six months, was work-shy and led very immoral life. She had many debts and wanted to escape them by fleeing the Republic'; 'Returned from West Germany in January 1959 . . . Fled Republic again probably for family reasons, because he did not get along with his mother'.[27]

Of course these myriad individual motives for leaving did not exist in a vacuum, and cannot be understood outside of their broader context. Quite obviously, internal economic and political pressure within the GDR was a major factor behind flight, as the record peak of emigration in spring 1953 clearly shows (see Figure 11.1). The effects of different policies on particular social or occupational groups can also be read from the refugee statistics. For instance, the two collectivization pushes in 1952–53 and early 1960 led to marked increases in the number of farmers leaving (see Figure 9.1). The *Hochschulreform* of 1958 similarly prompted many students and members of the intelligentsia to emigrate. And as we have seen, the recruitment campaigns for the KVP and NVA in 1952 and 1955 also resulted in increases in the number of young men leaving for the West (see Figure 10.1). Changes in emigration laws were another important backdrop. The so-called *'Paßgesetz'* of 11 December 1957 sharpened the punishment for any unauthorized attempt to leave the GDR to up to three years imprisonment, and also outlawed both the preparation and assistance of *Republikflucht*. Combined with the practice of confiscating the property of illegal emigrants, the sharper punishment for attempted *Republikflucht* and the uncertainty as to when one might legally be able to visit friends and family again were powerful deterrents that are often overlooked as factors behind the drop in emigration in the years 1958–59.[28]

But what the East German internal reports, as well as many Western analyses, generally failed to take into account was the broader context *beyond* the GDR. The changing international context of German

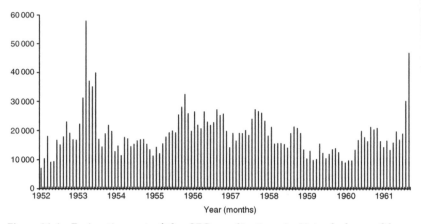

Figure 11.1   Emigration out of the GDR, applications in *Notaufnahmeverfahren*

Source: Bundesministerium für gesamtdeutsche Fragen (1961), *Die Flucht aus der Sowjetzone.*

division also played an important role, as suggested by the timing of the second and third highest peaks: the summer of 1961 and latter half of 1955, respectively. In summer 1955 the Geneva Conference (which had raised hopes for a solution to the problem of German division[29]) ended without any tangible results, and was followed shortly thereafter by the Soviet declaration of full sovereignty for the GDR. The year 1955 also saw the integration of both German states into their respective military alliances, and it seems only natural that some East Germans who were disenchanted with the GDR, who harboured hopes for reunification and who had seriously considered leaving for the West at some time would be prompted by such events into finally taking the big step. Other less dramatic peaks of emigration followed similar international political disappointments or moments of exceptional tension which might have meant a worsening of inter-German relations and travel opportunities: Khrushchev's declaration in March 1959 that the Germans could manage without reunification; the abysmal failure of the Paris Summit in May 1960; and finally, the meeting between Kennedy and Khrushchev in early June 1961, followed first by East German announcements of a solution to the West Berlin problem by the end of the year and later by Kennedy's announcement of his 'three essentials' on 25 July, which together generated an almost tangible sense of '*Torschlußpanik*' over the summer of 1961.

The simple juxtaposition of 'push' versus 'pull' factors is always a false dichotomy, even in the unique case of the inner-German migration of the 1950s and 1960s, where the latter were particularly important. It is impossible to decouple the decision to pack up and leave the GDR from the unique circumstance of having what was in many ways an *alternative homeland* in the West which offered a more or less identical language community, instant citizenship and even financial and other forms of aid to ease integration. Without this immensely magnetic 'pull', many of the irritating 'push' factors within the GDR would have lost some of their significance as causes for flight.

However impressionistic an analysis of the reasons and motives for flight must inevitably remain, the above sketch nonetheless serves to illustrate that the mass emigration out of the GDR cannot be explained monocausally, but was based on a broad range of overlapping, cross-cutting factors – a fact which in some ways qualifies the widely-held notion that it represented a siphoning-off of potential troublemakers. Undoubtedly the vast bulk of those who left the GDR in the 1950s were discontented with certain aspects of life there; but so, too, were most of those who stayed. There was a wide range of factors that kept people in the GDR, some of the most important being such personal matters as extended family, possession of a house or land, a good job, not wanting to uproot one's children, etc. Certainly many of the most vociferous persons left the GDR for the West. Yet whether or not one was a potential 'troublemaker' was not the only factor. A sizeable proportion of the East Germans who stayed not only continued to complain loudly about life in the GDR and oppose various state policies that infringed upon their lives. They also, as we will now see, quite skillfully used the open border to their own advantage.

Popular responses and the uses of the open border

Popular responses in the GDR towards the mass emigration to the West are extremely difficult to judge due to both the dearth of sources at hand as well as the immense spectrum of circumstances under which cases of *Republikflucht* occurred. The most valid generalization – and one which could just as well apply to the Federal Republic – is that there were mixed feelings. It is crucial to bear in mind that *Republikflucht* was not merely an abstract political phenomenon to East Germans in the 1950s and early 1960s, but rather a part of everyday life. The sheer scale of the exodus before 1961 (a net loss of around one-sixth of the population) meant that the vast majority of East Germans personally knew at least one person who left, and had a good idea of why she or he did. In many cases there was widespread sympathy with those who left; comments such as 'if I did not have my family and livelihood here, I would leave too' can be found in numerous party and union reports. This was especially true in cases of undue economic hardship such as the loss of a family business, farm or sizeable decrease in one's wages. When, for instance, work-loads were arbitrarily increased in some of Leipzig's textile factories, union officials reported a certain *Schadenfreude* among the discontented workers whenever any of their colleagues left. In discussions with union officials the workers could barely disguise their satisfaction that someone had the courage to leave the 'so-called intolerable conditions' in the factories.[30]

However, under certain circumstances there was also considerable disapproval or resentment of *Republikflucht*. Though frequently motivated out of envy towards those who were not tied down by family or business matters or vague feelings of being 'left behind', most often this resentment emerged in cases where one felt personally disadvantaged or left in the lurch by someone's departure, especially when 'big wigs' left. For example, at the Gaswerk Dimitroff-straße in Berlin, workers were reportedly angry that so many of '*die Großen*' were disappearing across the border. Not only did the loss of engineers mean longer working hours for them, it also compromised safety. It would be no wonder, workers complained, if 'the whole place would blow up'.[31] Expressions of disapproval were also relatively common when the values of a particular profession were seen to be breached. Although few physicians were enamoured with life in the GDR, equally few appear to have approved of flight if it in any way jeopardized patients' health.[32] And quite naturally, there was no sympathy whatsoever for those who left as a means of escaping debts or punishment for having committed a crime.

In contrast to the issue of people leaving the GDR, there were no mixed feelings at all concerning the preferential treatment of those who came back from the West. The practice of offering returnees prioritized housing (which they did not always get) was, given the dire shortage, a particularly sore point. It was broadly viewed not only as unjust, but as patently absurd to effectively punish those who remained in the GDR by allowing a supposed 'traitor' to jump the queue. Thousands of East Germans defiantly pointed out the farcical logic of this practice to their local housing authority as a means of lending additional legitimacy to their petitions for new housing. Gerda S. of Lautawerk, for instance, complained of a certain family B. who came from the Federal Republic in 1955, got a new flat and suitable employment, even a loan to furnish the flat, but then left the GDR a little over a year later: '... large sums of money were paid out for nothing. We who haven't left the GDR since 1945 are getting pushed up against the wall...'[33] Others adapted the practice for their own ends by threatening to use it as a means of acquiring a flat for themselves. At the Sachsenwerk Niedersedlitz in Dresden, where 300 workers were in search of accommodation in 1954, such threats were reported as common: 'First we will leave the GDR for the West and after we come back someone will have to give us a flat'.[34] A show at the Erfurt Youth Theatre satirized the problem in verse: 'If you want a flat, I'll tell you what's best, you travel to the West. As a reward for coming back, you get yourself a flat'.[35] All humour aside, there was widespread *Schadenfreude* when returnees were given poor accommodation. Six months after the engineer K. and his five-member family returned from West Germany to Jena in 1955, triggering a storm of publicity in the local press, they were still in their provisional one-room flat. As a police report remarked, such incidents 'do not help put a stop to *Republikflucht* or strengthen trust in the GDR'. On the contrary, 'the populace is making fun of the case'.[36]

Even apart from the issue of preferential treatment for returnees, threatening to leave for the West was a fairly common strategy in attempts to procure new housing. Such threats, which were fairly common at least as early as 1954, were usually conveyed via written petitions (*Eingaben*) to various levels of the state apparatus.[37] Most were apparently bluffs, or to use Albert Hirschman's terms again, attempts to give added force to 'voice' through the threat of 'exit', indeed the ultimate form of exit, emigration. As an analysis of the petitions sent to President Pieck during January 1957 explained: 'in the majority of cases the threat is only made to underpin the demand', citing as an example the case of the family K. in Großlindow, who requested that their petition for an emigration permit be disregarded after receiving a new flat. But at the same time it noted that such threats were to be taken seriously in other cases, such as that of a mining-brigadier's wife who suffixed her desperate-sounding complaints about her miserable flat with the remark that, as a *Meister*, her husband could 'get work in West Germany any time he wished'.[38]

Whether taken seriously or not, the realities of the housing shortage meant that most of the thousands of petitions simply could not be honoured. In fact, threatening to leave the GDR as a means of acquiring a new flat could be counter-productive. Fearing a kind of 'domino-effect', some local officials were determined not to give in to such blackmail. In Karl-Marx-Stadt, where requests for flats were reportedly accompanied 'almost without exception' by threats to leave the GDR, the chairman of the district VII municipal council refused to budge on the issue: 'if you allow one [such threat] to work, you immediately get three or four parallel cases, because these things get spoken around'.[39]

Of course the success or failure of using the open border to one's advantage depended to a large extent on the person doing it. Emigration by members of the intelligentsia in general, and those in technical fields in particular, was considered no less than 'a great danger to society',[40] and they, more than any other segment of the population, were well placed to exploit the situation to their own advantage. Although it was generally assumed that most complainants had no serious intention of leaving the GDR, 'insofar as this deals with members of the intelligentsia, the problem requires special attention'.[41] And although the outlawing of even planned *Republikflucht* under the *Paßgesetz* of December 1957 curtailed *open* threats of leaving for the West, the precarious labour market caused by the open border meant that complaints made by doctors, scientists and engineers were still frequently successful not only in acquiring accommodation, but also in unburdening them from excessive bureaucratic work, in obtaining permission to receive professional journals from the West, even gaining permission to travel west for professional conferences.[42]

The clearest example were physicians, who were in especially short supply ever since the end of the war. There were grave concerns about the lack of doctors throughout the 1950s, and the rapid increase in the flight of medical personnel to the West after the Third *Hochschulkonferenz* in 1958 led to a potential crisis in medical provision in the GDR (Figure 11.2). This prompted the *Politbüro* to steer a more liberal course towards physicians, who were given special privileges in September 1958 and again in December 1960, including higher pay, eased restrictions on travel and against doctors'

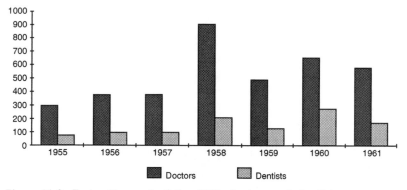

Figure 11.2 Emigration out of the GDR, doctors and dentists

Sources: SAPMO-BA DY30/IV2/19/53, 'Übersicht Republikflucht', 31 Oct. 1960, p. 1; 'Die Lage unter der medizinischen Intelligenz', 21 June 1958, p. 5; 1961 statistics.

children entering higher education, even the ability to bequeath medical practices to one's children.[43] But the privileges failed to make much of an impact since most doctors sceptically viewed them as mere stop-gap measures designed to keep them in the GDR until the party leadership could afford to treat them differently. As a report from the outpatients' clinic in Senftenberg put it: 'In the People's Democracies doctors earn no more than their drivers. It is generally assumed that as soon as the Berlin-Question is solved in the interests of the GDR the position of doctors will be revised and all the privileges cancelled'.[44] It was precisely such fears of an eventual change in their fortunes that prompted so many doctors to leave for the West. Although the westward drain of medical personnel slowed somewhat in 1959, it increased again considerably in 1960 and even further in 1961 (prior to 13 August), as many were gripped by '*Torschlußpanik*'.

The *Politbüro* thus found itself at an impasse. Cracking down in 1958 only drove up the numbers of emigrant doctors, and subsequent liberalization and granting of privileges had little appreciable effect. What is more, the open admission that physicians were precious commodities only amplified the demands for such things as better housing, automobiles, holiday accommodation and even written guarantees that they could retain their practices permanently.[45] As a report from October 1958 explained: 'There has recently been an increase in the number of petitions from physicians demanding a change to their poor housing conditions with reference to the *Politbüro* communique'.[46] Even worse from the perspective of the SED leadership, the 'physician communiqués' also raised expectations among other groups of the intelligentsia who resented the special treatment for doctors. A report from Bautzen summed up the mood thus: 'You ve made concessions to the doctors, now you'll have to make some to us'.[47] Although it is impossible to quantify, it seems from the attention given them in internal reports that demands for flats, better holiday accommodation, automobiles and other perks were increasing in the late 1950s, and this despite the sharper regulations imposed by the *Paßgesetz* in late 1957.[48] As regarded the possibilities of the open border, East Germans had an intuitive feel for what Hirschman explicitly theoritized over a decade later: namely, that 'the chances for voice to function effectively... are appreciably strengthened if voice is backed up by the *threat of exit*, whether it is made openly or whether the possiblity of exit is merely well understood to be an element in the situation by all concerned'.[49]

It was not necessary, then, to play the 'trump card' of the open border – that is, leave for the West – in order to make use of it. Many East Germans who might never have considered emigrating could still find ways of profiting from it: perhaps a better flat, better working conditions, avoiding military service by making a quick trip westwards, the list goes on. Considering both the myriad factors that underlay the decision to emigrate and the rather self-interested ways many East Germans who remained in the GDR took advantage of the open border, the idea that those who stayed were, on balance, significantly more pliable or less *'aufmüpfig'* than those who left seems somewhat exaggerated. While the problem of emigration to the West may indeed help explain the relative lack of an East German counter-elite compared to other 'People's Democracies' in Eastern Europe, at least in terms of the departure of a vociferous minority who might serve as crystallization points for political dissent, when applied to the broad mass of emigrants this old dualistic myth of the enterprising and freedom-seeking refugee and the hapless, indecisive East German who stayed is based as much on processes of West German self-legitimation and the efforts of refugee organizations to cultivate understanding and tolerance in the Federal Republic as on any balanced judgement of the motives of flight and the sociopolitical landscape in the GDR. Whether or not patterns of popular opinion and dissent changed *after* August 1961 as the possibility of flight vanished is another question, to which we now turn.

Part 4

East Germans, the Wall and the Prospects of the 1960s

The construction of the Berlin Wall on the night of 12–13 August 1961 is more or less universally viewed as a principal caesura in the political, economic and social history of the GDR. It is generally accepted that it marked the beginning of a period of greater domestic stability in East Germany with the end of the mass population drain westwards, as well as greater international stability in Europe as a whole by seemingly laying to rest the question of German unification once and for all. It is likely that it rescued the regime in the short-term from economic collapse, and there can be little doubt that the economic growth and improving material situation of the 1960s were to a large extent predicated on the relative normalization of the labour supply and enhanced control of goods and currency after 1961. For all of these reasons, some historians have gone so far as to regard the erection of the Wall as the 'secret founding of the GDR'.[1]

But beneath the level of high politics and macro-economics, the construction of the Wall also had far-reaching effects at the grassroots. It had hitherto been regarded as either impossible or imprudent from the party leadership's point of view to force through certain changes so long as the border was open, as Ulbricht complained in a letter to Khrushchev just days before the barbed-wire went up.[2] In Ulbricht's view, the problem with the open border was not just limited to the effects of the mass emigration (whose costs in terms of production losses alone were estimated at around DM 2.5 to 3 billion), but rather involved the entire 'construction of socialism' in the GDR. The living standard was singled out as one important problem: 'Simply put, the open border forced us to raise the living standard faster than our economic capabilities allowed'. So, too, were the difficulties associated with raising productivity in the state-owned factories and stopping individual farming practices in the supposedly '*vollgenossenschaftlich*' villages:

> The entire situation, influenced by the open border, hindered us from implementing adequate measures to eliminate the disproportions in the wage structure and to create a proper relationship between wages and performance... Of course we had similar difficulties with the transition to agricultural co-operatives as in other People's Democracies. But one should not overlook the fact that some things are much more complicated here... In all the other People's Democracies, in the context of their closed borders, such political–economic issues could be tackled differently than was possible under our political circumstances.[3]

The sealing of the border to West Berlin changed these 'political circumstances' dramatically, and indeed solved some of the problems Ulbricht mentioned. But as we will see in the following two chapters, other problems could only be cemented in.

12
The Grass-Roots Effects of the Berlin Wall

Popular opinion and the sealing of the border

The sealing of the border to West Berlin was arguably the single most invasive and brutal intervention into the lives of East Germans in the entire history of the GDR, profoundly affecting their ability to maintain contact with relatives and friends, as well as to travel, shop, and sample western culture. The images of families waving to each other across no-man's-land – in different worlds only metres apart – number among the most memorable and saddening in post-war history. The Wall was an unprecedented and shockingly bold political measure, as well as a geographical absurdity and human rights monstrosity.

But there were no major strikes, large-scale protests, demonstrations or any kind of broadly coordinated resistance to its construction within the GDR. Those strikes that did take place in the wake of the Wall were small, spontaneous and unorganized, and many were not primarily motivated by the border closure in the first place. Instances of industrial sabotage, the classic form of anonymous protest, indeed leapt from only six in the second quarter of 1961 to 83 in the third quarter, and there were widespread rumours of a general strike.[1] As one person looking on at the Brandenburg Gate was overheard saying on 13 August: 'Just wait – today everything is quiet, in the next few days things will look different'.[2] But things changed very little in the following days and weeks, and rumours remained just that.

Such opposition as emerged was decidedly small in scale and was generally confined to individual acts of protest or at the most small groups of young people. Internal reports more or less unanimously agree that youths were by far the most open in protesting against the sealing of the border. At the Wollankstraße crossing point in Pankow it was reported that there was a gathering of some 500–600 youths 'provoking' the guards with shouts and threats: 'into the middle of the street, let's make a forceful breakthrough, we're all Germans, we just want to cross over to our brothers'; 'it's a disgrace what you [guards] are doing . . . You're no Germans'.[3] At other crossing points in East Berlin, groups of youths, some of them on motorcycles, were reportedly organizing onlookers for the purpose of hurling abuse and threats at guards. After being dispersed by *Kampfgruppen*, they simply relocated to another crossing point.[4] There were also isolated cases of young 'rowdies' beating up party agitators or other individuals involved in carrying out the 'measures,' as well as attempts to stir up anger among people riding on public transport or in train stations. One youth, for instance, tried to provoke his fellow passengers on the *S-Bahn* by pointing to the rolls of barbed wire and proclaiming, 'Such is the democracy that is so clearly expressed today'. But such open criticism was the exception, not the rule, and moreover was essentially without practical effect. Although such 'provocations' occurred at a number of *S-Bahn* stations in East Berlin, it is characteristic of the popular response that the majority of those present were reported to have behaved 'quietly' and not responded either positively or negatively to the youth's overtures.[5]

Broadly speaking, there have been two different explanations of the remarkable quiet in the GDR in the wake of the construction of Wall. Emphasizing the legitimatory successes of the regime during the 1950s, Heinz Niemann has argued on the basis of East German opinion surveys from the latter half of the 1960s that only a 'majority acceptance of this measure' could explain why 'an unprecedented operation like 13 August 1961 came off so smoothly'.[6] Judging from both the internal reports written at the time as well as countless anecdotes from East Germans, it would seem that this interpretation has little to recommend it. There is precious little evidence of 'acceptance' – even in the most passive sense of the term – apart from the declarations of support that SED agitation troops demanded people sign. On the contrary, as the BGL chairman of the Firma Frank in Berlin warned a union official: 'If you want to talk to the colleagues, they'll probably throw you out. Ninety per cent of all people are against these measures anyway'.[7]

The more common and convincing explanation emphasizes the

massive apparatus of control and repression in the GDR. In this view, most East Germans only maintained their outward conformity under the pressure of the well-coordinated security forces, which by and large intervened rapidly to deal with unrest of any kind before it could escalate into any wider protest. An important difference between the events of 13 August 1961 and 17 June 1953, so this argument goes, was that there were no longer any uncertainties and apparent splits of opinion within the apparatus of power to lame its organizational capacity and ability to control the situation.[8] In the event, the NVA troops, *Kampfgruppen* and party agitators carried out their duties in exemplary fashion. Even the *Volkspolizei*, which largely failed the 'test' of 17 June, also proved itself a loyal and reliable instrument of coercion.[9] Certainly the crackdown after the sealing of the border was comparable in both scale and intensity to that following the June 1953 uprising. Whereas 6171 persons were arrested between 17 and 30 June 1953, between 13 August and 4 Sept 1961 the number was 6041, with 3108 of them incarcerated.[10] In some ways the crackdown after the Wall was even more swift and thorough. Whereas it took five days for the first convictions after 17 June 1953, this took only two days after the construction of the Wall.[11]

While repression, or more importantly the *fear* of repression, no doubt goes a long way towards explaining why the closing of the border met with no more grass-roots opposition within the GDR than it did, this nonetheless overlooks other important factors. For one thing, it was not necessarily clear at first that the 'measures' would last very long. After all, there had been earlier attempts to control all movement to West Berlin, most notably the so-called '*Aktion Schiebertod*' ('Operation Death to Smugglers') on 13 October 1957. The barbed wire that went up on the night of 12–13 August could, many East Germans hoped, quickly be dismantled again once the party leadership had made its point. Not untypical were the comments of one Berlin woman who was overheard saying that she regretted not being able to see her relatives in West Berlin for a while, but was certain that the measures were just temporary.[12] Of course there were plenty of East Germans who took what appeared to them the last opportunity to leave for the West by jumping from windows or leaping over barricades. But for many East Germans, it seems that the construction of the Wall was soon *remembered* as more of a caesura than it was actually *experienced* at the time.

Secondly, a not insignificant minority of East Germans agreed with the official argument that Berlin's special status constituted a serious problem for the East German economy that had to be solved, and thus felt a certain sense of relief, however little one approved of the harshness of the measures, that the harmful effects of the open border were being eliminated. There is evidence of this in both internal reports as well as post-1989 survey results.[13] As a pharmacist in Belzig was quoted as saying: 'The West Berlin question had to be solved, otherwise the GDR would have been bled dry'.[14] There was also a certain feeling of *Schadenfreude* that the much-maligned *Grenzgänger* (with the exception of those who had begun working in West Berlin before the currency changes of 1948) now had to work in the GDR like everyone else, though the fact that West Berliners were still allowed to travel East was totally inconsistent with official explanations about protecting the GDR from an attack and prompted considerable envy.[15]

Perhaps most importantly, there seems to have been a kind of shock with the suddenness and brutality of the border closure. In marked contrast to the problems associated with the implementation of measures against *Republikflucht* in the 1950s, the sealing of the border was done with legendary Prussian efficiency. Most Berliners awoke on the morning of 13 August to find there was little they could do. Rolls of barbed wire guarded by armed sentries at close intervals offered little chance of escape, and many East Germans were too afraid of the possible ramifications of the measures to think of much else. There were widespread fears of the response from the West, rumours of an impending war and a planned currency reform, as well as an epidemic of panic shopping over the following two weeks.[16] The mood in the Gaswerk Dimitroffstraße on the morning of 13 August was hurriedly summed up by a union secretary thus: 'Wait-and-see attitude, what will happen now? Main concern: hopefully there won't be trouble (*hoffentlich knallt es nicht*)'.[17]

Once the initial shock had worn off, the vast majority of reported opinions were decidedly negative and concerned with the broader implications, both personal and political, of the newly sealed border. There were numerous overlapping strands of disapproval, ranging from objections against the abrogation of the principle of free travel to desires for German unification to the more prosaic matter of no longer being able to visit relatives, shop, or go to the cinema in the West. Although the SED tried to portray the construction of the Wall as a sign of their strength, as a decisive victory for peace in Europe and a blow against the expansionist plans of the 'warmongers' in the West, internal reports leave no doubt that the vast majority of East Germans were of a different opinion. Even those who agreed in principle with the necessity of stricter border controls viewed the Wall rather as a sign of weakness. As a doctor in Frankfurt/Oder succinctly put it: 'The barbed wire was unrolled because we're at the end of our tether'.[18] Furthermore, the particular means chosen for closing the border were generally viewed as anything but 'peaceful'. Comments such as 'we're against barbed wire, army and tanks'; 'why are so many armed soldiers deployed?' and 'with tanks one cannot be for peace' were extremely common and can be found in most of the mood reports during the days following 13 August.[19] The fact that the *Kampfgruppen* stood with their backs to the Brandenburg Gate and weapons pointed eastward obviously undermined the claim that these were 'protective measures' directed against western agents and smugglers. Instead, comparisons with a jail or concentration camp were almost immediate.

It speaks volumes for the popular mood in the weeks following 13 August that many low-level party and union functionaries were showing signs of 'capitulation': suddenly falling ill, avoiding all discussions with employees and resigning from their functions. Some union secretaries simply could not bring themselves to support the 'measures' in front of their non-affiliated colleagues or to mouth their approval to superiors, choosing instead to remain silent: 'If I told you my genuine opinion, you would not approve'. Others found themselves unable to keep their genuine opinions to themselves: 'Our government can kiss my . . .'[20]

Undermining the *Produktionsaufgebot* on the shopfloor

Clearly, the construction of the Wall did little to reduce the many 'ideological unclarities' among union functionaries in the factories; if anything it had precisely the opposite effect. But the sealing of the border did significantly alter the parameters of shopfloor politics in the GDR. Much of the cause for the aggravating labour shortage in the GDR was eliminated, and workers could no longer simply leave for the West in search of a better living standard or if they got into trouble at work. It did not take long for the party leadership to make use of its enhanced position *vis-à-vis* the industrial workforce, and it did so in two ways. First, in the immediate wake of the building of the Wall there was a general crackdown against supposed 'internal enemies' of all kinds, including so-called 'work shy' elements. But more importantly, it took the bold step of trying once again to raise industrial work norms in a blanket fashion, something which it had not dared since June 1953. Thus what had been only tentatively and periodically attempted in the intervening years via such devices as the production brigades and piecemeal norm-tinkering was now to be quickly taken care of in the shadow of the Wall. Loafing, absenteeism and all other forms of industrial indiscipline were to be swept out of the republic on a tide of 15 per cent norm increases.

The campaign, known as the *Produktionsaufgebot*, began in typical fashion with a somewhat less than spontaneous resolution by a brigade of workers at the VEB Elektrokohle in Berlin-Lichtenberg to raise their own norms by some 15 per cent (less difficult than it sounds, as norms at this factory were at the time overfulfilled by an average of 195 per cent), and soon became a carefully staged and widely publicized movement.[21] But no matter how the FDGB tried to package it, the *Produktionsaufgebot* essentially amounted to a centrally-directed wage freeze, as the slogan 'to produce more in the same time for the same pay' clearly indicated.

As one could only expect, the *Produktionsaufgebot* was poorly received by most industrial workers: 'the *Produktionsaufgebot* is just a wage scissors'; 'now come adminstrative wage-cuts'; 'here they come with their norm-scissors'.[22] Both party and union reports clearly show that workers themselves were no less aware than the party leadership of the direct connection between their virtual house arrest and this latest campaign to boost work productivity. A reportedly 'common argument' in Cottbus was that 'they've closed the border on 13 August in order to revise the norms and carry out a wage freeze'. In Berlin-Treptow a lathe-operator was overheard by a union functionary comparing the situation to June 1953: 'Another 17 June will have to come so that the measures of 13 August will be undone. What couldn't be pushed through back then is now supposed to happen through the *Produktionsaufgebot'*. One worker in Potsdam was even more to the point: 'For years you were too cowardly to change the norm, and now you come up with this ploy'.[23]

Coming so close on the heels of the exceedingly unpopular 'measures' of 13 August, the *Produktionsaufgebot* created a potentially explosive situation. It disrupted the informal arrangements in the factories; not since June 1953, the last time the regime had introduced a blanket norm increase by fiat, was the SED made so conscious of where the limits of willingness to compromise lay. The sheer number of reports keeping track of the situation in the factories at this time clearly testifies to the nervousness of the party leadership. Yet there were, despite the vehement criticism and threatening invocations of 17 June, few signs of mass protest among workers beyond mere verbal rejection. As we have seen, there were no large-scale strikes; indeed there was no significant change in the number, scope or nature of work stoppages at all. The total number of strikes reported by the FDGB had actually decreased from 166 in 1960 to 135 in 1961, to rise again only slightly to 144 in 1962.[24] And of these, the vast majority were still small, spontaneous and unorganized. Why?

There were a number of reasons for this. First, as I have already noted, after the experience of June 1953 the improved security forces intervened rapidly to deal with industrial unrest before it could escalate into any wider protest. The flip-side of this was that workers were commensurately less willing or able to stage large-scale strikes than in 1953, not least because they could no longer escape to the West if things went awry. Second, there were a number of important structural factors including both the obvious lack of an independent union that could coordinate worker protest across a broad front as well as the ever-growing divisions *within* the East German workforce created by the widespread use of performance-enhancing bonuses and perks, the constant competitions, generational tensions, resentments between skilled and unskilled, the distortions of the brigade system and above all the policy of wage differentiation across industrial sectors and geographic regions.[25] Perhaps most importantly, the fact that the *Produktionsaufgebot* only managed to keep wages down very slightly,[26] combined with bits of evidence in the internal reports on its implementation, suggest that it was often gutted *en locale*; in other words that, much as with Order 234, the BKVs and the periodic attempts to raise the productivity-wage relation during the 1950s, a plethora of informal deals at the factory level was also crucial in keeping the potential for conflict below the threshold of open protest. Whatever the inflated reports of success in the official press, it seems that, for a number of reasons, the *Produktionsaufgebot* was never fully implemented on the shopfloor in the first place.

One reason for this was that workers *did* widely oppose it, if not in as spectacular and large-scale a fashion as in 1953. Despite the absence of broader strikes in autumn 1961, union reports nonetheless posit a sharp increase in 'sloppiness and breaches of the work ethic and work discipline', especially on the perennially problematic construction sites.[27] There was also a wave of alleged industrial sabotage in the third quarter of 1961 (though no doubt much of it was motivated by the construction of the Berlin Wall and not by the *Produktionsaufgebot* specifically): there were 83 cases of sabotage and 17 fires in factories across the GDR compared to only six cases of sabotage and three fires during the second quarter of the year.[28] Granted, the use of terms such as 'sabotage' was significantly broadened during the crackdown after 13 August, but the heightened discontent in the factories that cases of 'sabotage' were seen to reflect nonetheless comes through clearly in internal reports.

There were numerous symptoms of discontent and subtle opposition towards the *Produktionsaufgebot*. The reports complain time and again of workers refusing to pay their union dues, making resolutions only in the context of brigades in the hope of escaping into the anonymity of the collective, of high illness rates and lax observance of work-hours.[29] The minority of 'norm breakers' who actively supported the *Produktionsaufgebot* were still held in contempt and their efforts thwarted wherever possible. When the brigade '13th of August' at the VEB Walzlagerfabrik 'Josef Orlopp' tried to set an example by voluntarily raising its norm by 3 per cent, the other workers in the factory derided it as the 'barbed-wire brigade' and cursed the brigadier as a 'wage-cutter'. Similarly, when an SED member in a Potsdam textile factory wanted to establish a concrete norm-time and have a TAN calculated on it, 'she was thereafter cut-off by the arrangers; that is, she was forced to wait longer for work etc. than the other employees'.[30] Even the attempt to improve productivity and work discipline by deploying as many *Grenzgänger* as possible in the VEBs was undermined. Although the SED was keen to harness what was regarded as the superior work ethic the *Grenzgänger* brought with them from the capitalist West, their new colleagues in the VEBs often nipped such efforts in the bud. As union officials at the EAW in Treptow reported, *Grenzgänger* were greeted on the shopfloor with the advice that '"We don't do capitalist work here, but rather socialist" (that is, slow)'.[31]

These subtle forms of opposition to the *Produktionsaufgebot* on the shopfloor hardly diminished in the early months of 1962, and if anything got only stiffer with the growing shortages of consumer goods after the harsh winter of 1961–62. This was more the case in the provinces than in relatively well-supplied Berlin. By the spring of 1962, union functionaries in *Bezirk* Cottbus reported that many of the miners in the region simply refused to discuss raising work productivity until the questions of consumer provision were cleared up, and angrily complained to their superiors in the FDGB leadership that they had no convincing argumentation or explanations as to why there was no meat or eggs or even milk. By the summer, the connection between poor work morale and the continuing shortage of goods even found expression in a popular slogan in the region: *'Wie die Verpflegung, so die Bewegung'* ('As the provisions, so the effort').[32] As a frustrated *Kreisleitung* official at Schwarze Pumpe remarked in May 1962, 'The miners have driven us to the wall with questions about provision'.[33]

But subtle opposition on the part of workers was only one side of the problem. Many factory managers and union functionaries themselves were little more enamoured with the *Produktionsaufgebot* than the workers whom they supervised. Many were well aware that it was a risky venture, and there is plenty of evidence of managers afraid or unwilling to introduce it in undiluted form. There were any number of potentially detrimental consequences, not least the loss of workers to other enterprises. Although the end of the mass population drain to the West helped mitigate the overall labour shortage in the GDR, the labour market was still flush enough for dissatisfied workers to find jobs quite easily elsewhere.[34] Moreover, in the context of the 'Defence Law' (the legal forerunner to conscription) and latest recruitment drive for the NVA, the 50 000 additional workers whom the SED claimed to have won for the economy overnight through the 'measures' of 13 August made little difference.

Diluting the *Produktionsaufgebot* on the shopfloor was also motivated by the simple dread of having to sell an exceedingly unpopular policy to one's employees. The central thrust of the *Produktionsaufgebot* (to produce more in the same time for the same pay) was broadly considered a 'hot potato', and factory officials were often accused in instructors' reports of 'insufficiently dealing with' the lax observance of shift-starts and -ends, keeping breaks within prescribed limits and other general matters of work discipline.[35] Fairly typical was the situation at the VEB LTA in Berlin, where the production management was reportedly 'governed by the principle "not to tackle it so sharply right away"'. The situation was little different in the key industrial conglomerates of *Bezirk* Cottbus or the VEB Volksbau in Berlin, where it was reported that 'the discussion was badly hindered through the passive behaviour and reticence of many *Meister* and construction foremen. Most of the representatives (*Vertrauensleute*) also have not yet gone on the offensive by speaking out. The leading economic functionaries in the management have left the political discussions with the brigades to the societal organs'. Yet the 'societal organs' (the party and MOs) were often no better themselves. At the VEB Elektroprojekt Berlin, it was reported that, 'in spite of numerous instructions for the comrades in the party organization and the union functionaries, they nonetheless remained silent at the assemblies in their departments. We regard this as a sign of insufficient ideological steadfastness and insufficient knowledge of the issues being discussed, which leads to fear and to a shying-away from discussions'. Indeed, some SED functionaries failed to appear at all at the assemblies dealing with the *Produktionsaufgebot*.[36]

Eventually, of course, the *Produktionsaufgebot* had to be introduced in some form or another, though this meant little in practice. Caught between the demands of the party leadership to implement it and the imperative of retaining workers and maintaining the peace on the shopfloor, many managers once again steered a middle course as with Order 234, going through the motions and maintaining appearances without really observing the intended spirit of the campaign. Without wanting to descend too far into speculation, it seems that there was a kind of tacit understanding on the shopfloor that the *Produktionsaufgebot* should not be allowed to upset the existing *modus vivendi* any more than necessary. Here again we see a fault line of conflict running not so much between 'workers' and 'regime' as between the needs of the individual factories and the demands of the central economic authorities.

The most common means of diluting the *Produktionsaufgebot* on the shopfloor was the evasion of definite figures.[37] As I have already noted, workers as a rule offered only vague resolutions concerning working hours and production targets, usually making them only under the anonymity of the brigade and often with little intention of observing them in any event. For instance, although the brigade 'Free Cuba' was the first at the VEB Ziegelkombinat Bad Freienwalde to declare its participation in the *Produktionsaufgebot*, this did not keep its members from staging a short work stoppage on 6 November when their norms were *actually* changed.[38] The reports often accuse workers of not honestly divulging all of their efficiency 'reserves' for scrutiny, which for most were an integral part of their pay calculations and served as a buffer against the periodic shortages in supply and consequent down-time. A reportedly 'typical' attitude was that of a group of workers at the Brandenburger Traktorenwerk:

'We simply cannot lay everything on the table now, we have to retain something because . . . you'll certainly want to have something more again'.[39]

This kind of 'formalism', as it was called, was often complemented, and indeed made possible in the first place, by that of the factory managers and functionaries themselves.[40] There were occasional complaints of managers simply organizing the *Produktionsaufgebot* 'from their desks' without actually analyzing time and costs, and with apparently little intention to implement new measures in any event.[41] There were also cases of managers avoiding a confrontation with their employees by succumbing to worker demands to analyze and determine their work norms themselves, i.e. by giving them a blank cheque. Indeed, some functionaries even organized this so-called '*Selbstnormung*' themselves by putting a stopwatch in workers' hands and letting them take care of it.[42]

Even when definite figures and specific resolutions were established, they were often little more than a means of avoiding what one feared might be even greater wage losses. Many workers were, it is true, grudgingly willing to raise their norms by a certain percentage or give back a few minutes from their 'reserves'. But as a rule, this was less an expression of support for the campaign than a strategy for being left in peace without sacrificing any more than necessary. A report from the VEB Lederverarbeitung in Berlin offers an illustration:

> One colleague in the sport department voluntarily agreed to finish three more balls per hour. After he presented his resolution, a TAN-inspector was immediately called and the result of the investigation was that twelve more balls, not just three, could come out of his norm. This example of course taught everyone a lesson, and one does not need to wonder why we are not getting any further with the *Produktionsaufgebot*. One could cite similar examples from [the factories] Oberflächenveredlung, Druck- und Prägemaschinen, Libelle and Konsum-Großbäckerei.[43]

Moreover, the fact that the managers and union functionaries generally presented the *Produktionsaufgebot* to workers in terms of giving back a small percentage of their norm time – economic functionaries in Nauen were openly speaking of a 'Minute-Movement' by October 1961[44] – suggests that they, too, recognized this danger. As one party instructor in Potsdam concluded from his investigations: 'In carrying out the crux of the matter, it is important to make it clear in all factories that the point of the *Produktionsaufgebot* is not to exchange mutual gifts (this tendency is especially visible in the practice of returning norm-time), but rather not to demand any more from society than one contributes to it through one's own work.'[45]

The purpose in focusing on these problems of implementation and subtle worker opposition is not to portray the *Produktionsaufgebot* as an unmitigated failure. It did succeed in modestly raising work-productivity, if indeed far below the targets originally envisioned. Rather, the point is that its principal aims (the centralized regulation of wages and norms and the rapid increase of work productivity without corresponding wage increases) were at best only partially realized at the grass-roots, and foundered on the needs of individual enterprises to retain their manpower (a need which, even after the construction of the Wall, could only be met via precisely the decentralized mechanisms of wage regulation that it sought to end) and on the unwillingness of many managers and local functionaries to push it through against the wishes of their employees. It is difficult to pinpoint precisely how this happened in the factories, as such informal 'arrangements' left no paper trails. One catches only occasional glimpses, such as a work stoppage and compromise solution being unsuccessfully covered up by the party organization and factory management at the VAZ Schrott in Brandenburg; the SED *Kreisleitung* in Berlin-Lichtenberg discovering in July 1962 that workers at the VEB Herrenbekleidung were still overfulfilling their old norms by 200 per cent; or the matter-of-fact report from the regional union leadership in Cottbus: 'Distortion of the *Produktionsaufgebot*: in the BMK Lübbenau work norms were administratively reduced by 5–20 per cent by the labour department. Regional union functionaries put a stop to this'.[46] It is also difficult to say precisely how widespread they were. But if the initial reactions of managers, local functionaries and workers are any indication, they were more the rule than the exception. The construction of the Berlin Wall was of little help in the critical attempt to gain control over wages and productivity on the shopfloor, let alone win the hearts and minds of industrial workers.

The wall and the villages

It seems that the Wall had a greater immediate effect on the situation in the countryside. For several reasons, it more clearly augmented the SED leadership's ability to push through its agricultural policies, mostly by means of intimidating recalcitrant LPG farmers who were still working 'individually'. Not only was there less tendency among farmers than industrial workers to engage in strikes or slow-downs that would essentially be more detrimental to themselves than to the state, it was also more difficult to escape notice in the villages than in the relative anonymity of a large industrial factory. Only twelve days after the barbed wire went up around West Berlin the 'Order on Residence Restriction' came into force, which mandated 'work education' for the so-called 'work-shy elements' in the countryside. The object was not so much to arrest large numbers of LPG opponents as it was to scare them into toeing the line. The few convictions to which it led were widely publicized for effect, such as that of Oskar Stern from Potsdam-Bornim who was essentially charged with failing to cooperate with the rest of his LPG.[47] As a December report from the MfS and *Volkspolizei* in *Bezirk* Potsdam euphemistically put it, 'the struggle for the establishment of cleanliness, order and collective work as the basis of the LPG economy received a boost after the measures of 13 August'.[48]

But it is easy to overestimate the impact of the Wall and the legislation that followed it, as some scholars have done.[49] Despite such scare tactics the situation in the countryside remained unstable and the LPGs were only gradually consolidated over the following years. In fact, the very same MfS report that initially posits a 'boost' after the construction of the Wall goes on to leave little doubt about the continued unreliability of many local functionaries, widespread disaffection with the SED's collectivization policies and the myriad ways this was manifested: sabotage, arson, refusal to work collectively, rumours. The 'political mass-work' of rural functionaries was still deemed 'by no means satisfactory', the majority of local SED organizations were still 'ideologically insecure' and the village VdgB associations remained 'completely unsatisfactory' – indeed, most existed merely on paper. The LPGs' economic performance in *Bezirk* Potsdam was none too impressive either: 315 (53 per cent) were still operating in the red at the end of the year. As for the overall mood in the countryside, most farmers still had 'no interest in collective development' and were deeply alienated from the regime. Farmers in Pessin, *Kreis* Nauen, summed up the mood thus: 'if the border were open the whole village would be empty in 24 hours, including the party secretary and the mayor'.[50]

Such sentiments are anything but surprising given the bleak situation in the countryside at the time. The problems associated with collectivization were compounded by the unusually harsh winter of 1961–62. Many LPGs needed bridging-loans to stay financially afloat, and some were even decreasing the sizes of their livestock herds because of a shortage of feed. The tenuous economic situation of many farmers was made even more precarious by the harsher stipulations regarding the payment of debts before receiving bridging loans. Some responded by borrowing a page from the repertoire of industrial workers' protest: there were sporadic demands for wage guarantees, reports of work slow-downs in the LPGs and even isolated calls for strikes, some emanating from village party secretaries. Under the circumstances, it is no wonder that the *Produktionsaufgebot* was essentially a non-starter in the East German countryside. Most farmers understandably felt that there was simply nothing more to be squeezed out of agriculture. LPG incomes remained low throughout 1962. Although the introduction of a minimum annual salary of DM 3120 for LPG members (accompanied by a maximum salary of DM 8000, over which one was forced to reinvest one's income at a progressively increasing rate) guaranteed a subsistence income, it did little to improve the overall economic standing of many struggling LPGs, as the small wave of farm withdrawals in late 1962 amply illustrates.[51] And although the majority of LPGs were finally working according to plan by the end of 1962, so long as the overall situation in agriculture remained poor, so too did the prospects of any substantial improvement in the attitudes of most farmers towards the regime and its agricultural policies.

Youth from crackdown to conscription

The internal reports in the wake of the Wall unanimously agree that the greatest potential for protest against the sealing of the border was to be found among young people. Groups of youths were the instigators of most incidents of overt disapproval and opposition towards the border closure, at least in Berlin and the surrounding areas, and also were reportedly most open in expressing 'unclarities' and 'RIAS-arguments'. Comments such as 'Leave me alone with that rubbish – are you still Germans at all?'; 'You need not bother giving me those things [pro-SED flyers] at all. After all, we're living in a jail'; 'we want to go to West Berlin, because one can earn well there and here we get nothing'; 'we want to go to West Berlin cinemas because the GDR does not offer us an attractive cultural life' were reported time and again as characteristic of the mood among East German youth in the weeks following the erection of the Wall.[52]

Because of the fear of mass protest, the crackdown in the wake of the Wall was particularly harsh towards young people. It had two primary thrusts: first, to force young men into the military forces once and for all; and, second, to increase efforts towards rearing the diligent, disciplined species of youth symbolized by the notion of 'socialist morality', but undermined by the disruptive influence of 'western decadence'. But as was also the case with the crackdown in the factories and villages, sealing the border was of only limited use for achieving greater influence and control over youth. While it held great promise for mobilizing them against the military threat of the West – largely a matter of controlling bodies – it could do little to turn them into model socialist citizens.

A special focus of concern was, as always, what youths did in their free time. Although the cultural bridgehead West Berlin was now physically unreachable for all but the most daring, it still literally transmitted its 'poisonous influence' to tens of thousands of young people via radio and television. In September, 25 000 FDJ members were deployed in the 'Operation Strike against NATO-stations', and literally turned thousands of TV and radio antennae 'in the direction of socialism', much to the chagrin of many a party member tuned into the West. At the same time, pupils and apprentices were called on to give written declarations against listening to western stations. But in spite of such staged approbation, the FDJ still lost around 300 000 (or 9 per cent) of its members in the period immediately following 13 August,[53] and officials reckoned with continued protest among youth.

A particular incident of pranks and unguarded opinions at the upper school (*Erweiterte Oberschule*, or EOS) in Jüterbog is illustrative of both the problems the FDJ and party confronted in trying to control the behaviour of this most high-spirited age-group of the populace, as well as the harsh manner in which the leadership reacted during the months after the Wall. In late August, just over a week after the border was sealed, a group of 18 pupils attended a camp on the Baltic Sea with a group from the Karl-Marx-Oberschule in Leipzig. The two groups quickly made friends, and in the evening got rather drunk, danced without supervision until late into the night, and afterwards, in the typically disapproving words of the report, 'engaged in immoral activities in the tents'. Worse still, in a mood of irreverence a group of pupils carried out a ritual ceremony, burying a bottle containing pictures of Ulbricht and other communist leaders under a marker entitled 'pigswill'. This joke did not stop after one night, but continued with daily flag ceremonies (mocking the quasi-military discipline at FDJ meetings), anti-Soviet songs and Nazi salutes. A number of pupils from each school met again shortly after returning home from the camp. As the report remarked, 'although there was no "flag ceremony" on these occasions, there was nonetheless once more a lot of drinking and dancing to recordings of Bill Haley and Presley', which of course was deemed much of the reason for the pupils' rowdy behaviour in the first place.[54]

This rather innocuous incident, which in the overdrawn interpretation of the SED was regarded as no less than 'hostile to the state', had a chain of serious consequences. There followed a series of investigations and meetings with the school directors, teaching staff and parents, in the course of which, as always, a veritable nest of 'enemy ideology' was uncovered among both pupils and staff.[55] Despite copious 'self-criticism', the director, deputy director and party secretary of the Jüterbog EOS were all dismissed for downplaying the seriousness of the incident and failing to evince a 'party-minded attitude' towards the fact that 'their pupils "symbolically buried" comrade Walter Ulbricht'.[56]

News of the incident circulated rapidly, and led to a further crackdown in the other upper schools of *Bezirk* Potsdam. In Oranienburg, the school councillor thought it would be a good idea to give the pupils a 'test on how they stand by Walter Ulbricht' by assigning them a weekend project on the theme 'What do you know about our State Council Chairman Walter Ulbricht, the shining example to all Germans, especially the German youth?'.[57] The tightening discipline and political control at the Oberschule 4 in Potsdam was even more ridiculous. While waiting for a bus to take them home after a harvest deployment at the nearby LPG Schwanebeck, several pupils passed the time by pulling a few pictures of Marx, Engels and Stalin out of the clubhouse storage rooms, dusting them off and presenting them to each other as 'bonuses' for their work, finally setting them on chairs around the room as a 'picture gallery'. Understandably, neither the teacher nor the school FDJ secretary reported this harmless incident. Once the criminal police were informed by the LPG, however, the usual series of investigations and meetings began. The party assembly reached the usual conclusions: the teacher, who as it turned out was 'strongly connected to the church', was to be formally punished; the 'ringleaders' were to be 'exposed' and expelled from the school; and of course the 'political-ideological work' in the school needed to be improved by redoubling the efforts of the FDJ, hanging pictures of Ulbricht on the Walls, etc.[58]

Much of this heavy-handedness in the schools and towards young people in general after the Wall was in response to what was regarded as a far more dangerous display of youth dissent towards the ever-increasing pressure to undergo paramilitary training and enlist in the armed forces. On 21 September 1961, the day after the *Volkskammer* passed the Defence Law that paved the way for universal military conscription, the entire class 12b at the Oberschule in Anklam came to school wearing black as an expression of protest.[59] The uniformity and solidarity of this gesture, as well as the conciliatory stance adopted by a number of teachers, magnified the incident into a matter of concern at the highest political levels. For this 'counter-revolutionary' gesture, the pupils involved were expelled from school and forced to 'work in production', the two alleged ringleaders arrested and imprisoned, a number of teachers fired, and the pupils' parents forced to make public admissions of their parental failings. Numerous meetings were held to evaluate the incident, and a report was sent all the way to Ulbricht and Honecker. A party and *Stasi* investigation revealed that the teaching staff was politically unreliable (three teachers, including the school director, had taught there under the Nazis), that the SED organization was substandard and that even the FDJ secretary had played a 'politically negative role'. The reaction dwarfed the incident itself, and led to the major investigation into the situation in schools all across the GDR whose results we have just seen.

What the youths in Anklam were objecting to was not just the passing of the Defence Law, but the entire situation of being locked into their own state, coerced into doing something against their wishes or consciences, and generally feeling condemned to a life of increasing militarization and subordination. The life of young people, both men and women, who had grown up in the GDR of the 1950s was in a variety of ways characterized by military principles, rituals and organizational forms: uniforms for the *Junge Pionieren* and FDJ, frequent flag ceremonies at schools, '*Wehrerziehung*' both during and after school, pre-military training in the GST. After the Wall this encouragement of military discipline and behaviour was generally intensified, and was manifested most tangibly in the increasingly forceful methods of recruitment for formal military service. After the 'completely insufficient' recruitment results during the first half of 1961, the new border circumstances were the object of great hopes among the party and NVA leadership in terms of at least controlling young men's bodies, if not their minds.[60] But even this proved more difficult than expected at the grass-roots. Despite diffuse talk of a 'fundamental turnaround in recruitment' after the Wall and a sharp rise in the number of 'declarations of willingness' to enlist during September and October 1961, it did not take long to discover that this was more a reflection of the increasingly coercive tactics of recruiters than of any real turnaround in recruitment, much less a change of heart on the part of East German youths.

As the year-end report of the Central Committee's Security Department remarked, 'often the methods of administration, of coercion, of threats and defamation of youths were given priority over the methods of persuasion'.[61] This was especially the case in *Bezirke* Potsdam and Leipzig, which – and this was no coincidence – reported by far the highest number of resolutions to enlist. In these two regions 'it was not uncommon for youths who did not immediately declare themselves willing to perform their honourable service in the armed forces to be branded as "traitors to the Fatherland", "supporters of the Bonner-Ultras", "scoundrels", etc., sometimes even to be removed from their trained occupations and deployed as unskilled labourers'. In *Bezirk* Potsdam it was reported that a number of party and state functionaries thought that, in view of the 'measures' of 13 August, they could 'do away with the patriotic *Erziehungsarbeit* and give a new tone'. As the director of security at the SED *Bezirksleitung* remarked, all youths should have to enlist 'whether wooden leg or glass eye'. In a number of enterprises in the region, such as the Stahl- und Walzwerk Brandenburg, VEB Industriebau Brandenburg and RAW Brandenburg-West, some young workers were given the choice of signing up or being permanently laid off. In Oranienburg, a number of youths who had refused to appear at the municipal offices for a 'discussion' about joining the armed forces were sought out and delivered there by the police.[62] There were also 'a number of *Bürgermeister*' who sent written summons to youths to appear at the municipal offices where they were threatened with fines or arrest if they failed to enlist. The result of such coercive tactics was predictable: many youths appeared before the local recruitment commissions and gave statements of their willingness to enlist with absolutely no intention of carrying them out. This was even the case in the regions with poorer results: in *Bezirk* Erfurt only 181 of the 1432 resolutions made in October were honoured, and in *Bezirk* Magdeburg only 209 of 1835.[63]

An illustration of what this coercion looked like more concretely, how youths tried to escape it and how higher levels of the party and state apparatus responded was the case of 20-year-old Rainer O.

and eight other young men in Neu-Zittau. On 21 October, he and the others received letters summoning them to appear in two days at the local municipal council (*Gemeinderat*) and warning that if they failed to do so, they could be 'called to account' on the basis of the Defence Law. At the municipal council, they were all presented with NVA enlistment papers which the officials demanded they sign immediately; otherwise, they were told, they would be 'picked up' and taken to Fürstenwalde or Frankfurt/Oder for a 'discussion'. If they refused to sign at all, they would have to work in an LPG. In the event, all nine refused. The next day Rainer told the whole story to the BPO secretary at his workplace in Berlin-Schöneweide, explaining that they refused not because they were against service in the NVA 'in principle', but rather because of the appalling manner of recruitment. The secretary was obviously sympathetic to their plight, and brought the entire case to the attention of the Central Committee in a letter requesting that such 'methods' (quotation marks from the original) be examined and that the young men's case be quickly reviewed since they were due to be taken to Frankfurt/Oder within the next few days.[64]

On instructions from the Central Committee, the SED *Bezirksleitung* in Frankfurt/Oder indeed carried out an investigation of the local council in Neu-Zittau which both confirmed that such coercive tactics were being used and blamed them on the 'insufficient political and ideological clarity' of the *Bürgermeister* and his deputy. Were Rainer and the others off the hook? Hardly. Despite giving the local councillors a slap on the wrist, the *Bezirksleitung* instructors nonetheless recommended that they redouble their efforts with local youth, especially regarding the 'raising of their willingness to defend' the GDR. They also recommended that the Neu-Zittau officials carry out personal discussions with all who had received such a summons and present to them again, only this time in more proper form, the 'standpoint of the party and government'. The *Bezirksleitung* instructors tried but were unable to do this themselves with Rainer, who was attending night school on the evening they visited his home. Speaking with his father, they emphasized that the local council's actions were not approved of at higher levels. Yet even in assuring him of this, they nonetheless tried to drive home the message to Rainer by 'presenting to him [Rainer's father – CR] our standpoint on performing one's duty of honour in the armed forces of our republic'.[65]

Clearly, the problems of recruitment were not all solved with the construction of the Wall. The behaviour of would-be recruits did not change overnight from widespread refusal to resignation. Low-level party and economic functionaries did not all immediately metamorphosize into military enthusiasts. Coercive recruitment methods were not suddenly rendered unnecessary. In fact, they still backfired occasionally. Yet the sealed border did create the basic preconditions for solving the problem of personnel shortage by eventually making it possible to put an end to 'recruitment' as such (i.e. obtaining volunteers).

When universal conscription was finally introduced on 24 January 1962, popular responses were more ambivalent than they had been towards the earlier rearmanent pushes associated with the expansion of the KVP and founding of the NVA. There was an even more noticeable generation-cleft than before, and not just because older people were not personally affected. In view of the constant talk of the 'youth question' throughout the preceding years, it is scarcely surprising that, as one report put it, 'A large portion of older citizens say that it should have come much earlier . . . They say that through (conscription) the youth problem will be better solved and the youth educated to greater order and discipline'.[66] As welcome as such a 'positive' response from the older generation was for the party leadership, ironically it only made the task of winning support among young people more difficult. According to another report from Berlin: 'Remarks such as "a stint in the army is necessary to turn you into men", which are primarily uttered by older colleagues, often only lead to opposition and strengthen false attitudes among youths'.[67]

Although young people as a group tended to be less supportive than their elders, for several reasons conscription was not wholly unpopular among them either. A significant number of East Germans of all ages thought it would save the state money by making the high wages that had been used to attract recruits superfluous. There was also a pronounced sense of *Schadenfreude* among many who had already completed a stint in the NVA and who had 'very often been derided by other youths because of their supposed stupidity'.[68] And given the often appalling manner of recruitment up until then, the introduction of a compulsory 18-month period of service for all young men seemed to many people, even some church pastors, a vast improvement.[69] Fairly illustrative of the overall response was the vote taken at an assembly at the RAW Jena, where of the fifty employees present only five came out in favour of conscription,

six against it and the rest (especially youths, the report emphasizes) sullenly abstained.[70]

Yet whatever the perceived advantages of conscription, most East
Germans were anything but enthralled by it, especially the young
men who now knew with certainty that they faced a period of
military service. There was the predictable wave of 'provocations',
subversive flyers, graffiti, and 'hostile arguments' such as refusal
ever to shoot at West Germans. Notices of the conscription law
were destroyed, smeared with graffiti or covered by other 'malicious
posters'; there was widespread slandering of Heinz Hoffmann, the
Minister for National Defence; signs were hung on the doors of
draft boards proclaiming 'Caution! Danger to Life'; and at least one
industrial work stoppage was motivated by the introduction of conscription.[71] One young electrician even warned a recruiter that 'once
we all get guns we might just point them at you'.[72] Against the
background of such reports, concerns in army circles that conscription might put weapons into the wrong hands or dilute individual
units' fighting ability are understandable.[73]

But in the event such fears proved to be unfounded, for however
much youths might have disliked the idea of compulsory military
service, the vast majority complied with the new law without making much disturbance. This was true even of the majority of active
Christian youth, despite their concerns about being able to attend
services while in the army and their misgivings about the incom-
patibility of the oath of allegiance and the First Commandment.[74]
Draft boards reported precious few cases of 'provocations' upon
induction and only minor difficulties in registering conscripts, such
as alleged 'rowdy-groups' trying to avoid registration by switching
flats and jobs, isolated cases of recruits feigning illness or disabil-
ity, and a brief wave of enquiries about signing up for the *Volkspolizei*
as a way of avoiding military service.[75] A March 1962 report from
Bezirk Frankfurt/Oder summed up the situation thus: 'The conscripts
appeared punctually and in a disciplined fashion before the draft
boards, but showed great reservation, from which it was clear that
they are indeed willing to follow the law, but in large measure do
not recognize the necessity of the military strengthening of our
republic. A number of conscripts responded to the effect that they
were only prepared to fulfil their duty as citizens because they were
forced to do so by the law on conscription'.[76]

This lack of enthusiasm among the conscripts did not present a
serious problem; mere compliance was enough. The greatest problem

in filling out the ranks of the NVA and paramilitary forces in the months following the introduction of conscription was not presented by the conscripts at all, but rather by self-interested economic functionaries who reports complained were still showing a 'complete disregard' for military matters by applying for too many deferments and exemptions for their workers. Indeed, there were 7943 such applications during the three weeks in the middle of March alone. In *Bezirk* Magdeburg the number of applications for exemptions reached a total of 35.4 per cent of all conscripts (1009 applications for only 2848 conscripts). As one report succinctly concluded, 'This shows an underestimation of the necessity of strengthening the defence of the republic'.[77]

Although compulsory military service still ran against the grain of national sentiment among the majority of East Germans and was hardly something most youths wanted to do, it quickly became a taken-for-granted aspect of everyday life in the GDR, even to factory managers, who eventually calculated it automatically into their production plans.[78] Leaving for the West was no longer an option, and few young men were prepared to jeopardize their career prospects by refusing to comply. Perhaps more importantly, military service did not seem as unattractive once everyone had to do it and it was no longer paraded as a matter of 'showing one's colours'. The one issue that was still considered a 'question of loyalty' after the introduction of conscription was that of becoming a career soldier or officer. After ten years of rather disappointing recruitment experience since the initial expansion of the KVP, it could thus come as no surprise to the party leadership when in February and March 1962 the NVA only managed to achieve 53 per cent (6479 of 12 225) of the plan target for these career soldiers.[79] With the introduction of conscription it was possible to get the vast majority of young men to serve dutifully in the NVA, but not necessarily to believe in it.

13

Integration, Scepticism and Pragmatism: Patterns of Popular Opinion and Social Change in the Mid-1960s

The construction of the Wall did not completely revolutionize the SED leadership's ability to exert control at the grass-roots. To be sure, it ushered in a new relationship of power in the GDR; East Germans no longer had the 'trump card' of being able to leave. But this new relationship still had to be negotiated, it could not simply be dictated. The Wall may indeed have *enhanced* the regime's stability and ability to control matters at the grass-roots, but its power to do so was still limited in many of the same ways as before. As we have seen, shoddy work discipline remained a problem, industrial workers and pliant managers continued to make their informal wage and norm deals, reluctant farmers continued for a while to work 'individually' in the LPGs, many would-be soldiers still tried to escape recruitment. Apart from a general keeping-one's-head-down during the repressive atmosphere of the remainder of 1961, the overnight sealing of the border did not bring about a dramatic overnight transformation of social and political relations in the GDR.

But by no means is this to say that it had no consequences on the ground, especially in the long-term. There can be little doubt that the existence of the Wall fundamentally changed the parameters of social and political action for East Germans, which inevitably changed their expectations and frameworks of orientation. The point is rather that the effects were more indirect than direct, and took some time to emerge. As numerous observers have commented, over time the inability to leave for the West tended to foster a greater willingness to work within the system from which there was no longer any escape, a kind of passive pragmatism that made life easier for both rulers and ruled under 'real existing socialism'. Yet in itself, this pragmatism was not all that new; it was as much a matter of continuity as discontinuity. Certainly many East Germans came to terms and 'arranged themselves' with the regime in the shadow of the Wall. Yet for the vast majority it was not so much a matter of *making* their 'arrangements' after August 1961, as is so often implied, but rather *extending* and *modifying* those they had already made, still by and large grumbling and trying to make the best of the situation.

Arguably the main difference of the 1960s was less a change on the part of 'ordinary' East Germans than on the part of the party leadership, who, however grudgingly, tacitly came to accept their limited control at the grass-roots and the continuation of wayward impulses on the ground. The half-decade or so after the Wall was an important transitional period in terms of patterns of popular opinion and expectations. To put it crudely, there was a gradual shift from the widespread reluctance and scepticism that characterized the 1950s towards a more resigned pragmatism that by and large held sway until the latter 1980s. With all due caution regarding the increasing ritualization and correspondingly decreasing quality of internal reporting in the 1960s, it is significant that party reports posit this very development within a few years of the erection of the Wall. For the leadership this period was also one of changing expectations, though in the opposite direction: from ideological optimism and visionary enthusiasm to a more subtle and cautious pragmatism. Although this may, as numerous observers have commented, first have found open, programmatic expression with the 'unity of social and economic policy' under Honecker, the increasing willingness to experiment with the economy and to allow a careful thaw in the cultural sphere – indeed the very interest in more serious sociological research on popular opinion itself by the newly-founded Institute for Opinion Research[1] – all reflect a process of re-thinking soon after the initial crackdown following the construction of the Wall. No longer blindly expecting a change in popular attitudes as Marxist–Leninist theory postulated, the party leadership was also, it would seem, trying to make the best of the situation on the ground.

The NES in the factories

Summing up the attitude towards the *Produktionsaufgebot* on the shopfloor, a *Meister* at the RAW Brandenburg-West said that '. . . the colleagues declare themselves willing to produce more in the same time, but only for more money'.[2] While this attitude presented an obstacle to the SED's policies in the autumn of 1961, by 1963 it held some promise. The approach to constructing socialism in the factories of the GDR was partially revised with the advent in 1963 of the 'New Economic System' (NES), whose basic idea was to increase efficiency and productivity through greater flexibility and a new system of 'economic levers': prices, profits, credit, wages and bonuses. The binding principle was that of 'material interest': profits and bonuses were to serve as an incentive for greater performance. Among other things, this meant a new conceptualization of how to mobilize East German workers to increase productivity. The emphasis shifted from working harder for the glory of socialism in the future to efficiency, inward investment and the profit incentive in the present. To a certain degree, this change represents less an attempt to bring the circumstances on the shopfloor into line with official policy than of bringing policy into line with circumstances on the ground. This was clearly a new tack. But was the response at the grass-roots any different than before?

Not at first. Reports on the preliminary discussions of the NES with workers read like a paraphrase of those we have already seen. Again, there was widespread scepticism on the factory floor, as most workers quite understandably saw it merely as another attempt by the state, not unlike the *Produktionsaufgebot*, to reassert control over costs and ultimately to lower wages. Party agitators in *Bezirk* Potsdam reported making little headway against the almost universal argument that 'the increase of work-productivity is a never-ending spiral'.[3] The main point of contention was the new and extremely complex wage scheme, which most workers understandably regarded with suspicion.[4] Now that production costs, including labour, were to be as important a measure of productive performance as output, factory managers and engineers took them more into consideration. The immediate result was a new offensive of truly 'hard' norms.

It seems that the most vehement opposition was encountered on the perennially problematic construction sites. In Königs-Wusterhausen the anger among construction workers came through loud and clear in the reports: 'What does the FDGB say to the new wage form? If it represents our interests, it has to intervene so that we don't get exploited. Take our last shirts off our backs, then you'll have what you want!' On construction sites in Oranienburg the reception was so poor that union functionaries in the IG Bau/Holz even felt obliged to invoke the spectre of 17 June in advising caution about disrupting the material status quo: 'It would be better not to change the existing wage and bonus scheme. The comrades of the Office [for Industry and Construction – CR] should think of 17 June 1953'.[5] Given these initial responses, it can come as no surprise that when the new wage forms were actually introduced on construction sites in *Bezirk* Potsdam in June, the result was widespread and demonstrative work-restraint. As the party secretary at the Montagebau Teltow complained, 'Good brigades that used to fulfil their norms by 230–250 per cent are now only mustering up 101–102 per cent'. The workers at Montagebau, for their part, made no secret of the reason for this: 'Get rid of the new wage-forms, then we'll give you the old performance'.[6]

But such knee-jerk opposition was only short-lived since wages, bonuses and even vacation time improved for many workers with the new payment scheme. In order the absorb the predictable anger on the shopfloor resulting from the introduction of 'harder' norms, new bonuses were also introduced for overfulfilling them. During the course of 1963 and 1964, these bonuses enabled production workers to achieve significant wage increases; tariff wages were sometimes even below 50 per cent of real wages. But the effects of the new scheme varied for different occupations and different branches of industry. Salaried employees – engineers, technicians and *Meister* – could not make use of the new earning opportunities, which was rather demotivating for them and increased frictions on the shopfloor. Also, the difference between the low and high end of the wage spectrum grew significantly. Complaints about the new norms were loudest in the relatively disadvantaged light industries, which was a primary factor behind the partial re-levelling of the wage structure in 1967, against the principles of the NES.[7]

Generally speaking, however, the NES led to significantly higher incomes for industrial workers as well as greater pressure to improve performance – which, as we have seen in the case of the socialist brigades, many were willing to do so long as it was worthwhile for them. Reports from this period generally agree that the reforms were viewed positively on the shopfloor. A 1963 study on the 'consciousness development' of the populace in Berlin-Lichtenberg put this in rather abstract terms, reporting that workers were 'applying themselves with all their strength towards solving the economic tasks', though there were still, of course, numerous 'unclarified questions' concerning the 'nature of the state border' and the 'Wall'.[8] A report of November 1963 was more to the point, positing that shopfloor attitudes towards the perpetually thorny issue of raising work-productivity had begun to transform from an instinctive hostility into a more open-minded questioning of how it might benefit them personally in terms of higher wages and lower prices for consumer goods.[9]

Although there was some anger in factories where workers were actually underfulfilling their new norms (this amounted to around 25 per cent of industrial workers in February 1965) and were generally presented with 'done deeds' in terms of their calculation and implementation, on the whole the reports become more and more sanguine by 1964, especially in the better-paid branches of industry. Party functionaries in growth areas like the chemical industry not only claimed to discern a 'greater willingness to cooperate', a 'new attitude to work' and a 'vastly improved' work-morale, but also reported that work-time was becoming more productive, workers were tending to 'intervene more and more' in cases of shoddy work-discipline, and that criticisms and proposals from workers were 'more concrete' and 'less tolerant'.[10] The opportunity of significantly improving one's personal economic position proved an attractive feature of the new reform concept, and no doubt goes a long way towards explaining its relatively positive reception in comparison to previous campaigns to raise work productivity. With the NES, personal material interest now finally seemed to overlap somewhat with the state's new economic goals, though the reforms still failed to achieve the kind of productivity gains needed.

It is extremely difficult to say whether these improvements on the wages and norms front had any appreciable effect on more specifically political attitudes among industrial workers. Certainly many reports around this time posit a connection between the improving economic situation and workers' 'socialist consciousness'. The 'secure prospects' of the chemical industry had, in the words of one report, brought about a 'visible transformation' in the attitudes of many workers, even to 'the basic questions of our policies'.[11] A November 1964 study in Berlin-Prenzlauer Berg similarly reported that the NES was increasing workers' 'trust' in the party and that the improvements in work-morale were the result of a gradually crystallizing 'socialist consciousness'.[12] Yet such assertions must be taken with a hefty pinch of salt in view of the continuing stream of reports on 'enemy activities' and 'hostile attitudes' among workers towards the party leadership, the high pay of the intelligentsia, the FDGB's political dependence on the SED and, of course, the sealed border to the West. The sheer volume and frequency of these 'negative' reports leaves little doubt that such improvements in the general mood on the shopfloor as were perceived had more to do with the rising living standard or even the increasing ritualization and decreasing quality of internal reporting than with any changes to workers' 'consciousness'. In fact, despite its assertions about a gradually crystallizing 'socialist consciousness' among workers, the report from Prenzlauer Berg nonetheless makes precisely this suggestion in its more differentiated conclusions: whereas the small group of 'most progressive' workers found their previous political opinions confirmed in the successes of the NES, others simply saw in it the application of Western market principles.[13]

The NES, though widely welcomed on the shopfloor, did not represent any solid new social or political consensus. Whatever degree of 'loyalty' it generated was still of the rather passive variety we have already seen. The willingness of most East German industrial workers to accept the SED and its policies was still by and large determined by the opportunities it gave them to improve their standard of living. As for active political loyalty, this was essentially a non-starter. It was still hard to find many workers genuinely willing to carry SED banners on the first of May.

The 'socialist village' from collectivization to rationalization

The economic re-emphasis associated with the NES met with a similar mixture of initial scepticism and gradual assent in the villages. Although forced collectivization had taken its toll on agricultural productivity, the SED leadership was not about to revert to individual farming methods as the Polish communists had done. Instead, they looked to the 'rationalization' of East German agriculture as the key to improving the agricultural economy, and hence also as a means of convincing farmers of the correctness of the socialist course, of binding them more closely to the party and state. This rationalization, or 'industrialization' of agriculture had both ideological and practical motives. Ideologically, the further expansion of industrial methods and collective structures in agriculture was seen as a virtue in itself, a means of helping abolish the differences between town and countryside and thus facilitating the heralded alliance of workers and farmers. In practical terms, the idea was to improve yields with increased mechanization and specialization. In turn, this was to be made possible by the amalgamation of several LPGs into one, which would not only allow for a more efficient use of machinery, but also would have the desirable side-effect of forcing recalcitrant and 'uncooperative' (in every sense of the word) Type I LPGs finally to develop meaningful collective forms of organization.[14]

With hindsight it is clear that the SED's rationalization plans led to a rapid growth in agricultural output, which was a crucial prerequisite for the general rise in living standards in the GDR during the 1960s. At the time, however, East German farmers were still recovering from the massive upheavals of 1960, and were by and large sceptical of any new changes in agriculture. For most, all of this added up to yet another tightening of the state's grip on their lives, and there was, at least initially, an overwhelming desire simply to be left in peace. The emphasis on increased work productivity at the Sixth Party Convention in early 1963 found extremely little resonance among farmers, whose complaints that any rise in productivity would only be achieved 'on their backs' and would not benefit them personally in any event echoed the standard complaints of industrial workers on this issue.[15] The first attempts to integrate LPGs in 1963 were scarcely more popular; even official East German accounts spoke of 'no appreciation' (*kein Verständnis*) for them among farmers.[16] On the contrary, most were still convinced that the way to increase production was to return to traditional individual farming methods, and that further integration was thus going in the wrong direction. This was – ominously from the SED's point of view – not least the prevailing opinion in a number of the first large conglomerate LPGs, where in the summer of 1963 party functionaries were concerned that discussions with farmers about splitting them up into small units in order to make them more efficient 'should not take on an all-too-broad character – at least in terms of a wave of LPG separations being precipitated'.[17]

But rationalization in general and the principles of the NES in particular soon gained some acceptance. The principle of material interest was not at all unpopular among farmers, and was in fact viewed as a slight return to older market principles which most still espoused.[18] The new emphasis on investment, development and the use of new machinery – not to mention the abolition of different prices for quota deliveries and *freie Spitzen* (crops in 1964, livestock in 1969) and bonuses for increasing production and lowering costs – was also greeted with qualified approval, as it promised to yield income dividends in the future. In 1964 the idea of 'industrialized agriculture' gained increasing currency after being a central focus at the Eighth Farmers' Congress. Generally speaking, 'industrialized methods' and mechanization met with interest and qualified approval, not least because they offered the prospect of mitigating the continuing labour shortage in agriculture. The drain of youth to the cities and consequent age imbalance in the LPGs remained one of the main worries of farmers in the mid-1960s. By this time the average age of Type III LPG members in *Bezirk* Potsdam was between 50 and 60 years; the average percentage of members under 25 was only 6.9 per cent in Type III and a mere 4.8 per cent in Type I LPGs.[19] The dire prospects of securing an adequate supply of labour in the future was one of the primary reasons why, despite certain reservations and a lingering desire to return to older individual methods of farming, most farmers were showing an increasing openness to the SED's plans for agriculture.

In August 1964, the Department for Ideological Work in the Office for Agriculture conducted an in-depth study of farmers' opinions, questions and 'unclarities' towards the government's agricultural policies in six LPGs in *Kreis* Nauen, just north of Potsdam. The resulting document, though inevitably couched in SED-speak and with a degree of customary communist prejudice towards peasants as backward and self-interested, clearly represents a self-critical attempt to gain a realistic picture of the situation on the ground (not only in these six enterprises, but in LPGs in general) and as such offers a unique insight into farmers' opinion during a period of ever-decreasing quality of internal reporting.[20] On the whole, the report gives the impression of piecemeal approval for certain aspects of government policy against the overall backdrop of an essentially unchanged picture of political apathy and resignation mixed with defence of one's economic interests and a lingering bitterness about being forced into the LPGs.

Even in 1964, much of the problem facing the SED was how to overcome farmers' stubborn conservatism and scepticism towards any innovation that entailed any risks or that did not bring them obvious and immediate benefits. The report complains that the farmers in Nauen had certain ingrained characteristics and opinions that would conflict with the transition to industrial production: in particular a 'lack of creative initiative', a general scepticism about any claims to increase productivity – especially if levels were supposed to surpass that of individual farming methods – and a pronounced 'brigade-egoism', or disregard for developments at other farms or in other departments with no direct bearing on themselves personally. One might add to this list a deep-seated disapproval among many male farmers of female colleagues (who by the end of 1961 constituted 46.6 per cent of all LPG members[21]) gaining advanced qualifications and occupying leading positions in the LPGs, which came through loud and clear during discussions about the 1961 communique *'Die Frau, der Frieden und der Sozialismus'* and the women's advancement plans of 1963–64.[22] Yet at the same time the report acknowledges that most did not reject the principle of industrial production out of hand. While many felt anxious about the possibility of losing their jobs to mechanization and about the risks of specialization, especially monocultural farming, such fears co-existed with broad approval for using the existing technology to the fullest in order to raise production and incomes.[23] This cautious fear of the financial risks of specialization also appears in numerous other reports around this time, and farmers understandably demanded 'good preconditions' (i.e. improved buildings, credits and income guarantees) before taking such a step. As another report from *Bezirk* Potsdam put it: 'Farmers are, after all, practical (*realdenkend*) people . . . They tell us "what you say about industrial production is completely correct for the future. But if we go over to special branches of production under the current conditions, what do we do if we have low yields in our special branch?"'[24] But by and large this 'practicality', this self-interested pragmatism, eventually led farmers to adopt the regime's plans for specialization and mechanization, not to reject them.

Convincing farmers of the advantages of industrial farming methods was one thing; 'binding' them more closely to the party and state and generating a modicum of loyalty to the regime was another matter entirely. As disappointing as the political mood in the factories must have been to party officials, the villages of the East German countryside appeared even less promising in this regard. In the mid-1960s it seems that East German farmers were still by and large indifferent to any matters not directly affecting their economic interests. As the 1964 Nauen report put it, 'a large proportion of the farmers judge the results of their work merely according to the level of their personal income', adding that this had tradition- ally been the case with farmers. The authors could not help but notice that the farmers with whom they spoke were far more open to discussions about this issue than about ones from which they could discern no direct use to themselves. These same proximal economic criteria also formed the basis of farmers' opinions about the difference between the GDR and the Federal Republic: 'The dis- tinction is in the main measured not according to the structures and relations of society, but rather by the fact that in the West there are more cars, "one can buy everything", the "authority of the West-Mark is greater", etc.', an attitude that was, of course, only reinforced by the occasional difficulties in the availability of basic goods, spare parts and other necessities that the isolation from West Berlin had made only worse.[25]

This immovable pragmatism was all but impervious to the party's attempts at political mobilization. Reports during the 1963 *Volks- kammer* elections still complained of a general 'lack of influence on the village population', which was usually attributed to the fact that the party organization was still the 'least developed in the agricultural sector'.[26] Despite a broad attempt in 1963 to invigorate the party organization and enhance its influence in the country- side to match that of the towns and cities, reports in the summer were still forced to concede that 'there are no satisfying results to report', and in fact complained of regression in many areas.

Remarkably little progress had been made in this regard since the late 1940s. It was estimated that still only around one-half of all rural SED members actually participated in party life in 1963, and member assemblies were not regularly convened in most vil- lages.[27] This situation had not changed at all by 1964, and reports still complained of inactivity in rural GPOs (*Grundparteiorganisationen*, or basic party organizations), of the 'greatest unclarities' among farmers and of a broad range of factors and attitudes hindering the expansion of the party ranks: 'I'll become a socialist when I can travel where I want!'; 'leave us alone about the party . . . we'd have to go to more meetings'; 'I'd just be avoided by a whole string of people in the village'.[28] The vast majority of rural party members still had little political experience or party education, and mem- bers often would not act in their role as SED members because they could not – or would not – offer answers to other people's questions. While the vast majority of village comrades reportedly showed a great willingness and enthusiasm as regarded their farm work, 'in political questions they often differ little from those un-attached to a party'.[29] A year later in 1965 the picture still looked the same in *Kreis* Kyritz, where a party investigation into farmers' 'political consciousness' was forced to conclude that 'the farmers are moved by a number of questions, but really only economic ones'.[30] The report optimistically notes that the situation was better among younger farmers, who tended to have more faith in the underlying principles of collective farming. But as we have seen, there simply were not that many young farmers around.

Yet the situation in the countryside was not all bleak from the SED's point of view. The party leadership could take some consolation in the fact that the church was also finding it increasingly difficult to maintain its influence over the rural populace. The conflicts of the 1950s had taken their toll in terms of church membership and attendance, especially with the increasing pressure on individuals since 1958 to sever their ties with the church, which were increasingly viewed as a hindrance to one's educational and career advancement. The growth of non-church-affiliated clubs and organizations also meant that the church no longer had a monopoly on social life in the village.[31] More importantly, however, a new generation of agricultural experts trained in the agricultural colleges established in the 1950s and for the most part committed to the communist regime were rising to positions of influence in the countryside and gradually displacing some of the *Großbauern* who had managed the LPGs up until then. By the mid-1960s they had largely stabilized the collective farms and were poised to take control of them in the years that followed.[32] The rural state apparatus was also becoming more professionalized and reliable with the influx of these 'new men and women': of the 259 members of the *Ratskollektive* (collective council) in *Bezirk* Potsdam in 1965, 198 were SED members and 118 possessed a university degree.[33] The previous rift between the party and state leadership and their subordinates in the countryside was no longer so pronounced.

Youth and generational change in the 1960s

The mid-1960s was not just a period of economic experimentation, but also of cultural thaw. For a number of reasons, the main recipients of this careful opening within the GDR after the wave of repression and 'vigilance' following the construction of the Wall were the East German youth. By the mid-1960s, the younger generation had no personal memory of fascism and war, had been almost entirely socialized under the GDR (apart from occasional trips to West Berlin) and was therefore viewed as particularly 'educable'. Also, by this time most other issues regarding the socialization and disciplining of youth had been in some way or another solved: the school teachers were mostly all 'new' (even if this did not have all the desired results), the *Junge Gemeinden* had been weakened and the *Jugendweihe* pushed through, and military conscription had been introduced. The greatest remaining impediment facing efforts to 'educate' the younger generation into model socialist citizens was the 'outer' disruptive factor of Western culture, especially the ever-increasing popularity of beat-music.

In contrast to the previous tendency simply to tighten control, the party and FDJ leadership responded in 1963 with a policy of partial integration. Rock-and-Roll music and the entire subculture that accompanied it were as popular in the GDR as in West Germany, and clearly would not go away. The object was to co-opt these impulses, to keep them within the bounds of socialist propriety and steer them in a more acceptable direction through such measures as the establishment of the popular music radio station DT 64 (whose 60:40 format – that is, 60 per cent socialist and 40 per cent western music – hindered its popularity) and even the organization of a 'guitar band competition'. Though clearly a new policy departure, the effects on the activities of the FDJ at the grass-roots level were modest; in a sense, it did little more than give the official stamp of approval to what was already widely tolerated at many FDJ clubs.[34]

But unlike the growing pragmatism towards the situation on the shopfloor and in the villages, this tentative acceptance of the youth subculture, like the cultural 'thaw' of the mid-1960s more broadly speaking, was for a number of reasons rather short-lived. For one thing, it became mired in the broader generation conflict of the time. In this regard the GDR was not entirely unlike the West during the 1960s. The 'bumming around', 'dropping-out' and wild dancing that marked the subculture clashed with most older East Germans' notions of respectability and propriety. Given the general pressure on youths to conform in school and in the FDJ, there was a certain conflation of generational and political tension. Parents often came across to youths as representatives of the state, and educators and functionaries often came across as parents: both expected discipline, and both seemed to resent the freedoms enjoyed by the youth of the 1960s. As in the West, this conflation of parental and political control made beat-music all the more popular among young people as a symbol of self-realization and struggle against 'the powers that be'. What made it even more significant in the GDR was the fact that the entire 'scene' – the clothes, unkempt hair, informal style of social interaction, etc. – was obviously based on Anglo-American models which itself alarmed party officials, who had warned for years of the detrimental effects of 'western decadence' and 'American lack of culture'.

When in 1965 the FDJ and party leadership no longer deemed the opening towards youth subculture a success, the only remaining solution was to crack down again. Most performing licenses were revoked, rules on listening to western music in public were generally tightened and a spontaneous 'beat demonstration' by several hundred youths in Leipzig was ruthlessly crushed on 31 October 1965. But given the popularity of Western music and styles, there was little chance of changing more than public appearances. In fact, if anything the effects of this second crackdown on the attitudes and preferences of East German youths were the opposite of what was intended. The number of youths listening to Western music rose dramatically in the 1960s, as did the number of those who were open about doing so, which reflected the growing sense that such behaviour was becoming increasingly self-evident. Rather than trying to integrate the various impulses among youths into the FDJ and 'win them over' on their own ground, the party and FDJ leadership instead politicized all non-conformist behaviour and in the process strengthened the undercurrent of disaffection among young people that would plague the regime for most of the rest of its history.[35]

Although these problems of 'educating' youths into their prescribed role of model socialist citizens in the mid-1960s were in some ways very similar to those of the 1950s, there were also some important generational differences that point to subsequent developments in the GDR. For one thing, although the fascination with things Western had irritated party and FDJ officials from early on, by the mid-1960s this had become the dominant youth subculture, and would remain so until the demise of the regime. A far more important difference, however, was the gradually dwindling opportunities for upward mobility and advancement for young people by the mid-1960s. Earlier efforts to win the loyalties of the HJ- and

FDJ-generations (born from the late 1920s to early 1940s) were to a considerable extent aided by the unprecedented opportunities for social mobility resulting from the system of positive recruitment and advancement of people from 'working-class' backgrounds, the exigencies of denazification and the population drain to the West up to 1961.[36] Highly trained professionals were approximately doubly represented in the stream of refugees to the West, which left tens of thousands of vacancies for those willing and able to replace them.[37] Many who left were also skilled workers whose places were vacated for others to fill, and roughly half were young men under the age of 25 – that is, those most likely to gain further occupational qualifications. This massive population movement alone would have offered enormous opportunity for upward mobility. But it is only part of the story, as the absolute number of places in higher education more than tripled during the 1950s.[38]

It would be impossible to arrive at precise statistics on how many people achieved upward mobility in the GDR of the 1950s and early 1960s, not least because of the problems of adequately defining what 'upward mobility' would be. But the results of oral history projects in the GDR leave little doubt that rapid upward mobility was a key *experience* for both men and women (though for the former more than the latter) of the HJ and especially FDJ generations, and especially among those with solid socialist political credentials.[39] Whatever they may privately have thought about the SED and the Soviet-style socialism it espoused, many felt they had a stake in the system that was instrumental to their own social ascendency, and were basically willing to play along, however unenthusiastically, with the rules of the game.

But these social benefits of the population drain and post-war reconstruction were largely confined to the HJ- and FDJ-generations, and the situation was rather different for those born after the GDR was already founded. The period from the mid-1960s to the 1980s was marked instead by a certain consolidation and crystallization of the East German social hierarchy.[40] Among those born after the late 1940s who did not have the same life chances as their parents, the rather meagre prospects could in no way compensate for the inescapability of the GDR, and led to growing frustration and disillusionment, eventually to political instability. It was no coincidence that the majority of demonstrators in 1989 were the children of Ulbricht and Honecker, not of Hitler.

Retrospective and outlook onto 'real existing socialism'

By the mid-1960s the basic features of 'real existing socialism' (as Erich Honecker liked to call the society he governed from 1971 onwards) were in place. Starting from rather unpromising circumstances, the party leadership had managed to bring all basic industries under state control, to achieve SED predominance over political and economic life, to establish a near-monopoly on organizational life through the mass organizations, to push through collective forms of ownership in agriculture, to weaken the position of the churches in society and to mobilize the vast majority of young people for defence purposes either through paramilitary training or conscription for formal military service. Viewed from above, East German society had by and large been reshaped according to the communist leadership's plans – that is, apart from having to lock East Germans into their own country. At the grass-roots, however, the picture was rather more ambiguous. Many other basic features of 'real existing socialism' were rooted precisely in the problems and unintended developments that had emerged as a result of older continuities or the contradictions of the socialist transformation itself: the 'hidden bargaining' in the factories, a west-oriented youth broadly averse to being 'organized', a grumbling and politically apathetic countryside, widespread complacency and inactivity among the party and mass organizations at the grass-roots, widespread minor corruption and collusion, the 'shadow economy' as partial compensation for the contradictions and inefficiencies of the planned economy, the list goes on. Apart from the gradual improvement of basic living standards and social facilities (which after the dismantling of the NES at the close of the 1960s were based more on Western credits than productivity gains in the GDR), this basic picture at the grass-roots changed relatively little until the collapse of the regime two and a half decades later. The 'construction of socialism' in the GDR was essentially complete. But before closing this chapter it seems appropriate to ask what, more concretely, had been constructed.

The communist leadership's ability to realize its objectives and control social developments varied considerably in different spheres. The goal of reshaping the industrial shopfloor and bringing it under party control was by far the most problematic, and was especially disappointing for party officials given the high hopes initially placed on the role of the industrial workforce. Although the communist regime indeed managed to refashion the structures and culture of work in the factories in a number of ways, for the most part these were contrary to intentions. The initial hopes among broad sections of the industrial workforce for a socialist-inspired transformation of Germany after the horrors of Nazism quite rapidly turned into disillusionment and disinterest once the party began taking over the initially elected interest-representing bodies in the factories, the shop councils and union organizations. The work ethic on the East German shopfloor also changed considerably under the impact of Soviet industrial practices, post-war scarcity and the entry of a new generation into the workforce, many of them women and refugees from the East new to the world of the industrial worker. Without a clear wage incentive, many of the 'traditionally German' virtues of diligence and discipline on which the Soviets had initially placed such hope dissolved. As a result, the regime still had to wrestle with the problem of substandard productivity, poor industrial discipline and wage inflation in the mid-1960s and beyond. Recent research has shown that this had long-term political ramifications and was an important contributing factor to the ultimate demise of the regime, which found itself unable to respond to these problems effectively in the years that followed.[41]

In this context, managers and functionaries in the factories also developed distinct orientations, habits and expectations which influenced the manner in which – indeed, the very extent to which – the 'construction of socialism' on the shopfloor took place. Despite significant improvements in the reliability and training of union and party officials by the 1960s, most factory managers were still anxious to keep shopfloor discontent beneath the threshold of conflict even if this came at the expense of the planned economy (and it is worth noting that this was the essence of social and economic policy later on under Honecker). In economic terms, the result was an uneasy, and ultimately unviable compromise between the desires and expectations of workers and the needs of the economy. In political and organizational terms, the result was a fabric of local arrangements that ultimately had to be tolerated for maintaining the social peace, and thus also for upholding the appearance of a healthy and ideologically sound relationship between the workers and 'their' state. This problem was never solved, and 'real existing socialism' in the factories of the GDR was a far cry from what communist party leaders had initially envisioned. The best they could hope for, even twenty years after the end of the war, was widespread political indifference, incomplete control of the shopfloor, insufficient productivity gains and ultimately containing the potential for worker unrest.

Although the goal of transforming the East German countryside was in many ways less promising given the widespread conservatism and aversion to socialism among most farmers, this was, as it turned out, more successful than the control of the shopfloor. By the mid-1960s there was little evidence that farmers would present the regime serious difficulties. There was still a nominal identification with the party among some of those, particularly *Neubauern*, who had profited from its policies of land distribution and collectivization. More importantly, the political attitudes and behaviour of even the most anti-SED farmers were no longer characterized by resolute opposition, but more by resignation to their fate and making the best of the circumstances in the GDR – circumstances which, it should be noted, were slowly but steadily improving by this time. There were also, of course, the lessons drawn from the 'socialist spring': the threat of coercion in the countryside remained sufficient in the early- and mid-1960s to dissuade almost anyone from sticking his or her neck out. In any event, so long as farmers were grudgingly willing to cooperate with the main thrust of SED agricultural policies, their political attitudes were without much significance in terms of the stability of the regime.

There were a number of structural reasons for this beyond the dramatic decrease in the numbers of East Germans involved in agriculture by the mid-1960s.[42] For one thing, even farmers in the Type 3 LPGs still worked nominally for themselves, and thus were unlikely to stop work or slow down production as an expression of protest. Work-stoppages were in any event hardly a customary form of rural protest, and withholding produce under the police-state conditions of the GDR could have serious consequences for anyone involved. Moreover, besides having no formal alternative parties or organizations to represent their interests and fight their battles with the state, there was also no *informal* village equivalent to the brigades and established practice of 'wage-deals' in industry. Perhaps most importantly, in many areas the 'village' itself was gradually eroding. From around 1960 onwards the tight web of social bonds that for so long had resisted and refracted the attempt to transform the countryside were gradually breaking down under the force of migration to the cities and LPG conglomeration. There were, to be sure, still certain continuities in the villages: older tensions between 'new' and 'old' farmers, between rival families and to some extent between traditional village elites and relative 'have nots' that passed unscathed into many LPGs. But these hardly constituted a problem to a regime that was just as interested in keeping broader networks of solidarity from developing in any event. The behavioural result of agricultural collectivization in the villages was a certain retreat into the private sphere. Home and work became increasingly separate, and the former grew more important than the latter, where individual farmers no longer had much influence. With no easy alternatives, and with the shorter hours, vacation provision and child-care facilities of the LPG system, most eventually saw less to gain from opposition than from compliance with the rules of the game. Passivity and pragmatism thus became mutually reinforcing characteristics of life in the 'socialist village'.

Like the industrial workforce, the high hopes placed on young people were also for the most part disappointed, though this varied on different issues. The aim of mobilizing young people for military service was by and large fufilled with the introduction of conscription. Few were willing to risk their careers by refusing to enlist, and in any event it no longer seemed as unattractive once everyone had to do it. But this control of young people's bodies was a relatively easy task; convincing most of them of the threat of the 'imperialist West' and the reactionary character of the Federal Republic, let alone the necessity of their period of service, was another matter. Almost inevitably, the efforts to *persuade* young people were far less successful than efforts to *control* them, and in fact the latter by and large tended to undermine the former, as the ever-increasing interest in Western culture, clothes and music – not to mention the increasing trend towards 'dropping out' – from the 1960s onwards indirectly attests.

Although the party and FDJ organizations functioned more smoothly and were more viable at the local level by the mid-1960s, they were still of rather limited influence. According to a youth survey in 1969, only one-fifth of FDJ members based their membership on political conviction, only one-half found FDJ-life interesting and one-fourth reported that there had been no more than one local member assembly in the previous six months.[43] In any event, the apparatus for organizing young people's free time could have only a limited effect on the opinions and preferences of young people. As the same survey report complained, roughly 85 per cent claimed that they fulfilled their social needs 'in [non-organized] leisure groups not controlled and educationally directed' instead of in the FDJ-groups, which meant that they were 'frequently exposed to negative influences'.[44] In the latter 1960s there were also signs of an increasingly critical stance towards teachers and of a declining respect for authority more generally not at all unlike developments in the West at the time, all of which was symptomatic of a regime that had failed to 'win over' even those who were born under it.

In terms of building a new structure of consent, the construction of East German socialism was less the creation of positive approbation than, on the one hand, the containment and fragmentation of discontent via various social concessions and, on the other, the acceptance, even informal institutionalization, of an attenuated brand of social autonomy on the ground. This is not to say that the majority of East Germans were hopelessly alienated from the regime. Most rather exhibited what Alf Lüdtke has called a *'mißmutige'* or 'sullen' loyalty: a mixture of conformity, grumbling and defending their interests against the demands of the state when and where this was possible. However morose and disgruntled, this must not be confused with the term 'loyalty' in a more active sense. To quote Albert Hirschman again: 'Just as it would be impossible to be good in a world without evil, so it makes no sense to speak of being loyal to a firm, a party, or an organization with an unbreakable monopoly'.[45] It was more a matter of passive acceptance in the absence of any viable alternatives. Getting rid of the regime was not on many people's minds, at least not after June 1953 (or before autumn 1989, when alternatives once again appeared increasingly viable); securing a better material living standard, pursuing a fulfilling career and enjoying one's private interests – even if they might be politicized by the regime – were. After the initial hopes for a 'softer' socialist regime had dissipated, the vast majority were not as interested in the regime's ideological pronouncements as in its ability to 'deliver the goods' and offer reasonably promising economic and social prospects. The party leadership was well aware of this by the mid-1960s, and acted accordingly. In the sober words of a 1967 report on popular attitudes in Berlin-Weißensee: 'People often work hard, and great economic achievements are made; <u>yet the open conviction to work hard in order to strengthen the GDR because one supports the policies of the party is often still lacking</u>'.[46] There can be little better description of the pragmatic arrangements and rudiments of the 'consumer contract' of the Honecker era than this.

14
Conclusions

While the years after 1945 clearly witnessed a radical social and political transformation of East Germany at the macro-level – in patterns of ownership, exchange of social and political elites, recasting the political system and network of social organizations – this process was more a slow, patchy and inconsistent transition at the grass-roots. Although it has long been assumed that the strategic goals of the Soviets and SED were not always identical with the actual outcome of policies on the ground, this grass-roots perspective is one which few accounts of the SBZ/GDR have explored in any detail. There are, as was noted in the introduction, a number of reasons for this, above all the flurry of fascination with theories and models of 'totalitarianism' since the latter 1980s, especially since the collapse of the communist states of Central and Eastern Europe in 1989–91, which has left an indelible mark on the debate about the GDR's history. Eckard Jesse may have exaggerated in claiming that the notion of the GDR as a 'totalitarian system' has 'virtually canonical validity',[1] but the frequent use of the term and the discussion of various models and approaches has been remarkable indeed. The debate has been wide and varied, ranging from adaptations of the 'classic' models of Arendt, Friedrich and Brzezinski to issues of the relationship between 'totalitarianism' and 'modernity' to questions of the comparability of dictatorial regimes all the way to rather unreflective polemics.[2] Although the primary aim of this study has not been to engage in these debates, it nonetheless has something to say to them, not so much by consciously setting out to test these ideas against the empirical evidence,[3] but rather by its very portrayal of the socialist transformation of East Germany from a perspective that is missed by 'totalitarian' and 'top-down' models of all kinds.

As numerous scholars have pointed out, these models have a number of serious shortcomings, perhaps the most obvious being their static nature that does not adequately capture, let alone explain, processes of change.[4] Another serious drawback more pertinent to the story told here is their blindness vis-à-vis 'society', which appears as a dimension of historical reality wholly separate from 'politics', or in any event as little more than a mere object of dictatorial manipulation and control. As Klaus Schroeder has put it in a recent attempt at synthesis, the GDR was above all a 'political society'.[5] This notion is an inherent feature of the 'classic' models of totalitarianism, which focus above all on the formal mechanisms of exerting authority and power in a narrow sense. Though Sigrid Meuschel's broader conceptualization of the establishment of the East German dictatorial system as the arresting and reversal of the 'normal' process of modern functional differentiation of societal spheres (i.e. between politics, economics, law, leisure, etc.) manages to link political and social developments, here, too, 'society' is little more than an object of dictatorial political control.[6] Now, the intention here is not to cast doubt on the power of the SED-regime to shape processes of social change in the GDR; it was immense. But the problem with these various models is nonetheless twofold: first, they all tend to take the caesura of the communist societal project for granted, thus overlooking, or at least de-emphasizing, important threads of continuity with the pre-communist past; and second, they miss how everyday socialist 'reality' in the GDR was actually an unplanned mixture of ideologically-derived intervention on the one hand and the unpredictable, unplanned actions of people on the other.

This argument is by no means intended to downplay the total claims of the regime, the limitations it placed on civil rights and the public sphere, and the rejection of pluralism that distinguish it from liberal democratic polities. Obviously, decision-making in the GDR was highly centralized, the party leadership exercised formal control over most aspects of political and social life, and fundamental criticism of the official line – not to mention the possibility of viable alternatives to its rule – was largely prevented by the massive security apparatus. If we view the socialist transformation of East Germany solely or even primarily as a matter of policy formation and transformation of broad, formal social structures (merely as a piece of political history) it is hard not to conclude that East German society was 'shut down' by the total claims of the communist dictatorship. It is also hard in this view not to perceive meaningful human action as basically limited to those in positions of power and thus to dismiss the experiences and behaviour of millions who lived there as essentially irrelevant to this process. 'Totalitarianism' seems a very apposite epithet for political systems such as that in the GDR.

But the history of the GDR was more than the history of its formal system and apparatus of power, and 'totalitarian' models, however one might distinguish between 'total' and 'totalitarian' power, are not very helpful for understanding developments outside of this realm. Moreover, when one analyzes how the policies and authority of the central leadership were conveyed to the grass-roots, even the apparatus of power itself appears less sleek and controllable than such models suggest. For one thing, at the most basic level it is clear that the widespread unreliability, self-interest and divided loyalties among low-level functionaries at the periphery of the regime constituted a serious impediment to the party leadership's ability to realize many of its aims. Although enormous personnel problems had to be expected during the early years, many local functionaries continued to play a rather dubious role well after the regime was consolidated, as we have seen at length. For another, from this grass-roots perspective it would seem that the intended function of the 'mass organizations' to serve as 'transmission belts' from the party to the masses – that is, to convey the ideas and intentions of the communist party to 'target' sectors of society (workers, youth, farmers, women) – was never effectively realized. This programmatic statement of Lenin, which became a policy imperative in all Soviet-style socialist states, has often been taken as a more or less accurate description of the situation in the GDR from about 1950 onwards by scholars in both East and West viewing the system from the 'top down'.[7] Of course it is in one sense entirely correct: there is no question that the mass organizations were subordinated to and controlled by the party. But as we have seen, the more the leadership gained control over them in the factories, towns and villages (which itself took longer than most accounts have implied), the more they lost their connection with the masses. Or in other words, the more the party improved this 'transmission' function between itself and the mass organizations during the course of the 1950s, the less 'transmission' there was between the organizations and 'ordinary' East Germans. The shopfloor recognition initially enjoyed by the BGLs quickly turned to widespread indifference; the rather popular FDJ-as-dance-organizer alienated many of its members when it tried to recruit them for military service; the initially *Großbauer*-dominated VdgBs became insignificant in the villages and the DBD (German Democratic Farmers' Party) never had much influence at all. The mass organizations at the local level functioned like intermediary pulleys connecting the central party authorities (the engine) and the masses (the wheels), but the transmission connection tended only to work on one side or the other.[8]

Processes of social change at the grass-roots were strongly affected by a variety of threads of continuity from both the pre-communist past as well as from problems rooted in the chaos immediately after the war. Older social networks and ways of life in the villages; traditional notions of distinction, prestige and property; the culture of work as it developed under the impact of Soviet occupation and scarcity; the widespread pacifism resulting from the experience of war and defeat; the strong foothold of the churches in many areas – all of these factors played an important role in subsequent developments. This is not to say that the obstacles to the socialist transformation of East Germany remained unchanged from the 1940s to the 1960s. Rather, the point is that many of the efforts to transform and mobilize society in the 1950s and early 1960s proceeded along similar lines to the immediate post-war years. The communist regime still failed to overcome many of the understandable problems of this period of chaos well after it was established and consolidated at 'the top', as the history of agricultural collectivization in the villages and raising productivity in the factories amply testify. In this sense, the notion that 'against the will of the SED, society had attained a certain autonomy since the beginning of the sixties'[9] is only half correct: 'society' indeed possessed a certain autonomy, but it did so well before the beginning of the 1960s.

At the local level, the socialist transformation of East Germany always meant more than just recasting social structures. Millions of people lived there, people with their own lives, ideas and agendas which sometimes overlapped and often collided with the communists' plans, but were never reducible to them. This, too, was an important factor that distorted and impeded the socialist project. Although East European communism did indeed rest, as Charles Maier has argued, on 'repression tempered by enthusiasms'[10] for its various projects worthy of support (construction efforts, education reforms, peace initiatives, etc.), most East Germans showed little interest and even less inclination to be 'mobilized' for the

SED's projects that did not directly correspond to their own immediate concerns and interests.

Yet it would be one-sided to interpret this as a manifestation of 'opposition' or 'protest'. In the wake of the GDR's collapse, the moral wrestling with the legacies of this second German dictatorship has tended to pose these questions of political behaviour in terms that often seem too black-and-white. This is perhaps, somewhat ironically, a kind of backlash reflection of the SED's own dualistic official jargon of 'positive' versus 'negative' attitudes, 'loyal' versus 'hostile' behaviour which for forty years divided the world into friends and foes. But life is rarely so straightforward, and people everywhere are bundles of contradictions. The bipolar concepts of resistance/compliance, opposition/obedience, even political/apolitical, quite obviously fail to capture these complexities.

A more subtle problem of posing questions in this dualistic fashion is that it tends to reduce human action under dictatorial regimes to a matter of mere reaction. As we have seen, 'ordinary' East Germans were not as passive as these bipolar concepts would suggest. Although adopting a defensive posture in response to incursions 'from above' was common enough, this was not the whole story. Ordinary people also frequently played a more active role by using the structures and opportunites at hand (the land reform, the socialist brigades, the tensions between recruiters and economic functionaries, to list just a few) to make the best of the situation for themselves – actions which had consequences for the outcome of centrally-dictated policies. This is not to say that the majority of East Germans were somehow 'engaged' with the system in any positive sense of the term. Political indifference and apathy were, as we have seen, far more characteristic of the situation on the ground. But such 'apoliticism' and disinterest were not the same as total passivity. While Günter Gaus' famous concept of the 'niche society' neatly captures the dynamics of indifference, of opting out of civic participation and retreat into the sanctuaries of private life, it sheds little light on these more proactive, self-interested impulses at the grass-roots.[11] One could be completely indifferent to politics as such but still use the regime's policies to one's own advantage. The dynamics of this two-way process of action and reaction are perhaps better understood as a kind of 'creative accommodation' within the boundaries of the possible than through such concepts as 'niche society', resistance/compliance, or opposition/obedience.

Clearly, this 'creative accommodation' could only take place beyond the totalizing reach of the central authorities. Indeed, the key to understanding it, as with any kind of behaviour that deviated from the official line throughout this period, was that it was unorganized, with the mere fear of attention by the police usually enough to preclude any organized forms. Yet during the period covered here, there was considerable, albeit limited, room for it at the grass-roots. These semi-autonomous spaces commonly opened up as a result of the divided loyalties or self-interest on the part of individual officials at the local level. Most often, though, they resulted from the broader systemic contradictions within 'the regime' itself. In attempting to control every aspect of society, the East German dictatorship did not solve society's contradictions and conflicts (this basically would have been to realize its utopian goals) so much as it incorporated them into its own structures and policies. In turn, these contradictions presented certain opportunities for 'ordinary' East Germans to pursue their own agendas: the conflict of interest between factory managers and military recruiters helped disinclined young men to avoid military service; industrial managers' concerns about retaining scarce manpower against party demands for raising productivity presented opportunities for local wage bargaining; reference to the regime's own 'peace and bread' rhetoric served as a justification for refusing to join the army; complaining about the logical inconsistency of prioritized housing provision for returnees from the West, or even threatening to leave briefly and become one, could be used as a means of acquiring a new flat; the list goes on.

Of course all societies have their contradictions and conflicts, and we should not blow the GDR's out of proportion. Indeed, one might ask what was different about this picture from the situation in any Western country. On the face of it, not very much at the grass-roots level. People behaved in much the same self-interested fashion as anywhere else, using the opportunities presented by local circumstances for their own gain and generally getting on with their private lives as unmolested as possible by larger events and developments – a fact which should perhaps make Westerners less surprised that the system was as stable as it was. 'Creative accommodation' and '*Eigen-Sinn*' can be readily observed in most societies most of the time. Yet this should not obscure the glaring inequality of power between rulers and ruled under state socialism. The crucial difference from liberal Western societies lay not as much in the micro-milieu as in broader structures, in the absence of formal

channels for political feedback, of an independent institutional framework for civic activity and asserting interests, of a clear division
between state and private affairs in principle, and of course in the
contradictions and inefficiencies of the planned economy. Again,
the concept of 'totalitarianism' can, in a descriptive, taxonomical
sense, be useful for capturing these macro-structural characteristics
that differ so markedly from liberal-democratic polities. But as Ralph
Jessen has insightfully observed: 'The unique feature about this
political-social system was not that society was "shut down". Rather,
it seems much more as if the ever-expanding, undifferentiated,
unlimited state, precisely because it had lost its limits, in a certain
sense became increasingly *vergesellschaftet*'[12], (which one might rather
imperfectly translate as 'shaped by society'). This '*Vergesellschaftung*'
and overlap of state and society was clearly visible at the grass-
roots, whether in the form of undependable and self-interested
functionaries or ordinary people distorting and taking advantage
of the regime's structures and policies for their own benefit. Arguably, any regime that attempts to control and penetrate society to
the same degree as in East Germany will incorporate some of its
tensions and contradictions. East German society may formally have
been under party control, and the SED leadership may have made
all the major decisions, but the manner and extent to which these
decisions were actually carried out on the ground often lay beyond
the limits of its control.

At the same time, one should recognize that this local social
autonomy in the GDR was very attenuated. 'Creative accommodation' was only possible on an informal basis and extremely small
scale. Its primary manifestation was a kind of 'take the money and
run' strategy by individuals or at the most small groups of people,
which could only partially compensate for the absence of opportunities for broader collective action. This social autonomy was both
unintended and in many ways unwanted by the party leadership,
which at least initially hoped for a significant behavioural change
on the part of the populace with the transition to socialism, and
which in principle did not like to see any sphere of life beyond its
control. But in the event it actually lent a measure of stability to
the system by both mitigating some of contradictions of policies
dictated from above (for instance, maintaining agricultural production while collectivizing farms, or raising productivity at the same
time as raising an army), as well as channeling impulses that di-
verged somewhat from the party line into less politically dangerous

directions. There is a clear parallel to be drawn here with the building of the socialist system in the Soviet Union, where, as Merle Fainsod has argued in his classic study of Soviet Smolensk, 'paradoxically, it was the very inefficiency of the state machine which helped make it tolerable'.[13] If all the demands of the centre were faithfully transmitted to the ground, the result would undoubtedly have been more hardship and most likely stiffening popular resistance. The failures of local control acted as a kind of escape valve to help alleviate tension. Although these failures were slowly but surely diminished, they were never completely eradicated. Over time there developed a sort of tacit exchange of a certain amount of social autonomy at the grass-roots in return for the unquestioned political authority of the party leadership; a pragmatic, implicit arrangement which, though not without its problems, ultimately reinforced and stabilized the communist leadership's hold on power, at least in the short- and mid-term.

Was the regime then, in this sense, effectively undermining its own stability through the proliferation of the vast apparatus of cadre-screening, security and surveillance whose very purpose was to ensure the greatest possible control from the centre? Not really. Organs such as the *Stasi*, the party control commissions and the *Instrukteur*-brigades could, and sometimes did, function as a kind of 'short circuit' between the party leadership and the grass-roots. The fear and immense pressures of conformity this engendered determined the outer parameters of life in the GDR and no doubt precluded many wayward or threatening developments. But these organs, however inflated they became, were usually only switched on when troubles reached a certain point. Problems such as work stoppages or discord within the LPGs were often defused well before the threshhold at which they became involved. Many grass-roots functionaries were reluctant to call them in, not least because they themselves might get into trouble. After all, there was no shortage of complaints in the Central Committee about 'heartless and bureaucratic' behaviour, of 'insufficient attention to people's needs' and 'administrative excesses' on the ground, accusations that could have serious consequences for low-level officials. As in both the Soviet Union and Third Reich, local functionaries could be used as scapegoats for problems, as 'lightning rods' for popular discontent about such matters as the lack of housing or the coercion involved in collectivization, thus diverting it away from the party leadership. The function of grass-roots functionaries as a kind of buffer between the leadership and populace at large therefore had advantages for the former as well as the latter. Again, the very indirectness of control at the grass-roots made it more secure.

In practice (if not in theory), constructing East German socialism could not merely be a process of dictation, but also entailed a degree of negotiation, however implicit, informal and one-sided it may have been. As we have seen, the SED's various political interventions into society and efforts to mobilize East Germans were for the most part neither immediately *nor completely* realized on the ground, and in many cases only a more 'workable' version could ultimately be implemented. Recognizing this should not, however, obscure the decisive influence of dictatorial steering from the 'centre' in processes of social change in the SBZ/GDR. Older social networks, habits and orientations may have shown a high level of *'Resistenz'* (in Martin Broszat's immunological sense of the term)[14] to political intervention, but they were not impervious to it. Nor were the East Germans themselves immune to the mobilization efforts: hardly anyone who lived in the GDR escaped the pressure to make an arrangement, to participate and cooperate in some form with what has aptly been called the 'contagious state'.[15] It is more that political intervention was so reshaped when applied at the grass-roots as to become at least partially compatible with traditional social structures, with the wishes of the broader populace and with the interests and capabilities of local officials. Given the ambitiousness of the project, it arguably could not have happened otherwise. In the final analysis, East German socialism was not just a new 'totalitarian' construction, but a mixture of different structures and mentalities inherited from the German past, various Soviet imports, occasional dictatorial intervention as well as human actions – not only on the part of those in the halls of power, but also by 'ordinary' East Germans.

A final word on some of the connections between the *construction* and *dismantling* of East German socialism is necessary. It seems in some ways odd that notions of totalitarianism should have witnessed such a renaissance after the very collapse of the regimes that they seek to describe. When viewing the history of the GDR through the lens of its demise in 1989–90, what one sees is less the omnipotence of the communist regime (the feasibility of the entire 'totalitarian project' of shaping and controlling everything) and more the limits to its power, whatever the many revelations about the *Stasi*'s immensity since the opening of the archives. This is true not just of the external limits (i.e. the good graces of the Soviet Union) but also the internal ones: low productivity, poor work discipline, a west-oriented and uncontrollable youth, retreat into domestic 'niches', corruption and the 'shadow economy', the overburdening of the regime apparatus itself by its own profusion of competences, etc. These unintended consequences were at least as central to the face of 'real existing socialism' in the GDR of the 1970s and 1980s as the plans and intentions of the SED leadership, and what this study has attempted to show is how both continuities from the pre-communist past as well as unplanned human responses at the grass-roots level helped shape East German socialism during its two formative decades. Of course it would be far too simple to attribute the regime's ultimate collapse solely to these unintended developments (systemic economic problems were absolutely crucial) or to stylize them as a form of heroic 'resistance' or 'opposition'. Yet it nonetheless seems clear that, at the very least, they nourished and represented a widespread culture of disrespect for the SED's authority and contributed to the difficulties of the party leadership in overcoming the mounting political and economic problems in the GDR that together helped pave the way for the ultimate demise of the regime once the external guarantees were abolished and internal political mobilization against it spread out of control.

Notes

1 Introduction

1 I use this term loosely to refer to all those who were not full-time functionaries in the apparatus of party, state and affiliated mass organizations.

2 Carl Friedrich, Zbigniew Brzezinski, *Totalitarian Dictatorship and Autocracy* (Cambridge, MA: Harvard University Press, 1956); Hannah Arendt, *The Origins of Totalitarianism* (London: Secker & Warburg, 1951).

3 Eckard Jesse, 'War die DDR totalitär?', in: *APuZG*, B40/94 (7 Oct. 1994), pp. 12–23; Klaus Schroeder (ed.), *Geschichte und Transformation des SED-Staates. Beiträge und Analyse* (Berlin: Akademie-Verlag, 1994), p. 11.

4 Sigrid Meuschel, 'Überlegungen zu einer Herrschafts- und Gesellschaftsgeschichte der DDR', in: *GG*, vol. 19 (1993), pp. 5–14; cf. also *idem*, *Legitimation und Parteiherrschaft. Zum Paradox von Stabilität und Revolution in der DDR 1945–1989* (Fr./Main: Suhrkamp, 1992).

5 This is the case with most research on the GDR since 1989, as embodied by the recent synthesis by Klaus Schroeder, *Der SED-Staat. Partei, Staat und Gesellschaft 1949–1990* (Munich: C. Hanser, 1998).

6 Jürgen Kocka, 'Die Geschichte der DDR als Forschungsproblem. Einleitung', in *idem* (ed.), *Historische DDR-Forschung: Aufsätze und Studien* (Berlin: Akademie-Verlag, 1993), p. 11.

7 One might ask what is meant by the term 'socialism' here. Many socialists, ranging from social democrats to Trotskyists all the way to Maoists, do not consider the Soviet-style system that prevailed in the GDR to be 'true' socialism at all. This study is not concerned with definitions of the term, but rather simply uses the label that the East German communist leadership itself applied to the system it constructed in the GDR.

8 See esp. the various works by Peter Hübner, Arnd Bauerkämper and Jörg Roesler in the bibliography. For overviews, see Mary Fulbrook, *Anatomy of a Dictatorship: Inside the GDR 1949–1989* (Oxford: Oxford University Press, 1995); J. Kocka, *Historische DDR-Forschung*; Hartmut Kaelble, Jürgen Kocka, Hartmut Zwahr (eds), *Sozialgeschichte der DDR* (Stuttgart: Klett-Cotta, 1994); Richard Bessel, Ralph Jessen (eds), *Die Grenzen der Diktatur: Staat und Gesellschaft in der SBZ/DDR* (Göttingen: Vandenhoeck & Ruprecht, 1996).

9 This is particularly the case with Armin Mitter, Stefan Wolle, *Untergang auf Raten: Unbekannte Kapitel der DDR-Geschichte* (Munich: Bertelsmann, 1993).

10 See, for example, Ulrike Poppe, Rainer Eckert, Ilko-Sascha Kowalczuk (eds), *Zwischen Selbstbehauptung und Anpassung. Formen des Widerstandes und der Opposition in der DDR* (Berlin: Ch. Links, 1995); Ehrhard Neubert, *Geschichte der Opposition in der DDR 1949–1989* (Berlin: Ch. Links, 1997);

Christoph Kleßmann, 'Opposition und Resistenz in zwei Diktaturen in Deutschland', in *Historische Zeitschrift*, vol. 262 (1996), no. 2, pp. 453–79.

11 A valuable collection of essays that adopts this micro-historical approach is Thomas Lindenberger (ed.), *Herrschaft und Eigen-Sinn in der Diktatur. Studien zur Gesellschaftsgeschichte der DDR* (Cologne: Böhlau-Verlag, 1999).

12 These three demographic categories need defining. 'Workers' is used here to refer to blue-collar labourers in industrial factories, primarily the state-owned enterprises. There were of course a number of important differences between skilled and unskilled trades, different branches of industry, men and women and with regard to the residual private sector which will be taken into consideration where appropriate. 'Farmers' refers to those directly involved in agriculture, on whom this study will focus. Though of course not all of the rural populace were farmers, many were in related trades and all were affected in some way by the land reform and subsequent collectivization. 'Youth' is used here in accordance with the official East German definition as all those between 14 and 25 years of age.

13 See esp. P. Hübner, *Konsens, Konflikt, Kompromiß. Soziale Arbeiterinteressen und Sozialpolitik in der SBZ/DDR 1945–1970* (Berlin: Akademie-Verlag, 1995); Jörg Roesler, 'Die Produktionsbrigaden in der Industrie der DDR. Zentrum der Arbeitswelt?', in Kaelble, *et al.*, *Sozialgeschichte der DDR*, *op. cit.*, pp. 144–70; Alf Lüdtke, '"Helden der Arbeit" – Mühe beim Arbeiten. Zur mißmutigen Loyalität von Industriearbeitern in der DDR', in Kaelble, *et al.*, *Sozialgeschichte*, *op. cit.*, pp. 188–213. Particularly provocative are Jeffrey Kopstein, *The Politics of Economic Decline in East Germany, 1945–1989* (Chapel Hill: University of North Carolina Press, 1997); *idem*, 'Chipping Away at the State. Workers' Resistance and the Demise of East Germany', in *World Politics*, vol. 48 (April 1996), pp. 391–423. Useful pre-*Wende* studies include: Axel Bust-Bartels, *Herrschaft und Widerstand in den DDR-Betrieben. Leistungsentlohnung, Arbeitsbedingungen, innerbetriebliche Konflikte und technologische Entwicklung* (Fr./Main: Campus-Verlag, 1980); Siegfried Suckut, *Die Betriebsrätebewegung in der Sowjetisch Besetzten Zone Deutschlands, 1945–1948* (Fr./Main: Haag & Herchen, 1982).

14 For an excellent overview, see Arnd Bauerkämper (ed.), *'Junkerland in Bauernhand'? Durchführung, Auswirkungen und Stellenwert der Bodenreform in der Sowjetischen Besatzungszone* (Stuttgart: Franz Steiner, 1996).

15 See Joachim Piskol, 'Zum Beginn der Kollektivierung der Landwirtschaft der DDR im Sommer 1952', in *Beiträge zur Geschichte der Arbeiterbewegung*, vol. 37 (1995), no. 3, pp. 19–26; Elke Scherstjanoi, 'Die DDR im Frühjahr 1952: Sozialismuslosung und Kollektivierungsbeschluß in sowjetischer Perspektive', in *DA*, vol. 27 (1994), no. 4, pp. 354–63; Christian Krebs, *Der Weg zur industriemäßigen Organisation der Agrarproduktion in der DDR. Die Agrarpolitik der SED 1945–1960* (Bonn: Forschungsgesellschaft für Agrarpolitik u. Agrarsoziologie, 1989). The notable exceptions are: Jonathan Osmond, 'Kontinuität und Konflikt in der Landwirtschaft der SBZ/DDR zur Zeit der Bodenreform und der Vergenossenschaftlichung, 1945–1961', in Bessel and Jessen, *Die Grenzen*, pp. 137–69; T. Lindenberger, 'Der ABV als Landwirt. Zur Mitwirkung der Deutschen Volkspolizei an der

Kollektivierung der Landwirtschaft, 1952–1960', in *idem* (ed.), *Herrschaft und Eigen-Sinn*; Christel Nehrig, 'Zur sozialen Entwicklung der Bauern in der DDR 1945–1960', in *Zeitschrift für Agrargeschichte und Agrarsoziologie*, vol. 41 (1993), pp. 66–76. On the role of the criminal justice system in the process of collectivization, see Falco Werkentin, *Politische Strafjustiz in der Ära Ulbricht* (Berlin: Ch. Links, 1995). A rather one-sided account of the first collectivization 'push' is Armin Mitter, '"Am 17.6.1953 haben die Arbeiter gestreikt, jetzt aber streiken wir Bauern". Die Bauern und der Sozialismus', in Ilko-Sascha Kowalczuk, Armin Mitter and Stefan Wolle (eds), *Der Tag X – 17 Juni 1953. Die 'Innere Staatsgründung' der DDR als Ergebnis der Krise 1952/54* (Berlin: Ch. Links, 1995), pp. 75–128.

16 Among the best studies to date which successfully incorporate the view 'from below', see esp. Ulrich Mählert, *Die Freie Deutsche Jugend 1945– 1949. Von den 'Antifaschistischen Jugendausschüssen' zur SED-Massenorganisation: Die Erfassung der Jugend in der Sowjetischen Besatzungszone* (Paderborn: F. Schöningh, 1995); also Dorothee Wierling, 'Die Jugend als innerer Feind. Konflikte in der Erziehungsdiktatur der sechziger Jahre', in Kaelble *et al.*, *Sozialgeschichte*, pp. 404–25. Studies on the East German military have tended to focus on its organizational history, its role within the Warsaw Pact and its activities during the Prague Spring and revolution of 1989, with investigations of recruitment basically confined to Soviet and SED policies *vis-à-vis* military cadre and returning POWs during the 'hidden rearmament' before 1952. See esp. Bruno Thoß (ed.), *Volksarmee schaffen – ohne Geschrei! Studien zu den Anfängen einer 'verdeckten Aufrüstung' in der SBZ/DDR 1947–1952* (Munich: Oldenbourg, 1994).

17 See Volker Ackermann, *Der 'echte' Flüchtling: Deutsche Vertriebene und Flüchtlinge aus der DDR 1945–1961* (Osnabrück: Universitätsverlag Rasch, 1995); Helge Heidemeyer, *Flucht und Zuwanderung aus der SBZ/DDR 1945/ 1949–1961. Die Flüchtlingspolitik der Bundesrepublik Deutschland bis zum Bau der Berliner Mauer* (Düsseldorf: Droste, 1994); Sylvia Schraut, Thomas Grosser (eds), *Die Flüchtlingsfrage in der deutschen Nachkriegsgesellschaft* (Mannheim: Palatium-Verlag, 1996); Rainer Schulze, Doris von der Brelie-Lewien, Helga Grebing (eds), *Flüchtlinge und Vertriebene in der westdeutschen Nachkriegsgeschichte* (Hildesheim: A. Lax, 1987). The only exceptions to date are: Henrik Eberle, 'Weder Gegnerschaft noch Abwerbung. Zu den Motiven republikflüchtiger SED-Mitglieder aus dem Bezirk Halle im Jahr 1961', in Heiner Timmermann (ed.), *Diktaturen in Europa im 20. Jahrhundert – der Fall DDR* (Berlin: Duncker & Humblot, 1996), pp. 449–60; narrower and less substantial are Joachim S. Hohmann, '"Wenn Sie dies lesen, bin ich schon auf dem Weg in den Westen". "Republikflüchtige" DDR-Lehrer in den Jahren 1949–1961', in *ZfG*, vol. 45 (1997), no. 4, pp. 311–30; and John Connelly, 'Zur "Republikflucht" von DDR-Wissenschaftlern in den fünfziger Jahren, Dokumentation', in *ZfG*, vol. 42 (1994), no. 4, pp. 331–52.

18 On this concept, see Alf Lüdtke, *Eigen-Sinn. Fabrikalltag, Arbeitererfahrungen und Politik vom Kaiserreich bis in den Faschismus. Ergebnisse* (Hamburg: Ergebnisse-Verlag, 1993).

19 For oral interviews conducted before 1989, see Lutz Niethammer, Dorothee Wierling and Alexander von Plato, *Die Volkseigene Erfahrung. Eine*

Ärchaeologie des Lebens in der Industrieprovinz der DDR (Berlin: Rowohlt, 1991). Dagmar Semmelmann has also conducted numerous oral interviews, both before and after 1989: 'Zeitzeugen über ihren 17 Juni 1953 in Berlin', in *hefte zur ddr-geschichte*, no. 7, pp. 26–55; *idem, Schauplatz Stalinstadt/EKO. Erinnerungen an den 17 Juni 1953* (Potsdam, 1993). I have used two different kinds of survey material: the 'Infratest' surveys conducted in the 1950s and 1960s on GDR refugees in West Germany, and to a lesser extent the formerly classified opinion surveys conducted by the *Institut für Meinungsforschung* in the SED Central Committee. Both have their problems: for the former that of self-selection and for the latter that of self-censorship under dictatorial conditions. Yet both are nonetheless very useful sources on particular aspects of popular opinion in the GDR.

20 See, for example, Peter Hübner, 'Die Zukunft war gestern', in Kaelble *et al.*, *Sozialgeschichte*, pp. 171–87.

21 Although the cumulative area of these three districts does not correspond precisely to that covered by *Land* Brandenburg, it is nevertheless similar enough to refer to them collectively as 'Brandenburg' after the dissolution of the *Länder* in 1952.

22 This was also reflected in the remarkably diverse political landscape of the region before the Nazi takeover of power in 1933, ranging from 'Red' Berlin to the strongly nationalist/conservative eastern electoral district around Frankfurt/Oder. For electoral figures, see Broszat and Weber (eds), *SBZ-Handbuch*, 2nd edn (Munich: Oldenbourg, 1993), pp. 82–3.

23 Calculated from figures in *StJB* (Berlin, 1990), pp. 69, 75, 89.

24 *SBZ-Handbuch*, pp. 81, 104, 169. For the sake of comparison, such large estates accounted for 62 per cent of agricultural acreage in Mecklenburg and less than 1 per cent in the dwarf-agricultural economy of Thuringia.

2 The land reform and its effects

1 *SBZ-Handbuch*, p. 92. This included 2357 enterprises with a total of 733 621 hectares (609 000 from *Großgrundbesitz*).

2 See Norman Naimark, *The Russians in Germany: A History of the Soviet Zone of Occupation, 1945–1949* (Cambridge, MA: Harvard University Press, 1995), p. 153.

3 SAPMO-BA DY30/2022/53, 'Jahresbericht für die Bodenreform', 7 Dec. 1946, bl. 37.

4 BLHA, Ld. Br. Rep. 208, Nr. 185, 'Runderlass Nr. 372', 4 Jan. 1946, bl. 136–7.

5 Boris Spix, *Die Bodenreform in Brandenburg 1945–47: Konstruktion einer Gesellschaft am Beispiel der Kreise West- und Ostprignitz* (Münster, 1997), p. 87.

6 BAB DK1/8189, bl. 12.

7 BLHA, Ld. Br. Rep. 208, Nr. 251, bl. 22.

8 SAPMO-BA DY30/IV2/7/256, 'Betr.: Befehl 209', 3 May 1948, bl. 209–10.

9 SAPMO-BA DY30/IV2/7/256, 'Errichtung von Neubauernhöfen', 29 Jan. 1948, bl. 232–3.

10 Arnd Bauerkämper, 'Strukturumbruch ohne Mentalitätenwandel. Auswirkungen der Bodenreform auf die ländliche Gesellschaft in der Provinz Mark Brandenburg 1945–1949', in *idem* (ed.), *Junkerland*, pp. 67–86.

11 BLHA Ld. Br. Rep. 332, Nr. 638, 'Bericht über einige Zustände im Landkreis Cottbus', 16 Nov. 1948, bl. 147.

12 Quote from BAB DK1/8189, bl. 67; see also 'Zusammenstellung der Landzuteilungen, die nicht den gesetzlichen Vorschriften entsprechen', undated, 1948, bl. 7–11.

13 BLHA Ld. Br. Rep. 332, Nr. 638, bl. 147–8. The 'Kattlow case' was resolved in December 1948 with the eviction of the 'Hendrisch Clique' from the property. SAPMO-BA DY30/IV2/7/240, bl. 123–6.

14 In *Kreis* Calau-Senftenberg, only one in eight refugees received land, and even they were poorly provided with equipment, fertilizer and draft animals. Cf. P. Ther, 'Die Vertriebenenpolitik in der SBZ/DDR 1945–1953 am Beispiel des Kreises Calau-Senftenberg', in *Jahrbuch für brandenburgische Landesgeschichte*, vol. 46 (1995), p. 164.

15 SAPMO-BA DY30/2022/53, 'Jahresbericht für die Bodenreform', 7 Dec. 1946, bl. 40. Underline in the original. See also BLHA Ld. Br. Rep. 208, Nr. 185, Runderlass Nr. 372, 4 Jan. 1946, bl. 136–137; SAPMO-BA DY30/IV2/7/231, 'Betr.: Auszug aus einem Bericht des Ortsumsiedlerausschusses Wölsickendorf, Krs. Oberbarnim', 14 July 1948, bl. 129.

16 Cf. Gerald Christopeit, 'Die Herkunft und Verteilung der Evakuierten, Flüchtlinge und Vertriebenen in der Provinz Mark Brandenburg und ihr Verhältnis zu der einheimischen Bevölkerung', in Manfred Wille, Johannes Hoffmann and Wolfgang Meinicke (eds), *Sie hatten alles verloren. Flüchtlinge und Vertriebene in der sowjetischen Besatzungszone Deutschlands* (Wiesbaden: Harrassowitz, 1993), pp. 86–109. BLHA Ld. Br. Rep. 250, Nr. 255; Rep. 203, Nr. 339.

17 *Ibid.*, pp. 99–100, 106.

18 BLHA Ld. Br. Rep. 208, Nr. 2758, report of 16 March 1948, bl. 180–1.

19 B. Spix, *Bodenreform*, p. 87.

20 G. Braun, 'Determinanten der Wahlentscheidungen in der Sowjetischen Besatzungszone 1946. Problemskizze', in *Deutsche Studien*, vol. 24 (1986), pp. 346–54.

21 *SBZ-Handbuch*, p. 397.

22 SAPMO-BA DY30/IV2/7/227, bl. 70.

23 LAB C Rep. 900, IV/4/06/402, 'Bericht aus der Ostzone', 24 June 1948, unpag.; LAB C Rep. 411, Nr. 1306, Bd. 1, 'Bericht', 20 June 1949, pp. 1–2.

24 BLHA Ld. Br. Rep. 332, Nr. 638, 'Statistisches Material', May 1946, bl. 2; *SBZ-Handbuch*, p. 80.

25 On the position of rural women generally during the latter 1940s, see Jonathan Osmond, 'Geschlechtsspezifische Folgen der Bodenreform in der Sowjetischen Besatzungszone: Gutsbesitzerinnen, Bäuerinnen und Landarbeiterinnen nach 1945', in A. Bauerkämper, *Junkerland*, pp. 153–68.

26 See N. Naimark, *The Russians*, p. 145.

27 SAPMO-BA DY30/IV2/7/231, report to the Kreissekretariat VdgB in Burg, 15 July 1948, bl. 131.

28 A. Bauerkämper, 'Strukturumbruch', p. 72.

29 SAPMO-BA DY30/IV2/7/229, Provinzialverwaltung Mark Brandenburg to SED-ZK, 'Bericht über die Durchführung der Bodenreform in der Provinz Mark Brandenburg', 4 Dec. 1945, bl. 191–3.

30 SAPMO-BA DY30/IV2/7/231, Wilhelm Schneider to FDGB Vorstand, 25 May 1946, bl. 84–5.

31 SAPMO-BA DY30/IV2/7/231, report of July 1948, bl. 131. See also Naimark, pp. 159–60.

32 See, for instance, the numerous complaints in the file SAPMO-BA DY30/IV2/7/231; also BAB DK1/8189, bl. 204.

33 N. Naimark, *The Russians*, pp. 158–60.

34 SAPMO-BA DY30/2.022/53, 'Jahresbericht für die Bodenreform', 7 Dec. 1946, bl. 26. Underline in the original.

35 SAPMO-BA DY30/IV2/7/240, report of 23 Jan. 1948, bl. 39–40. Underline in the original.

36 SAPMO-BA DY30/IV2/7/240, 'Sonderbericht von der Kontrollreise vom 22–27.5.1948 in dem Kreise Teltow, Land Brandenburg', 31.5.48, bl. 67–8.

37 BLHA Ld. Br. Rep. 332, Nr. 219, 'Auszug aus dem Arbeitsbericht des Sekretariats des Kreisvorstandes Oberbarnim für den Monat Mai 1949', 16 June 1949, bl. 90.

38 BLHA Ld. Br. Rep. 332, Nr. 413, 'Vorläufiger Bericht über die Ortsgruppe Görlsdorf', 4 July 1949, bl. 33; 'Auszug aus dem Bericht des Kreises Angermünde vom 10.5.49', 29 May 1949, bl. 35.

39 LAB C Rep. 900, IV/4/06/403, undated report, around May 1947, unpag.

40 SAPMO-BA DY30/IV2/7/231, Wilhelm Schardt to SED-ZK Abt. Landwirtschaft, 12 Apr. 1947, bl. 86–7.

41 By July 1949, 10.7 per cent of the new farms in the SBZ had been formally returned to the land commissions. By Dec. 1951, 2906 farms with a total of 23 500 hectares had been abandoned in Brandenburg alone. Figures from A. Bauerkämper, 'Die Neubauern in der SBZ/DDR 1945–1952. Bodenreform und politisch induzierter Wandel der ländlichen Gesellschaft', in Bessel and Jessen, *Die Grenzen*, pp. 123–4.

42 In April 1949, 91 per cent of the *Großbauern* in the GDR were members of the VdgB (159 had still been elected to the local executives), compared with 83 per cent of mid-sized farmers and merely 56.2 per cent of small farmers. Arnd Bauerkämper, 'Transformation or Transition? Rural Elites under the Impact of Land Reform and Collectivisation in the GDR' (Ms. 1997), p. 7.

43 SAPMO-BA DY30/IV2/7/231, bl. 3–7.

44 Cf. generally, Joachim Piskol, 'Zur sozialökonomischen Entwicklung der Großbauern in der DDR 1945 bis 1960', in *ZfG*, vol. 39 (1991), pp. 419–33.

45 F. Werkentin, *Politische Strafjustiz*, p. 57

46 See esp. Christel Nehrig, 'Bauern zwischen Hoffnung und Wirklichkeit. Die modifizierte Agrarpolitik von 1950/51', in Elke Scherstjanoi (ed.), '*Provisorium für längstens ein Jahr'. Protokoll des Kolloquiums Die Gründung der DDR* (Berlin: Akademie-Verlag, 1993), pp. 236–42.

47 Cf. generally, Wolfgang Bell, *Enteignungen in der Landwirtschaft der DDR nach 1949 und deren politischen Hintergründe. Analyse und Dokumentation*

(Münster: Landwirtschafts-Verlag, 1992).

48 A. Bauerkämper, 'Von der Bodenreform zur Kollektivierung. Zum Wandel der ländlichen Gesellschaft in der Sowjetischen Besatzungszone Deutschlands und DDR 1945–1952', in Kaelble *et al.*, *Sozialgeschichte*, pp. 119–43.

49 Dieter Schulz, 'Ruhe im Dorf? Die Agrarpolitik von 1952/53 und ihre Folgen', in Jochen Cerny (ed.), *Brüche, Krisen, Wendepunkte. Neubefragung von DDR-Geschichte* (Leipzig: Urania, 1990), pp. 103–9. For a concise yet lucid account of the inner-party debate about the nature and timing of collectivization in the GDR, see N. Naimark, *The Russians*, pp. 150–66.

3 Recasting the factories after the war

1 Wolfgang Zank, *Wirtschaft und Arbeit in Ostdeutschland 1945–1949* (Munich: Oldenbourg, 1987), p. 67.

2 LAB C Rep. 900, IV/4/06/403, undated report, around May 1947.

3 N. Naimark, *The Russians*, pp. 194–5.

4 BAB DC15/759, DWK, bl. 92.

5 There was even talk within the Central Committee during the summer and autumn of 1947 as to whether or not 'work shy' elements could be arrested by the police and forcibly taken to employment offices. This was in the end deemed beyond the mandate of the police. SAPMO-BA DY30/IV2/2027/22, bl. 12–13.

6 SAPMO-BA DY30/IV2/2027/22, bl. 66–7.

7 BLHA Ld. Br. Rep. 332, Nr. 565, 'Bericht zur Durchführung des Befehls 234', undated, autumn 1947, bl. 112.

8 SAPMO-BA DY34/20738, 'Bericht über die Belegschaftsversammlung der Rüdersdorfer Kalkwerke am 6.11.1947', unpag.

9 On the shop-council movement generally, cf. S. Suckut, *Die Betriebsrätebewegung*; Dietrich Staritz, *Sozialismus in einem halben Lande* (Berlin: Wagenbach, 1978).

10 S. Suckut, *Die Betriebsrätebewegung*, p. 196.

11 SAPMO-BA DY30/IV2/2027/22, bl. 119.

12 *Ibid.*, bl. 121; SAPMO-BA DY30/IV2/2027/27, 'Entschliessung zur Lohnpolitik des FDGB', 10 April 1948.

13 SAPMO-BA DY30/IV2/2027/22, bl. 27.

14 LAB C Rep. 900, IV/4/06/403, 'Bericht über die Stimmung der Bevölkerung der russischen Besatzungsmacht gegenüber', 10 Oct. 1947, unpag.

15 On opposition to dismantling and reparations in the SBZ, see Rainer Karlsch, '"Arbeiter, schützt Euere Betriebe!" Widerstand gegen Demontagen in der SBZ', in *Internationale wissenschaftliche Korrespondenz zur Geschichte der deutschen Arbeiterbewegung*, vol. 30 (1994), no. 3, pp. 380–404. See also N. Naimark, *The Russians*, pp. 178–89. Despite Soviet promises to end dismantling in both 1946 and 1947, it was only finally stopped in 1948.

16 SAPMO-BA DY34/20738, Warnke to Landesvorstand FDGB Brandenburg, 1 Nov. 1947, unpag., underline in the original.

17 LAB C Rep. 900, IV/4/06/402, 'Stimmungsberichte aus der Berlin

Bevölkerung!', 7 July 1948; LAB C Rep. 900, IV/4/06/403, 'Betr.: Abzug der Westmächte aus Berlin etc.', 4 April 1948.

18 LAB C Rep. 900, IV/4/06/402, report of 6 April 1948, unpag.
19 SAPMO-BA DY30/IV2/2027/22, bl. 140–1. In the event, however, receiving extra clothing allotments probably would have made less difference than many of them thought, for as local functionaries complained, the extra deliveries were often comprised mostly of women's and children's clothing of little use for a predominately male workforce. See BAB DC15/776, bl. 159.
20 See Petra Clemens, 'Die "letzten". Arbeits- und Berufserfahrungen einer Generation Niederlausitzer Textilarbeiterinnen', in J. Kocka (ed.), *Historische DDR-Forschung*, pp. 245–61.
21 BLHA Ld. Br. Rep. 332, Nr. 535, IG Textil to SED Landesvorstand, 20 Jan. 1948, bl. 122.
22 *Ibid.*, bl. 178.
23 N. Naimark, *The Russians*, pp. 196–7.
24 J. Kopstein, *The Politics*, ch. 1.
25 SAPMO-BA DY30/IV2/2027/22, report to Ulbricht, 6 April 1948, bl. 151.
26 SAPMO-BA DY30/IV2/2027/22, 'Bericht über die bisherige Verwirklichung des Aufbauplans 234', 8 April 1948, bl. 119.
27 BLHA Ld. Br. Rep. 332, Nr. 437, 'Betr.: Durchführung des Befehls 234', 4 June 1948, bl. 6–8.
28 BLHA Ld. Br. Rep. 332, Nr. 437, letter from Sharov to Steinhoff, 5 June 1948, bl. 18.
29 BAB DC 15/776, DWK report, 27 Sept. 1948, bl. 123.
30 *Ibid.*
31 SAPMO-BA DY30/IV2/2027/27, letter from Perelivchenko to Rau, 23 Dec. 1948, bl. 47–52. BAB DC15/777, bl. 5, 35.
32 SAPMO-BA DY30/IV2/2027/22, bl. 113–4, 152.
33 SAPMO-BA NY 4177/3, Nachlaß Hennecke, bl. 43. The literal translation of the poem is: 'Hennecke, you are the man who inspires us! Hennecke, with you we will overcome our distress! Hennecke, we swear to you that we will work hard! Hennecke, through you our economy will blossom again! Hennecke, you are a hero of our class! Hennecke, with us you are the powerful masses! Hennecke, we want to hold you up as a model! Hennecke, you will also destroy the enslavement of the brothers in the West!'
34 BLHA Ld. Br. Rep. 202G, Nr. 48, 'Stimmen zur Hennicke [sic!] – Bewegung aus Potsdam', 10 Dec. 1948, bl. 42.
35 *Ibid.*
36 A. Hennecke, 'Der Durchbruch aus dem Teufelskreis', in Erwin Lehmann *et al.* (eds), *Aufbruch in unsere Zeit: Erinnerungen an die Tätigkeit der Gewerkschaften von 1945 bis zur Gründung der Deutschen Demokratischen Republik*, 2nd edn (Berlin, 1975), p. 197.
37 K. Grünberg, *et al.*, *Helden der Arbeit: Aus Ihrem Leben und Wirken* (Berlin, 1951), p. 23.
38 Klaus Ewers, 'Aktivisten in Aktion. Adolf Hennecke und der Beginn der Aktivistenbewegung 1948/49', in *DA*, vol. 14, no. 9 (Sept. 1981), pp. 947–70.

39 A. Hennecke, 'Der Durchbruch aus dem Teufelskreis'.
40 SAPMO-BA NY 4177/3, bl. 64, 66, 69.
41 See Klaus Ewers, p. 952.
42 A. Lüdtke, 'Helden der Arbeit', p. 192; P. Hübner, 'Umworben und bedrängt: Industriearbeiter in der SBZ', in Alexander Fischer (ed.), *Studien zur Geschichte der SBZ/DDR* (Berlin: Duncker & Humblot, 1993), pp. 205–6.
43 Protokoll der Verhandlungen des II. Parteitages der SED (Berlin, 1947), p. 321. Research on this 'transitional elite' is just beginning. For an overview, see Arnd Bauerkämper, 'Die tabuisierte Elite. Problembereiche, Fragen und Hypothesen der Zeithistorischen Forschung über Führungsgruppen in der DDR', in *Potsdamer Bulletin für Zeithistorische Studien*, no. 9 (April 1997), pp. 19–33. For industrial managers, see the case study by Frank Schulz, 'Elitenwandel in der Leipziger Wirtschaftsregion 1945–1948. Von den Leipziger "sächsischen Industriefamilien" zu Kadern aus dem Leipziger Arbeitermilieu', in *Comparativ*, vol. 5, no. 4 (1995), pp. 112–26.
44 See R. Karlsch, 'Arbeiter, schützt Euere Betriebe!'
45 LAB C Rep. 411, Nr. 1310, BGL Protocol, 23 Sept. 1947, unpag.
46 LAB C Rep. 401–05, Nr. 6, IG-Metall report of 4 Jan. 1948, bl. 4.
47 LAB C Rep. 411, Nr. 1310, BGL Protocol, 14 June 1946, 11 Mar. 1948, 11 May 1948.
48 LAB C Rep. 910, Nr. 1658, Instrukteurbericht, 'Der Betrieb Kälterichter', 21 Nov. 1950, p. 1.
49 For a useful statistical insight into FDGB personnel patterns and trends during these early years, see Sebastian Simsch, '". . . was zeigt, daß sie ideologisch zurückgeblieben sind." Personelle Grenzen der frühen DDR-Diktatur am Beispiel der FDGB-Funktionäre in und um Dresden, 1945–1951', in P. Hübner (ed.), *Eliten im Sozialismus. Studien zur Sozialgeschichte der DDR* (Cologne: Böhlau-Verlag, 1999).
50 LAB C Rep. 900, IV/4/03–96, 'Bericht über die Kreis-Funktionär-Sitzung am 8.9.48', 16 Sept. 1948, pp. 5, 7–8.
51 *Ibid.*, p. 5.
52 LAB C Rep. 421, Nr. 210, 'Bericht über die Entwicklung des Werkes "Siemens-Plania" in gesellschaftlicher, kultureller, sozialer und sonstiger Hinsicht in den Jahren 1946–1953', bl. 14–15.
53 LAB C Rep. 411, Nr. 1312, 'Niederschrift über die Sitzung der BGL am 20.4.49'; 'Niederschrift 10.5.49'; 'Protokoll der außerordentlichen BGL-Sitzung am 26.8.1949'.
54 See *Protokoll des 3. Kongress des FDGB vom 30 August–3 September 1950* (Berlin, 1950), pp. 5–6.
55 LAB C Rep. 900, IV/4/07–164, 'Kontrolle über den Stand der Gewerkschaftswahlen der IG-Metall', 23 Jan. 1953, p. 9.
56 A. Bust-Bartels, *Herrschaft*, p. 44.
57 For all the differences between the Third Reich, Soviet Union and GDR, it is striking how this tendency towards unofficially satisfying some of the needs and demands of workers under the Nazis and also to a large extent the Soviets was repeated under the SED. See Hiroaki Kuromiya, *Stalin's Industrial Revolution: Politics and Workers, 1928–1932* (Cambridge: Cambridge University Press, 1988); Lewis Siegelbaum, *Stakhanovism and*

the *Politics of Productivity in the USSR, 1935–1941* (Cambridge: Cambridge University Press, 1988); Detlev Peukert, *Volksgenossen und Gemeinschaftsfremde. Anpassung und Aufbegehren unter dem Nationalsozialismus* (Cologne: Bund-Verlag, 1982), p. 134.
58 See P. Hübner, *Konsens*.

4 The origins and effects of 17 June in the factories

1 SAPMO-BA DY30/IV2/5/302, 'Vorläufige kurze Zusammenfassung...', 14 July 1952, p. 4.
2 SAPMO-BA DY34/15/61a/1191, 'Instrukteurbericht', 28 June 1952, pp. 5–7; also DY30/IV2/5/302, 'Vorläufinge kurze Zusammenfassung...', 14 July 1952. Despite the deliberate recruitment of manual labourers into the new professional elite, such feelings of injustice were a perpetual problem. The introduction of the new bonus scheme in 1957 and *Gesetzbuch der Arbeit* in 1961, both of which were widely perceived as benefitting the intelligentsia more than workers, aroused similar feelings of anger in the factories. See SAPMO-BA DY34/22673, 'Information Nr. 28/57', 21 June 1957, p. 6; SAPMO-BA DY34/22231, 'Einschätzung der bisherigen Ergebnisse der Diskussion des AGB Entwurfs', 10 Feb. 1961, p. 13. See also Viggo Graf Blücher, *Industriearbeiterschaft in der Sowjetzone* (Stuttgart: Enke, 1959), pp. 25–7.
3 SAPMO-BA DY30/IV2/5/267, '2. Bericht über die Diskussion und Stimmung der Bevölkerung zum Referat des Genossen W. Ulbricht auf der II. Parteikonferenz', 11 July 1952, p. 1.
4 Cf. generally, Dietrich Staritz, *Geschichte der DDR 1949–1985* (Fr./Main: Suhrkamp, 1985), p. 80.
5 SAPMO-BA DY30/IV2/5/525, 'Bericht über die Feindtätigkeit im Monat Mai', 12 June 1953, p. 2.
6 P. Hübner, *Konsens*, p. 150.
7 SAPMO-BA DY30/IV2/5/524, 'Tagesbericht Nr. 5', 14 June 1953, pp. 3–4.
8 See esp. Torsten Diedrich, *Der 17 Juni in der DDR. Bewaffnete Gewalt gegen das Volk* (Berlin: Dietz, 1991); Mary Fulbrook, *Anatomy*, ch. 5, 6; Manfred Hagen, *DDR – Juni '53: die erste Volkserhebung im Stalinismus* (Stuttgart: Franz Steiner, 1992); Ilko-Sascha Kowalczuk, Armin Mitter, Stefan Wolle (eds), *Der Tag X. 17 Juni 1953: die 'Innere Staatsgründung der DDR als Ergebnis der Krise 1952–54* (Berlin: Ch. Links, 1995); Armin Mitter, Stefan Wolle (eds), *Der Tag X: Quellen und Forschungen zum 17 Juni 1953* (Berlin: Ch. Links, 1995).
9 SAPMO-BA DY30/IV2/5/544, DFD 'Stimmungsbericht von den Ereignissen des 17.6 in Berlin', undated, p. 5.
10 Cf. SAPMO-BA DY30/IV2/5/304, *passim*.
11 LAB C Rep. 900, IV/4/07–155, 'Auswertung der Bericht über BMHW', 15 July 1953, pp. 2–4.
12 SAPMO-BA DY30/IV2/5/544, DFD 'Stimmungsbericht von den Ereignissen des 17.6. in Berlin', undated, p. 3.
13 BLHA Bez. Ffo. Rep. 730, Nr. 728, 'Analyse über die Entstehung und der Entwicklung des faschistischen Abenteuers im Kreis Fürstenberg/ Oder am 17 Juni 1953', 26 June 1953, unpag.

14 Cf. SAPMO-BA DY30/IV2/5/544, 'Stimmungsbericht über die Lage in den Stadtbezirken', 18 June 1953, p. 1; SAPMO-BA DY30/IV2/5/549, 'Bericht über auftretende Argumente und Stimmungen unter der Bevölkerung', 25 June 1953, p. 2.

15 SAPMO-BA ZPA JIV2/202/15, 'Analyse', 20 July 1953, bl. 19. It is estimated that around 500 000 people participated in the strikes and 400 000 in the demonstrations. T. Diedrich, *Der 17 Juni*, p. 132ff.

16 SAPMO-BA DY30/IV2/5/549, 'Analyse über die Entstehung und Entwicklung der faschistischen Provokationen im Bezirk Cottbus', 23 June 1953, pp. 18–19; SAPMO-BA DY30/IV2/5/549, 'Bezirksleitung Cottbus – Tagesmeldung', 25 June 1953, pp. 2–3.

17 The slogan rhymes in German: 'Gebt uns mehr zu fressen, oder habt ihr den 17. Juni vergessen?'. SAPMO-BA DY30/IV2/5/660, *Bezirksleitung* Frankfurt/Oder to ZK, 'Wochenbericht vom 3.6–9.6.55', 9 June 1955, p. 8; 'Informationen über die Auswertung des 24 Plenums des ZK', 15 June 1955, p. 7.

18 See esp. T. Diedrich, *Der 17 Juni*; M. Fulbrook, *Anatomy*, ch. 5, 6; I. Kowalczuk *et al.*, *Der Tag X*.

19 SAPMO-BA DY30/IV2/5/975, *Bezirksleitung* Berlin to ZK.

20 Ernst Wollweber, 'Aus Erinnerungen. Ein Porträt Walter Ulbrichts', in *Beiträge zur Geschichte der Arbeiterbewegung*, no. 3 (1990), pp. 350–78.

21 For a neat listing of the 'successes' of 17 June, see A. Bust-Bartels, *Herrschaft*, pp. 63–4. The wave of strikes only gradually abated into a surface calm over the summer of 1953. In the words of one report from September 1953, although the 'frankly irritated mood' of the previous months had subsided with the 'extraordinarily improved delivery' of consumer goods and the lowering of prices, the ubiquitous 'enemy' was still propagating the argument that DM 10 for a pound of butter, DM 8 for chocolate and DM 100 for a pair of shoes was too much for ordinary workers to afford. LAB C Rep. 900, IV2/4/06/381, 'Einschätzung der Lage im Kreis Prenzlauer Berg', 26 Sept. 1953, p. 1.

22 SAPMO-BA DY30/IV2/5/544, 'Situationsbericht über die Lage in den Stadtbezirken', 18 June 1953, p. 2; 'Stimmungsbericht von den Ereignissen des 17 Juni in Berlin', undated, p. 1; SAPMO-BA DY30/IV2/5/549, 'Bericht über auftretende Argumente und Stimmungen unter der Bevölkerung', 25 June 1953, p. 1.

23 Cited in M. Fulbrook, *Anatomy*, p. 158.

24 P. Hübner, *Konsens*; J. Roesler, 'Die Produktionsbrigaden'.

5 The 'unforced' collectivization, 1952–53

1 On the formation of collectivization policy, see J. Piskol, 'Zum Beginn der Kollektivierung'.

2 BLHA, Ld. Br. Rep. 332, Nr. 395, 'Bericht über die Meinung der Bauern zur Bildung der Produktionsgenossenschaften', 1 Aug. 1952.

3 SAPMO-BA DY30/IV2/5/302, '2. Bericht über die Stimmung und Stellungnahmen der Bevölkerung zu den Ausführungen des Genossen W. Ulbricht auf der 2 Parteikonferenz', 17 July 1952.

4 SAPMO-BA DY30/IV2/5/687, Bezirk Frankfurt/Oder, 'Informationsbericht für den Zeitraum 10.1.56 bis 24.1.56'.

5 Cf. J. Osmond, 'Konflikt', p. 151.

6 SAPMO-BA DY30/IV2/5/267, 'Bericht über die Stimmung der Bevölkerung zu den Beschlüssen der 2 Parteikonferenz', 26 Aug. 1952.

7 SAPMO-BA DY30/IV2/5/267, 'Bericht über die Stimmung der Bevölkerung zu den Beschlüssen der 2 Parteikonferenz', 26 Aug. 1952.

8 BAB DK1/5893, 'Beispiele über Erscheinungen des Klassenkampfes auf dem Dorf', 27 Nov. 1952.

9 SAPMO-BA DY30/IV2/5/303, 'Betr.: Feindliche Tätigkeit im Kreis Neuruppin', 6 Nov. 1952.

10 SAPMO-BA DY30/IV2/5/303, Volkspolizei report from Kreis Pritzwalk, 8 Sept. 1952.

11 N. Naimark, The Russians, p. 156; J. Osmond, 'Konflikt', p. 146.

12 BLHA Bez. Pdm. Rep. 401, Nr. 11045, Rat des Bezirkes Potsdam, statistical report of 15 Sept. 1953.

13 Cited in A. Mitter, 'Am 17.6.1953 haben die Arbeiter gestreikt', p. 93.

14 BAB DK1/5893, Hauptabteilung örtliche Organe to Ministry of Agriculture, 'Bericht über die Untersuchung der Arbeit der örtlichen Organe der Staatsgewalt zur Bildung und Unterstützung der landwirtschaftlichen Produktionsgenossenschaften', 25 Nov. 1952, p. 2.

15 Ibid., pp. 3–4.

16 BLHA, Ld. Br. Rep. 530, Nr. 1421, 'Bericht zur Entwicklung der landwirtschaftlichen Produktionsgenossenschaften und der Arbeit der Kreisleitungen Königs-Wusterhausen, Jüterbog und Luckenwalde', 28 Nov. 1952.

17 BLHA Bez. Pdm. Rep. 530, Nr. 2187, report of 17 July 1953, bl. 132–4.

18 BLHA Bez. Pdm. Rep. 530, Nr. 2187, 'Bericht über die Einhaltung der Vereinbarung vom 10 Juni 1953 seitens der Kirche über feindliche Tätigkeit durch einzelne Pfarrer, besonders auf dem Dorf', 17 Dec. 1953, bl. 207–10.

19 BLHA Bez. Ffo. Rep. 730, Nr. 876, 'Analyse zur Kaderstatistik über die Zusammensetzung der haupt- und ehrenamtlichen Sekretäre der Grundorganisationen', 20 May 1958, unpag.

20 BAB DK1/5539, 'Betr.: Materialen über die wesentlichen Mängel bei der Festigung der landwirtschaftlichen Produktionsgenossenschaften', 22 Apr. 1953.

21 Ibid., pp. 1, 8.

22 Ibid., pp. 2, 4–7.

23 The measures included a substantial increase in insurance payments and income-taxes as well as the withdrawal of ration-cards from all self-employed citizens and their dependents over 15 years of age. Cf. D. Staritz, Geschichte der DDR, p. 79.

24 See F. Werkentin, Politische Strafjustiz, p. 81; see also Dieter Schulz, 'Ruhe', pp. 105–7.

25 Calculated from figures in Bundesministerium für gesamtdeutsche Fragen, Die Flucht aus der Sowjetzone und die Sperrmaßnahmen des kommunistischen Regimes vom 13 August 1961 (Bonn/Berlin, 1961). There was little clear pattern in the social profile of those farmers who were leaving. One report from summer 1952 acknowledged that many were model farmers,

some deeply in debt, some fulfilling their quotas and others not, some 'new' and some 'old', but the majority economically weak. BAB DO1/ 11/961, Anlage', 2 Aug. 1952, bl. 118–20.

26 See 'Kommuniqué des Politbüros vom 9 Juni 1953', in *Dokumente der SED*, vol. 4 (Berlin, 1955), p. 429.

27 SAPMO-BA DY30/IV2/5/544, DFD report of 9 June 1953, pp. 1–2; 'Stimmungsbericht zum Kommuniqué des Politbüros der SED', 15 June 1953, p. 4.

28 SAPMO-BA DY30/IV2/5/524, 'Tagesbericht Nr. 4', 12 June 1953; 'Tagesbericht Nr. 5', 14 June 1953; DY30/IV2/5/528, report of 13 June 1953.

29 SAPMO-BA DY30/IV2/5/544, 'Stimmungsbericht zum Kommuniqué des Politbüros der SED', 15 June 1953, pp. 5, 6.

30 BLHA Bez. Ctb. Rep. 931, Nr. 117, KL Lübben, report of 19 June 1953, pp. 1–2.

31 SAPMO-BA DY30/IV2/5/544, VdgB report, 'Bericht: Demonstration am 17.6.53 im Kreis Jessen', undated.

32 SAPMO-BA DY30/IV2/7/354, 'Die Lage in den Landwirtschaftlichen Produktionsgenossenschaften und die Vorbereitungen zur Durchführung der Ernte', 7 July 1953, bl. 10–11. The report lists several examples of villages where feed grain quotas were indeed lowered, but bread grain quotas raised such that the total grain quotas were even higher than before.

33 SAPMO-BA DY30/IV2/5/251, 'Monatsbericht der Korrespondenzabteilung für Juli 1953', undated. SAPMO-BA DY30/7/354, 'Die Lage in den Landwirtschaftlichen Produktionsgenossenschaften und die Vorbereitungen zur Durchführung der Ernte', 7 July 1953, bl. 7. SAPMO-BA DY30/IV2/ 5/546, 'Analyse der Ereignisse vom 16. bis 22 Juni 1953', p. 1. See also A. Mitter, 'Am 17. 6 haben die Arbeiter gestreikt', p. 113.

34 SAPMO-BA DY30/IV2/5/544, 'Tagesmeldung, Bezirksleitung Cottbus', 25 June 1953, p. 1.

35 BAB DK1/5895, 'Analyse über die Vorkommnisse in der Zeit vom 16–18.6.53', 1 July 1953.

36 SAPMO-BA DY30/IV2/7/354, 'Die Lage in den Landwirtschaftlichen Produktionsgenossenschaften und die Vorbereitungen zur Durchführung der Ernte', 7 July 1953, bl. 7.

37 SAPMO-BA DY30/IV2/5/525, 'Bericht über die Stimmung der Bevölkerung am heutigen Tage', undated; 'Situationsbericht, KL Beeskow', 15 June 1953; IV2/5/524, 'Tagesbericht Nr. 5', 14 June 1953.

38 SAPMO-BA DY30/IV2/5/526, 'Telefonische Durchsage', KL Seehausen, 12 June 1953.

39 SAPMO-BA DY30/IV2/7/354, 'Die Lage in den Landwirtschaftlichen Produktionsgenossenschaften und die Vorbereitungen zur Durchführung der Ernte', 7 July 1953, bl. 13–14.

40 SAPMO-BA DY30/IV2/5/549, 'Tagesbericht der Bezirksleitung Cottbus', 27 June 1953.

41 BAB DK1/5895, 'Analyse über Austritte, Auflösungen und beabsichtigte Auflösungen', 10 Aug. 1953; 'Analyse über die Vorkommnisse in der Zeit vom 16–18.6.53', 1 July 1953.

42 Figure from A. Bauerkämper, 'Von der Bodenreform', p. 136.

43 This view is even represented in Norman Naimark's excellent account of the Soviet Zone. See *idem, The Russians*, p. 166.

6 Mobilizing East German youth

1 Helmut Schelsky, *Die skeptische Generation. Eine Soziologie der deutschen Jugend* (Düsseldorf: Diedrichs, 1957).
2 See generally, Bruno Thoß (ed.), *Volksarmee.*
3 SAPMO-BA NY 36/396, bl. 26, cited in R. Wenzke, 'Auf dem Weg zur Kaderarmee. Aspekte der Rekrutierung, Sozialstruktur und personellen Entwicklung des entstehenden Militärs in der SBZ/DDR 1947–1952', in Bruno Thoß (ed.), *Volksarmee*, p. 261; see also Rolf Stöckigt, 'Direktiven aus Moskau, Sowjetische Einflußnahme auf DDR-Politik 1952/1953', in J. Cerny, *Brüche*, pp. 81–7.
4 T. Diedrich, *Der 17 Juni*, pp. 22–3.
5 *Ibid.*
6 *Ibid.*, p. 262.
7 BAB DO1/11/1634, 'Werberichtlinie 3', 25 Jan. 1952, p. 15.
8 LAB C Rep. 900, IV/4/06-379, 'Bericht über die VP-Werbung in den Betrieben', 26 Nov. 1952, p. 2.
9 Cf. generally Michael Buddrus, *Die Organisation 'Dienst für Deutschland'* (Weinheim: Juventa, 1994).
10 J. Kocka, 'Eine durchherrschte Gesellschaft', in H. Kaelble *et al.*, *Sozialgeschichte*, pp. 547–53.
11 See R. Wenzke, 'Auf dem Weg', pp. 217–19; also N. Naimark, *The Russians*, p. 371.
12 For KVP wages, see T. Diedrich, *Der 17 Juni*, p. 25.
13 SAPMO-BA DY30/IV2/5/319, 'Einige Diskussionen und Stellungnahmen zur Frage der Nationalen Streitkräfte', 26 June 1952, p. 5.
14 *Ibid.*, p. 7.
15 SAPMO-BA DY34/15/61a/1191, 'Bericht über die Arbeitsbesprechung am 24.6.52'.
16 'Die neue Lage und die Politik der SED', in *Dokumente der SED, Bd. 5* (Berlin, 1956), p. 471.
17 On FDJ statistics and their problems, see Edeltraud Schulze (ed.), *DDR-Jugend: ein statistisches Handbuch* (Berlin: Akademie-Verlag, 1995).
18 SAPMO-BA DY30/IV2/5/319, 'Einige Diskussionen...', pp. 5, 6. The *Abzeichen für gutes Wissen* was a badge honouring outstanding technical knowledge and skills.
19 SAPMO-BA DY30/IV2/16/84, bl. 173–4.
20 SAPMO-BA DY30/IV2/5/302, 'Kurzinformation über aufgetretene gegnerische Arbeit', 21 May 1952.
21 *Ibid.*
22 SAPMO-BA DY30/IV2/5/319, 'Einige Diskussionen...', p. 5.
23 *Ibid.*, p. 1; see also Infratest GmbH, *Angestellten in der Sowjetzone Deutschlands: Verhaltensweise und gesellschaftliche Einordnung der mitteldeutschen Angestellten* (Munich: Infratest-Verlag, 1958), p. 182.
24 SAPMO-BA DY30/IV2/5/303, report of 20 November 1952.

25 On church–state relations generally, see Robert Goeckel, *The Lutheran Church and the East German State* (Ithaca, NY: Cornell University Press, 1990); Horst Dähn, *Konfrontation oder Kooperation? Das Verhältnis von Staat und Kirche in der SBZ/DDR 1945–1980* (Opladen: Westdeutscher Verlag, 1982); Martin Georg Goerner, *Die Kirche als Problem der SED* (Berlin: Akademie-Verlag, 1997).
26 Brigitte Hohlfeld, *Die Neulehrer in der SBZ/DDR 1945–1953: Ihre Rolle bei der Umgestaltung von Gesellschaft und Staat* (Weinheim: Deutsche Studien-Verlag, 1992), pp. 52–3, 342.
27 N. Naimark, *The Russians*, p. 456.
28 See Christoph Kleßmann, 'Zur Sozialgeschichte des protestantischen Milieus in der DDR', in *GG*, vol. 19 (1993), pp. 29–53.
29 Zentralrat der FDJ, *IV. Parlament der Freien Deutschen Jugend*, p. 238.
30 H. Dähn, *Konfrontation*, pp. 42–44.
31 Hermann Wentker, '"Kirchenkampf" in der DDR. Der Konflikt um die Junge Gemeinde 1950–1953', in *VfZ*, vol. 42 (1994), pp. 95–127, here p. 107.
32 *Ibid.*, p. 109.
33 See BAB DO4/2916, *passim*.
34 H. Wentker, 'Kirchenkampf', pp. 110–11, 116–7.
35 SAPMO-BA DY30/IV2/5/302, reports of 24 June 1952, 10 July 1952, 25 September 1952.
36 These figures from H. Wentker, 'Kirchenkampf', pp. 126–7.

7 'Republikflucht': fleeing the construction of socialism

1 See Richard Bessel, 'Grenzen des Polizeistaates: Polizei und Gesellschaft in der SBZ und frühen DDR, 1945–1953', in Bessel and Jessen, *Die Grenzen*, pp. 224–52, esp. pp. 231–4.
2 See generally, SAPMO-BA D430/JIV2/202/68, Büro Ulbricht.
3 In SAPMO-BA DY30/IV2/13/393, Abt. Bevölkerungspolitik.
4 A number of letters and other pieces of correspondence between Dahlem and Barth pertaining to the document can also be found in SAPMO-BA DY30/IV2/13/393.
5 SAPMO-BA DY30/IV2/13/394, Dahlem to Barth, 5 Jan. 1953, unpag.
6 SAPMO-BA DY30/IV2/13/394, bl. 27.
7 SAPMO-BA DY30/IV2/13/394, 'Bericht über die Durchführung von Maßnahmen gegen die Republikflucht und zur Werbung von Fachkräften in Westdeutschland gemäß dem Beschluß des Politbüros vom 6.1.53', 29 March 1953.
8 SAPMO-BA DY30/IV2/13/394, 'Einschätzung über den Stand der Republikflucht...', 22 Apr. 1953, bl. 156–7, 159.
9 SAPMO-BA DY30/IV2/13/394, 'Bericht über illegale Abwanderungen nach dem 9.6.53', 21 Nov. 1953. Ulbricht's files contain a copy of the original letter from the Soviets as well as the German translation, SAPMO-BA DY30/JIV2/202/68.
10 SAPMO-BA DY30/IV2/13/395, 'Bericht über die Durchführung des Beschlusses des Präsidiums des Ministerrates vom 28.1.1954', 19 May 1954, p. 3.

11 SAPMO-BA DY30/IV2/13/396, 'Bericht über die illegalen Abwanderungen aus der DDR und den Kampf gegen die Republikflucht im Jahre 1954', p. 6.

12 SAPMO-BA DY30/IV2/13/395, 'Gekürzter Bericht über die Überprüfung eines Hinweises der ZKK über die Republikflucht im VEB Bagger-Förderbrücken- und Gerätebau (BFG) Lauchhammer', 3 June 1954, pp. 1–5.

8 The factories from 17 June to the socialist brigades

1 LAB C Rep. 470-02, VEB Herrenbekleidung Fortschritt, Nr. 155, bl. 654–5, Protokol über die Versammlung der A-Schicht am 26 Juni 1953.

2 BLHA, Bez. Pdm. Rep. 531, KL Brandenburg, Nr. 329, 'Protokoll über die Kaderkonferenz am Mittwoch, dem 29.12.1954', Beitrag Gen. Weiß, RAW.

3 LAB C Rep. 900, IV/4/03-106, KPKK, 'Bericht über den VEB Akkurat', 23 Feb. 1954, pp. 1–7.

4 LAB C Rep. 470-02, Herrenbekleidung Fortschritt, Nr. 158, Bd. 1, 'Protokol vom 6.1.55', bl. 193.

5 LAB C Rep. 900, IV/4/03-128, 'Brigadebericht für die Zeit vom 12 bis 26.9.1959 im VEB Elektroprojekt', 2 Oct. 1959, p. 5.

6 LAB C Rep. 470-02, Herrenbekleidung Fortschritt, Nr. 155, 'Protokoll über die Versammlung vom 27 Juni 1953', bl. 657. On the problems of 'Intrigantentum' in the BGLs, see LAB C Rep. 900, IV/4/07-164, '1. Informationsbericht zum Stand der Gewerkschaftswahlen im Kreis', 11 June 1959, pp. 8–9; also IV/4/03-129 'Zwischenbericht über die Arbeit der Brigade der Kreisleitung Lichtenberg zur Veränderung der politischen Situation im VEB Elektrokohle', 6 Mar. 1958, pp. 9–10.

7 LAB C Rep. 900, IV/4/03-129, 'Zwischenbericht über die Arbeit der Brigade der Kreisleitung Lichtenberg zur Veränderung der politischen Situation im VEB Elektrokohle', 6 March 1958, p. 40.

8 See, for instance, LAB C Rep. 900, IV/4/02-249, 'Protokoll über die Aussprache mit den Sekretären der Grossbetriebe des Kreises Köpenick am 5.5.56, Zimmer 8 der Kreisleitung Köpenick', p. 3.

9 *Ibid.*, p. 10.

10 LAB C Rep. 900, IV/4/03-129, 'Zwischenbericht über die Arbeit der Brigade der Kreisleitung Lichtenberg zur Veränderung der politischen Situation im VEB Elektrokohle', 6 March 1958, pp. 5, 11.

11 LAB C Rep. 900, IV/4/03-128, 'I. Zwischenbericht der Brigade im VEB Wälzlager', 7 Feb. 1959, p. 3.

12 It was hardly surprising that Fritsch was later rejected by the employees as BGL chairman, 'because they lack trust in him'. LAB C Rep. 900, IV/4/07–131, 'Aussprache mit den Genossen des VEG Baumschule, Johannisthal', 18 Sept. 1954, p. 1; report of 22 Oct. 1954, p. 1.

13 LAB C Rep. 900, IV/4/02-249, 'Protokoll über die Aussprache mit den Sekretären der Grossbetriebe des Kreises Köpenick am 5.5.56', p. 3.

14 SAPMO-BA DY30/IV2/6.11/66, bl. 34. The causes for strikes in the GDR also recall those in the Third Reich. See Günter Morsch, 'Die kalkulierte Improvisation. Streiks und Arbeitsniederlegungen im "Dritten Reich"', in *Vierteljahreshefte für Zeitgeschichte*, vol. 36 (1988), no. 4, pp. 649–89. Warnke's quote from P. Hübner, *Konsens*, p. 209.

15 SAPMO-BA DY30/IV2/5/574, '3. Kurzinformation', 24 Oct. 1956, p. 7; '9. Information', 2 Nov. 1956, p. 11.
16 There were reportedly a total number of only 1400 participants in the 135 strikes in 1961; *ibid.*, bl. 29.
17 P. Hübner, 'Arbeitskonflikte in Industriebetrieben der DDR nach 1953. Annäherungen an eine Struktur- und Prozeßanalyse', in Ulrike Poppe *et al.*, *Zwischen Selbstbehauptung*, pp. 178–91.
18 BAB, ZStA E-1, Nr. 8773, 'Bericht über die Fluktuation der Arbeitskräfte in der sozialistischen Wirtschaft', 30 Jan. 1959, bl. 73–84.
19 This was a decades-old aspect of working-class life, and there were of course a variety of reasons for switching jobs. In the mid-1960s, Dieter Voigt found that 25 per cent of the workers at the large construction sites in *Bezirke* Cottbus and Halle had left their previous jobs to escape shift-work and the assembly line, while 50 per cent wanted more vacation and 32 per cent higher wages. D. Voigt, *Montagearbeiter in der DDR* (Darmstadt: Luchterhand, 1973), pp. 126–7.
20 Rüdiger Soldt, 'Zum Beispiel Schwarze Pumpe: Arbeiterbrigaden in der DDR', in *GG*, vol. 24 (1998), pp. 88–109, here p. 93.
21 Albert Hirschman, *Exit, Voice and Loyalty: Responses to Decline in Firms, Organizations and States* (Cambridge, MA: Harvard University Press, 1970).
22 LAB, Rep. 411, Nr. 1306, Bd. 1, 'Protokoll zur Parteiaktivtagung am 14 April 1953', p. 2.
23 R. Soldt, 'Schwarze Pumpe', p. 95.
24 SAPMO-BA DY34/22673, 'Information Nr. 50/57', 21 Dec. 1957, pp. 5–6.
25 This was a continual source of friction in the factories during the 1950s. See A. Lüdtke, 'Helden der Arbeit', p. 199.
26 LAB C Rep. 900, IV2/4/02/256, 'Betrifft: Einschätzung der politischen Situation im Kreis Köpenick', 16 Nov. 1956.
27 BLHA, Bez. Pdm. Rep. 530, Nr. 836, 'Informationsbericht', 8 Feb. 1955, pp. 2–3.
28 SAPMO-BA DY30/IV2/5/435, 'Informationsbericht über den Stand der Vorbereitung der Volkwahlen', 5 Oct. 1954, pp. 13–14. The slogans in English are 'Soldiers of all lands storm Moscow' and 'No Oder-Neisse, but rather our Memel' (a river in the former German province East Prussia).
29 BLHA, Bez. Pdm. Rep. 530, Nr. 822, 'Informationsbericht', 12 Oct. 1955, p. 5.
30 This campaign has recently received considerable attention for the role these brigades eventually assumed in offering their members a structural framework for articulating material interests to management officials – completely contrary to the intentions behind it. The fact that much of the difficulty of getting this movement started in the first place had to do with precisely the type of *non*-economic unwillingness to participate on the part of workers described above has, however, received little notice. See esp. the work of J. Roesler and P. Hübner in the bibliography.
31 SAPMO-BA DY30/IV2/5/422, report of 8 July 1959, bl. 54.
32 *Ibid.*, 'Informationsbericht über den Stand des Wettbewerbes um den Titel "Brigade der soz. Arbeit" in Berlin', 19 Aug. 1959, bl. 82.
33 *Ibid.*, bl. 47, 54, 60, 84.

34 At Schwarze Pumpe, the second enterprise in the GDR to join the 'movement', only 60 of the 300 brigades willing to compete for the title 'brigade of socialist work' made concrete obligations. R. Soldt, 'Schwarze Pumpe', p. 91.

35 BLHA Bez. Pdm. Rep. 530, Nr. 1218, 'Betr.: Argumentation im BTW', 28 Oct. 1961.

36 SAPMO-BA IV2/6.11/52, 'Zu einigen Fragen der sozialistischen Gemeinschaftsarbeit', 18 May 1960, report from SED-ZK Abt. Gewerkschaften und Sozialpolitik to Alfred Neumann, bl. 223–8.

37 See also Jörg Roesler, 'Probleme des Brigadealltags: Arbeitsverhältnisse und Arbeitsklima in volkseigenen Betrieben', in *APuZG*, vol. 47 (1997), no. 38, pp. 3–17.

38 See, for example, Ulbricht's criticism in *Neues Deutschland*, 10 June 1960, p. 4.

39 J. Roesler, 'Probleme des Brigadealltags', p. 10.

40 James Scott, *Weapons of the Weak* (New Haven: Yale University Press, 1985).

41 From J. Kopstein, 'Chipping Away at the State'.

9 The villages from stalemate to collectivization

1 BAB DO1/11/963, bl. 84.

2 Dieter Schulz, 'Ruhe im Dorf?', p. 104.

3 BLHA, Bez. Pdm. Rep. 530, Nr. 817, 'Stimmungsbericht über Äußerungen der Bevölkerung der DDR zur Entwicklung auf dem Lande', undated, ca. February 1954.

4 BAB DO1/11/963, bl. 84; BLHA, Bez. Pdm. Rep. 530, Nr. 822, 'Informationsbericht', 30 Sept. 1954, unpag.

5 T. Lindenberger, 'Der ABV als Landwirt'. Though most cases apparently involved the cooperation of VEAB officials, in some it was a matter of hiding produce from them. Typical of an unsuccessful attempt was an instance in Herbersdorf, *Kreis* Jüterbog, where one farmer told the local state buyer that his potato harvest was so poor he could not even feed his livestock. The buyer, with the help of the village mayor, searched his premises and soon discovered that L. had stashed 840 one-hundred-kilo sacks of potatoes in pits in the woods behind his barn. BLHA, Bez. Pdm. Rep. 530, Nr. 822, 'Informationsbericht', 30 Oct. 1954.

6 BLHA, Bez. Pdm. Rep. 530, Nr. 836, 'Informationsbericht', 10 Feb. 1955; BLHA, Bez. Pdm. Rep. 530, Nr. 817, 'Informationsbericht', 27 Feb. 1954, p. 2; 2 Mar. 1954, p. 2; Nr. 836, 'Informationsbericht', 4 Feb. 1955, p. 7; SAPMO-BA DY30/IV2/5/507, 'Frankfurt/Oder: Bericht zur Volksbefragung', 21 June 1954.

7 SAPMO-BA DY30/IV2/5/252, 'Bericht der Korrespondenzabteilung für das 1. Quartal 1956, Abt. Landwirtschaft', pp. 1–2.

8 These were precisely the same problems that thwarted previous and subsequent attempts to recruit agricultural cadre from among the industrial workforce. See BLHA Ld. Br. Rep. 332, Nr. 765; BLHA Bez. Pdm. Rep. 530, Nr. 1371.

9 BLHA Bez. Pdm. Rep. 530, Nr. 2045, 'Textbericht', 15 May 1959, unpag; Nr. 836, 'Stimmungsbericht über Äußerungen aus der DDR zur politischen und wirtschaftlichen Lage auf dem Lande', 16 Feb. 1955; 'Informationsbericht zum 30.1.1956; SAPMO-BA DY30/IV2/5/549, 'Bericht über auftretende Argumente und Stimmungen', 25 June 1953.

10 BLHA, Bez. Pdm. Rep. 530, Nr. 735, 'Informationsbericht zum 9. April 1956', p. 3; BLHA, Bez. Pdm. Rep. 530, Nr. 735, 'Informationsbericht zum 14 Mai 1956', pp. 10–11.

11 BLHA, Bez. Pdm. Rep. 530, Nr. 735; *ibid.*, 'Informationsbericht zum 21.12.56', p. 8; SAPMO-BA DY30/IV2/5/687, 'Informationsbericht', Kreis Seelow, 10 Dec. 1952, p. 11.

12 BLHA, Bez. Pdm. Rep. 530, Nr. 822, 'Informationsbericht', 30 Sept. 1954, p. 3.

13 A. Mitter, 'Am 17.6.1953 haben die Arbeiter gestreikt', pp. 77–8.

14 BLHA, Bez. Pdm. Rep. 530, Nr. 822, 'Informationsbericht', 30 Sept. 1954, p. 3.

15 SAPMO-BA DY30/IV2/5/435, 'Argumente der Bevölkerung, besonders der Arbeiter, der Bauern, der Mittelschichten und der Jugend', 28 Sept. 1954; see also 'Informationsbericht über den Stand der Vorbereitung der Volkswahlen', Oct. 1954; SAPMO-BA DY30/IV2/5/443, 'Information über die Weiterführung der Wahlarbeit', 28 Oct. 1958; SAPMO-BA Nationalrat der NF 4533, report of 21 Oct. 1958.

16 BLHA, Bez. Pdm. Rep. 530, Nr. 822, 'Informationsbericht', 14 Oct. 1954.

17 D. Staritz, *Geschichte der DDR, Erweiterte Neuausgabe*, p. 128.

18 SAPMO-BA DY30/IV2/5/443, 'Information über die Weiterführung der Wahlarbeit', 28 Oct. 1958, p. 16; IV2/5/664, 'Tagesinformation Nr. 5', 11 July 1958, p. 4; 'Tagesinformation Nr. 6', 12 July 1958, p. 3.

19 SAPMO-BA DY30/IV2/7/354, Mückenberger to agricultural secretaries of *Bezirksleitungen*, 8 Sept. 1958, bl. 351.

20 *Ibid.* See also Hermann Wegner, 'Die Kollektivierung wird vorangetrieben', in *SBZ-Archiv* (1958), p. 354; SAPMO-BA DY30/IV2/13/414, 'Bewegung der Kriminalität im Jahre 1958'.

21 *Ibid.*, bl. 351.

22 SAPMO-BA DY30/IV2/5/664, 'Tagesinformation Nr. 5', 11 July 1958, p. 4.

23 SAPMO-BA DY30/IV2/5/664, 'Tagesinformation Nr. 15', 23 July 1958, p. 3

24 SAPMO-BA DY30/IV2/5/664, 'Bericht über den Stand der Auswertung des 5. Parteitages im Bezirk Frankfurt/Oder', 26 July 1958, pp. 2–3.

25 *StJB* (Berlin, 1990), pp. 36, 128.

26 SAPMO-BA DY30/IV2/7/354, Mückenberger to agricultural secretaries of *Bezirksleitungen*, 8 Sept. 1958, bl. 350.

27 SAPMO-BA DY30/IV2/5/667, 'Informationsbericht vom 24.8.59'; 'Informationsbericht vom 10.8.59'.

28 BLHA Bez. Ctb. Rep. 930, Nr. 772, Generalstaatsanwaltschaft to SED-BL Cottbus, 3 Dec. 1959, unpag.

29 *Ibid.* The SED Central Committee was itself made aware of such methods by the State Attorney's office: SAPMO-BA DY30/IV2/13/415, report of 5 Dec. 1959, F. Werkentin, *Politische Strafjustiz*, p. 96.

30 Cf. Mitter and Wolle, *Untergang*, pp. 310–11.

31 See, for instance, BLHA Bez. Pdm. Rep. 531, KL Pritzwalk, Nr. 193, *passim*.

32 SAPMO-BA DY30/IV2/7/408, 'Bericht über die sozialistische Umgestaltung der Landwirtschaft im Kreis Senftenberg', undated, late March 1960, p. 30.

33 SAPMO-BA DY30/IV2/7/354, bl. 351; see also Christel Nehrig, 'Industriearbeiter im dörflichen Milieu. Eine Studie zur Sozialgeschichte der Niederlausitzer Nebenerwerbsbauern von 1945–1965', in P. Hübner, *Niederlausitzer*, p. 189.

34 SAPMO-BA DY30/IV2/5/725, 'Ergänzung zum Informationsbericht', 16 Feb. 1960, pp. 42–3. *Kreis* Eilenburg was the first to become fully collectivized in the GDR on 13 Dec. 1959.

35 SAPMO-BA DY30/IV2/7/408, 'Bericht über die sozialistische Umgestaltung der Landwirtschaft im Kreis Senftenberg', p. 29.

36 SAPMO-BA DY30/IV2/5/725, 'Ergänzung zum Informationsbericht', 16 Feb. 1960, pp. 42–3.

37 *Volks- und Berufszählung der DDR* (Berlin, 1964), p. 100.

38 SAPMO-BA DY30/IV2/13/622, 'Analyse der Republikflucht in der Landwirtschaft', 12 May 1960, bl. 89.

39 SAPMO-BA DY30/7/376, 'Die Entwicklung der genossenschaftlichen Arbeit in der Landwirtschaft', undated, ca. summer 1960, p. 2.

40 SAPMO-BA DY30/IV2/2023/9, 'Analyse der Kriminalität in der Landwirtschaft', 28 July 1960, p. 1.

41 SAPMO-BA DY30/IV2/13/367, 'Information Nr. 1/60', 18 Mar. 1960, pp. 1–3. The number of such 'crimes' increased in the second half of March: by the end of the month there was a total of 109 cases. *Ibid.*, 'Information Nr. 3/60', 1 Apr. 1960, p. 2.

42 For general overviews, see esp. Robert Conquest, *Harvest of Sorrow: Soviet Collectivization and the Terror-Famine* (London: Hutchinson, 1986); Moshe Lewin, *Russian Peasants and Soviet Power* (London: Norton, 1968).

43 SAPMO-BA DY30/IV2/2023/61, 'Bericht der Gruppe Bachmann, Ulrich und Meusel aus der Arbeit im Kreis Zerbst', undated, Mar./Apr. 1960, p. 1.

44 SAPMO-BA DY30/IV2/2023/61, 'Bericht über die Brigadetätigkeit im Kreis Haldensleben vom 22.3 bis 14.4.60', p. 2; SAPMO-BA DY30/IV2/7/408, 'Information', 23 Mar. 1960, p. 54.

45 SAPMO-BA DY30/IV2/2023/61, 'Abschlußbericht vom Einsatz zur Festigung der genossenschaftlichen Entwicklung in Reitwein, Kreis Seelow', 22 Apr. 1960, p. 4; BLHA, Ld. Br. Rep. 530, Nr. 734, '2-tägier Bericht zur politischen Lage', 25 Mar. 1960, p. 7; SAPMO-BA DY30/IV2/13/367, 'Information 1/60', 18 Mar. 1960, p. 6; HVDP 'Information Nr. 10/60', 19 May 1960, p. 3.

46 SAPMO-BA DY30/IV2/7/405, bl. 85.

47 BLHA Bez. Ctb. Rep. 930, Nr. 772, 'Sekretariatsvorlage', 5 June 1961, unpag.

48 SAPMO-BA DY30/IV2/7/406, 'Bericht über die Aussprache mit den Bauern in Lubolz, Kreis Lübben', 29 Mar. 1961, bl. 8–11.

49 SAPMO-BA DY30/IV2/7/406, 'Bericht über die Lage in der Gemeinde Lubolz, Kreis Lübben', 24 Apr. 1961, bl. 12–15.

50 BLHA Bez. Ctb. Rep. 930, Nr. 772, 'Sekretariatsvorlage', 5 June 1961, unpag.

51 Siegfried Prokop, *Unternehmen 'Chinesischer Wall' – Die DDR im Zwielicht der Mauer*, 2nd edn (Fr./Main: R. G. Fischer, 1993), p. 113.
52 *Ibid.*, p. 97.
53 *Ibid.*, p. 115.
54 SAPMO-BA DY30/IV2/2023/62, 'Zu einigen Problemen der Führungstätigkeit der Partei im Kreis Belzig, Bezirk Potsdam', 13 April 1960, p. 2. SAPMO-BA DY30/IV2/2023/61, 'Bericht der Brigade des Instituts für Gesellschaftswissenschaften beim ZK über den Einsatz im Kreis Cottbus-Land', 11 April 1960, pp. 2–3.
55 BLHA Bez. Pdm. Rep. 401, Nr. 11026, 'Büro-Vorlage über den Einsatz der Kader in den LPG-Zentren', 30 April 1960, unpag.
56 SAPMO-BA DY30/IV2/7/376 'Bericht über den Einsatz im Bezirk Cottbus vom 20–23.7.1960', bl. 36. Some local officials even refused to be involved at the risk of losing their positions in the state apparatus. BLHA Bez. Pots. Rep. 401, Nr. 11026, 'Büro-Vorlage', 30 April 1960, unpag.
57 BLHA Bez. Pdm. Rep. 401, Nr. 4371.
58 BLHA Bez. Pdm. Rep. 401, Nr. 4373.
59 SAPMO-BA DY30/IV2/2023/62, 'Zu einigen Problemen der Führungstätigkeit der Partei im Kreis Belzig, Bezirk Potsdam', 13 April 1960, pp. 5–6; 'Ergänzung zum Bericht über den Einsatz im Kreis Brandenburg-Land, Bezirk Potsdam'; D430/IV2/2023/61, 'Bericht über die Arbeit der Brigade des IGW Beelitz'.
60 SAPMO-BA DY30/IV2/7/405, 'Probleme in den LPG Typ I im Bezirk Cottbus Frankfurt (Oder)', undated, summer 1960, bl. 124.
61 SAPMO-BA DY30/IV2/7/376, 'Bericht über den Einsatz im Bezirk Cottbus vom 20–23.7.60', bl. 28–34.
62 BLHA Bez. Pdm. Rep. 404/15, Nr. 27, 'Analyse über die Lage in den LPG – Typ I – des Bezirkes Potsdam', 27 Sept. 1960, bl. 220.
63 BLHA Bez. Ctb. Rep. 930, Nr. 772, 'Sekretariatsvorlage', 5 June 1961, unpag.; SAPMO-BA DY30/IV2/7/376, 'Einschätzung der Lage und Stimmung der Bauern zu den politischen Grundfragen', undated, ca. July 1961, p. 4.
64 SAPMO-BA DY30/IV2/2023/61, 'Bericht über die Brigadetätigkeit im Kreis Seehausen/Altmark', undated, Mar./Apr. 1960, pp. 4–6.
65 SAPMO-BA DY30/IV2/2023/61, 'Bericht der Brigade des Instituts für Gesellschaftswissenschaften', 11 April 1960, p. 6.
66 SAPMO-BA DY30/IV2/7/376, 'Die Entwicklung der genossenschaftlichen Arbeit in der Landwirtschaft', undated, spring/summer 1960, p. 2; D430/IV2/2023/61, bl. 5.
67 SAPMO-BA DY30/IV2/2023/61, 'Bericht über die Brigadetätigkeit im Kreis Haldensleben vom 22.3–14.4.60', p. 3.
68 SAPMO-BA DY30/IV2/2023/61, 'Bericht über die Brigadetätigkeit im Kreis Seehausen/Altmark', undated, Mar./Apr. 1960, p. 4; SAPMO-BA DY30/IV2/9.02/92, 'Einschätzung der politischen Massenarbeit im Bezirk Frankfurt/Oder', 18 Oct. 1960, p. 2.
69 SAPMO-BA DY30/IV2/5/672, 'Informationsbericht', 24 July 1961.

10 Youth and the threats to socialism

1 See Ulrich Mählert, '"Die gesamte junge Generation für den Sozialismus begeistern"'. Zur Geschichte der Freien Deutschen Jugend', in *APuZG*, B49–50/93, p. 8f.
2 SAPMO-BA DY30/IV2/2/337, 'Anlage Nr. 3 zur Sitzung des Politbüros', 15 Dec. 1952, bl. 27, cited in R. Wenzke, 'Auf dem Weg', p. 264.
3 *Frankfurter Allgemeine Zeitung*, 3 Aug. 1957.
4 SAPMO-BA DY34/22672, 'Information Nr. 10', 3 Feb. 1956, p. 2.
5 SAPMO-BA DY34/20780, report of 16 Feb. 1956, pp. 5–6.
6 SAPMO-BA DY34/22083, report of 17–21 Jan. 1956.
7 BA-MA DVH3/2062, bl. 1–3.
8 V. Ackermann, *Der 'echte' Flüchtling*, p. 198.
9 *Ibid.*
10 Cited in M. Buddrus, '"Kaderschmiede für den Führungsnachwuchs"?', p. 176.
11 BAB DO1/11/1634, bl. 93; V. Ackermann, *Der 'echte' Flüchtling*, p. 198.
12 SAPMO-BA DY30/IV2/5/725, report of 23 Feb. 1960.
13 SAPMO-BA DY30/IV2/12/58, 'Betr.: Maßnahmen zur Sicherung der Werbung', 12 June 1961, bl. 189.
14 BLHA Bez. Ffo. Rep. 730, Nr. 1100, 'Einschätzung der Werbung zur NVA', 8 Nov. 1960, unpag.
15 BAB DO1/11/967, bl. 80.
16 SAPMO-BA DY30/IV2/12/58, letter of 15 Sept. 1960, bl. 129.
17 This figure from SAPMO-BA DY30/IV2/12/58, bl. 187.
18 Infratest GmbH, *Angestellten*, p. 183.
19 See V. Ackermann, *Der 'echte' Flüchtling*, p. 178.
20 BLHA Bez. Pdm. Rep. 530, Nr. 2045, 'Textbericht', 29 April 1959, unpag.
21 See, for instance, LAB C Rep. 900, IV/4/07–191, 'Protokoll über die erzielten Ergebnisse der VP Werbekommission', 31 Oct. 1952, p. 3.
22 V. Ackermann, *Der 'echte' Flüchtling*, p. 198.
23 See BA-MA DVH3/2683, *passim*; BAB DO1/11/351, reports of 31 July 1952, 23 Dec. 1954.
24 Cited in M. Buddrus, '"Kaderschmiede für den Führungsnachwuchs"?', p. 176.
25 BAB DO1/11/1635, 'Betr.: Werbearbeit', 1 Oct. 1952.
26 SAPMO-BA DY30/IV2/5/267, report of 13 Nov. 1952.
27 BLHA Bez. Pdm. Rep. 530, Nr. 2052, bl. 77–81; Nr. 2035, report of 14 Oct. 1952; also LAB C Rep. 900, IV/4/07–191, 'Bericht zur Werbung für die Volkspolizei', 15 Sept. 1952, pp. 1, 4.
28 BA-MA VA-01/2904, 'Analyse über die bisherigen Erfahrungen in der Werbung von Reservisten', 30 July 1958, bl. 163; VA-01/2900, 'Betr.: Maßnahmen zur Erhöhung der Einsatzbereitschaft der Verbände und Truppenteile des MB V', 13 May 1957, bl. 1–3; BAP DO1/11/1634, bl. 88.
29 SAPMO-BA DY30/IV2/13/397 'Wie ist die gegenwärtige Lage in der Abwanderung nach Westdeutschland?', undated, p. 11.
30 BLHA Bez. Pdm. Rep. 530, Nr. 2052, bl. 140.
31 R. Wenzke, 'Auf dem Weg', p. 264.
32 BA-MA VA-01/2900, bl. 1–3.

33 BAB DO1/11/1634, bl. 88.
34 LAB C Rep. 900, IV/4/07–191, 'Bericht über die bisherige Arbeit der Registrierabteilung', 15 March 1953.
35 BA-MA VA-01/2900, 'Textbericht', 22 April 1959; BLHA Bez. Ffo. Rep. 730, Nr. 1100, 'Einschätzung', 8 Nov. 1960; BAB DO1/11/967, bl. 78.
36 SAPMO-BA DY30/IV2/12/58, 'Kurzinformation', bl. 212–3.
37 LAB C Rep. 900, IV/4/07–191, 'Protokoll der VP und NVA Werbekommission', 25 July 1958, p. 3.
38 SAPMO-BA DY30/IV2/12/58, bl. 243.
39 BA-MA VA-01/1832, bl. 171–5, 176–81; VA-01/2029, bl. 73–4.
40 SAPMO-BA DY30/IV2/12/55, report of 19 April 1960, bl. 125–9.
41 BA-MA VA-01/25099, 'Das Problem der personellen Auffüllung der Nationalen Volksarmee auf der Grundlage des Freiwilligensystems von 1956 bis 1961 und nach Einführung der allgemeinen Wehrpflicht', here bl. 11–13.
42 See Hermann Wentker, 'Die Einführung der Jugendweihe in der DDR: Hintergründe, Motive und Probleme', in H. Mehringer, *Von der SBZ zur DDR*, pp. 139–65, here p. 154.
43 See SAPMO-BA DY30/IV2/14/25, *passim*.
44 SAPMO-BA DY30/IV2/14/27, 'Analyse über die feindliche Tätigkeit der evg. und kath. Kirche gegen die Jugendweihe', 2 Feb. 1956, p. 13.
45 SAPMO-BA DY30/IV2/14/25, 'Einschätzung der Jugendweihe 1955', p. 2.
46 H. Wentker, 'Jugendweihe', p. 154.
47 H. Wentker, 'Jugendweihe', pp. 158–60, 162–4.
48 The *Volkspolizei* confiscated on average around 500 such books per month in the Leuna-Werke alone. SAPMO-BA DY30/IV2/16/103, 'Beispiele was die Jugend in ihrer Freizeit macht, von Jugendlichen aus dem Leuna Werk', undated, ca. 1958–59.
49 *Ibid.*
50 See SAPMO-BA DY30/IV2/16/230, 'Einschätzung der gegenwärtigen Bandentätigkeit und strafbaren Handlungen die gegen den Staat gerichtet sind', 4 Dec. 1959.
51 SAPMO-BA DY30/IV2/611/65, bl. 204.
52 SAPMO-BA DY30/IV2/16/90, 'Bericht über die Jugendkriminalität und das Rowdytum', Jan. 1960, bl. 28–57.
53 *Ibid.*
54 SAPMO-BA DY30/IV2/16/103, 'Betr.: Der negative Einfluß W-Berlins', 29 Jan. 1959.
55 SAPMO-BA DY30/IV2/16/228, 'Einschätzung der Fragebogen', undated, ca. 1961; 'Bericht der Brigade der Arbeitsgruppe für Jugendfragen', 27 April 1960, p. 6.
56 SAPMO-BA DY30/IV2/16/91, bl. 14.
57 SAPMO-BA DY30/IV2/16/90, 'Bericht über die Jugendkriminalität und das Rowdytum', Jan. 1960, bl. 50–1.
58 Youths were found on the whole to be more supportive of various aspects of the East German regime and society than older people, which no doubt reflected their political socialization via the school system. V. Blücher, *Industriearbeiterschaft*, p. 13; Infratest GmbH, *Angestellten*, p. 34; *idem, Die Intelligenzschicht*, p. 45; *idem, Jugendliche*, pp. 18, 67.

11 The problems and possibilities of the open border

1 For typical examples, see BAB DO1/11/963, bl. 70, 74. To be fair, the notion of *Abwerbung* was not complete fantasy when taken to include such factors as the influence of West German relatives and the efforts of West German firms to attract skilled labour. The West German government was well aware that work opportunities conveyed by the West German media or relatives certainly constituted a powerful attraction to many East Germans, and the business community in West Germany quite naturally tried to take advantage of this as it could. BAB DO1/11/965, bl. 70.

2 See, for instance, SAPMO-BA DY30/IV2/13/401, 'Informationsbericht über die Methoden der Abwerbung von Bürgern der DDR', 30 Sept. 1960, bl. 117–25. A distinction was sometimes made between 'passive *Abwerbung*', or the opportunities many East Germans saw in the West, and 'active *Abwerbung*' organized by western agents. BAB DO1/11/963, bl. 225–9.

3 BAB DO1/11/962, bl. 67; SAPMO-BA DY30/IV2/5/566, 'Durchführung des Beschlusses des Politbüros über weitere Maßnahmen gegen die Republikflucht vom 15.12.53', 11 Feb. 1954. The ritualization of language in internal reporting in the GDR was of course a general phenomenon and has already been the subject of scholarly attention. See Ralph Jessen, 'Diktatorische Herrschaft als kommunikative Praxis. Überlegungen zum Zusammenhang von "Bürokratie" und Sprachnormierung in der DDR-Geschichte', in A. Lüdtke and P. Becker (eds), *Akten*, pp. 57–75.

4 See esp. SAPMO-BA DY30/IV2/13/397, 'Niederschrift über die Sitzung der Kommission zu den Fragen der Republikflucht am 23 Nov. 1956', 4 Dec. 1956, bl. 446–7.

5 BAB DO1/11/967, bl. 66.

6 SAPMO-BA DY30/IV2/13/395, 'Material für die Besprechung mit den Abteilungsleitern der Bezirksleitungen', undated (ca. May 1954), p. 3.

7 SAPMO-BA DY30/9.04/669, 'Bericht an das Sekretariat des ZKs über die Republikflucht', 19 Aug. 1955.

8 This was occasionally recognized by party instructors. For instance, the flight of one university librarian was intentionally *not* condemned in a resolution prepared by instructors because the letter she left for her colleagues listed these resolutions as one of her main reasons for leaving. SAPMO-BA DY30/9.04/669, 'Analyse der Republikflucht', 8 Aug. 1959, p. 3.

9 SAPMO-BA DY30/9.04/669, 'Analyse der Republikflucht', 8 Aug. 1959.

10 LAB C Rep. 900, IV/4/07–196, undated report, ca. June 1956.

11 SAPMO-BA DY30/IV2/13/397, 'Niederschrift über die Überprüfung der Probleme des Kampfes gegen die Republikflucht im Bezirke Leipzig vom 26–27.1. und vom 8–10.2.1956, undated, p. 3.

12 See, for instance, LAB C Rep. 900, IV/4/07–196, 'Protokoll über die Zusammenkunft der R-kommission in der Kreisleitung am 7.6.1956'; BLHA Bez. Pdm. Rep. 531, KL Neuruppin, Nr. 103, 'Bürovorlage', 16 Mar. 1961; BLHA Bez. Pdm. Rep. 401, Nr. 6644, 'Bericht über die am 24. und 25.10.57 durchgeführte Überprüfung im Kreis Belzig bezügl. Republikfluchten und anderen Fragen des innerdeutschen Reiseverkehrs', 7 Nov. 1957.

13 LAB C Rep. 411, Nr. 197, 'Bericht über den Brigadeeinsatz im VEB TRO

vom 19.1.–31.1.1959'; 'Einschätzung der Arbeit der betrieblichen RF-Kommission und Analyse der Republikfluchten, Rückkehrer und Neuzuzüge', 13 May 1961.

14 BAB DO1/8/291/2.

15 SAPMO-BA DY30/IV2/13/398, 'Bericht der Brigade über die Ergebnisse des Einsatzes im Bezirk Halle', undated, ca. 1957–58.

16 SAPMO-BA DY30/IV2/13/397, document of 17 Feb. 1956, MdI, bl. 67–8; also *ibid.*

17 BLHA Bez. Pdm. Rep. 401, Nr. 6696, report of Nov. 1958.

18 SAPMO-BA DY30/IV2/13/397, document of 17 Feb. 1956, MdI, bl. 67–8.

19 Such an impression among the police is hardly surprising given that around 22.6 per cent of returnees and 25.5 per cent of first-time immigrants in the years before 1961 had a previous criminal record. BAB DO1/8/291/2, 'Erläuterung und Ergänzung zur Übersicht über Rückkehrer und Zuziehende aus Westdeutschland und Westberlin', 31 May 1961, p. 3. This quote from BAB DO1/11/965, 'Informationen über die Entwicklung der Behandlung von Rückkehrern in den Aufnahmestellen und Volkspolizeikreisämtern', 24 Oct. 1958, bl. 91.

20 For a regional case study, see H. Eberle, 'Weder Gegnerschaft noch Abwerbung'.

21 See, for example, Bundesministerium für gesamtdeutsche Fragen, *Die Flucht aus der Sowjetzone und die Sperrmaßnahmen des kommunistischen Regimes vom 13 August 1961* (Bonn/Berlin, 1961); Bundesministerium für Vertriebene, Flüchtlinge und Kriegsgeschädigte, *Flucht aus der Sowjetzone* (Bonn/Berlin, 1964); Johannes Klein, 'Ursachen und Motiven der Abwanderung aus der Sowjetzone Deutschlands', in *APuZG*, B 24/55 (15 June 1955), pp. 361–83. Figure from H. Heidemeyer, *Flucht und Zuwanderung*, p. 54.

22 See, for example, Dietrich Storbeck, 'Flucht oder Wanderung?', in *Soziale Welt*, vol. 14 (1963), pp. 153–71.

23 Ernst Richert, *Das zweite Deutschland* (Gütersloh: Mohn, 1964), p. 82.

24 As the director of the VEB Elektro-Öfen und Gerätebau in Meiningen wrote to his colleagues after leaving for the West, 'All the initiatives that I developed in order to help the enterprise grow are stifled by the absolutely insurmountable bureaucracy'. SAPMO-BA DY30/13/397, 'Wie ist die gegenwärtige Lage in der Abwanderung nach Westdeutschland?', undated, ca. Feb. 1956, p. 5. See generally, SAPMO-BA DY30/9.04/668–669; also DY30/9.04/62, 'Probleme, die in der Arbeit mit der wissenschaftlichen Intelligenz eine Rolle spielen', 2 Dec. 1960, pp. 1–2.

25 V. Ackermann, *Der 'echte' Flüchtling*, pp. 126–95.

26 BAB DE1/11835, Duscheck to Leuschner, 25 Sept. 1956, bl. 5–8.

27 LAB C Rep. 411, Nr. 197, 'Aufstellung von R-Fluchten ab 1.1.1959'.

28 The decreasing number of refugees in these years has often been interpreted instead as a reflection of political and social consolidation in the GDR. See, for instance, H. Weber, *DDR, Grundriß der Geschichte 1945–1990*, p. 88; also D. Staritz, *Geschichte der DDR*, pp. 170–1.

29 There is more than ample documentation of such hopes in summer 1955. See, for example, the numerous opinion reports during the Geneva Conference in SAPMO-BA DY30/IV2/5/573 and DY34/20774.

30 SAPMO-BA DY34/22673, report of 9 Aug. 1957.

31 SAPMO-BA DY34/20772, report of 25 Apr. 1955.

32 SAPMO-BA DY34/21500, 'Informationsbericht über den Einsatz in der Universität Jena zur Untersuchung der Situation unter der Intelligenz', 16 Jan. 1961.

33 SAPMO-BA DY30/IV2/5/252, bl. 210.

34 SAPMO-BA DY30/IV2/13/396, 'Bericht über die illegalen Abwanderungen aus der DDR und den Kampf gegen die Republikflucht im Jahre 1954', p. 13.

35 The text in German is as follows: 'Wenn du mal eine Wohnung suchst, dann ist es wohl am besten, du reist mal nach dem Westen. Bei deiner Rückkehr als Belohnung, bekommst du eine Wohnung'. SAPMO-BA DY30/ IV2/5/252, 'III. Quartal 1956', 2 Oct. 1956, bl. 112.

36 BAB DO1/11/963, bl. 74.

37 See SAPMO-BA DY30/IV2/5/251, 'Monatsbericht der Korrespondenzabteilung für den Monat April 1954', undated, bl. 472. Housing problems were by far the single greatest source of complaint in these petitions, comprising 30–40 per cent of all those received by the state. On *Eingaben* generally, see the somewhat problematic overview by Felix Mühlberg, 'Konformismus oder Eigensinn? Eingaben als Quelle zur Erforschung der Alltagsgeschichte der DDR', in *Mitteilungen aus der kulturwissenschaftlichen Forschung*, vol. 19, no. 37 (Feb. 1996), pp. 331–45. For a better analysis of petitioning, albeit focusing on the final years of the GDR, see Jonathan Zatlin, 'Ausgaben und Eingaben: Das Petitionsrecht und der Untergang der DDR', in *ZfG*, vol. 45 (1997), no. 10, pp. 902–17.

38 SAPMO-BA DY30/IV2/5/252, 'Eingabenanalyse', 17 Jan. 1957, bl. 165–6.

39 *Ibid.*, bl. 166.

40 BAB DO1/11/728, 'Halbjahresbericht', 30 July 1958, p. 99. It is telling that the *Volkspolizei* made regular special reports on *Republikflucht* among the intelligentsia, which it did not do for any other social groups. See BAB DO1/11/962–968, *passim*. This was true of all groups within the intelligentsia, but especially of the most highly-trained such as university teachers and researchers. Incoming reports about the mass exodus of chemists to the West during the late 1950s were alarming enough for Ulbricht himself to oversee efforts to stem the tide, which merited the involvement not only of the usual state authorities, but also of Erich Mielke and his *Stasi* lieutenants. See SAPMO-BA DY30/9.04/669, 'Bericht über die Republikabgänge aus der chemischen Industrie', 23 April 1959.

41 SAPMO-BA DY30/IV2/5/252, 'Bericht der Korrespondenzabteilung für das I. Quartal 1956', 12 April 1956, bl. 46.

42 For example, in response to tightened regulations on travel for professional purposes in 1956, SAPMO-BA DY30/IV2/19/58, 'Betr.: Protestbewegung unter den Ärzten im Bezirk Halle wegen Einschränkung der Besuchsmöglichkeiten wissenschaftlicher Kongresse in Westdeutschland', 4 June 1956, pp. 1–2.

43 In *Neues Deutschland*, 18 Sept. 1958, p. 2; 20 Dec. 1960, p. 1.

44 SAPMO-BA DY30/IV2/13/401, bl. 28.

45 SAPMO-BA DY30/IV2/902/6, 'Zur Einschätzung der Arbeit mit der

Intelligenz', 4 April 1961, p. 1; SAPMO-BA DY34/22231, 'Anlage zur Information Nr. 3/61', Jan. 1961, pp. 1–2, 4.
46 SAPMO-BA DY30/IV2/5/253, report on third quarter 1958, 29 Oct. 1958, bl. 48.
47 SAPMO-BA DY30/IV2/5/443, 'Information über die Weiterführung der Wahlarbeit', 28 Oct. 1958, p. 17.
48 See generally the files SAPMO-BA DY30/IV2/902/58; DY34/21500.
49 A. Hirschman, *Exit, Voice and Loyalty*, p. 82. Italics in the original.

Part 4

1 For example, D. Staritz, *Geschichte der DDR*, p. 196. For new evidence on the decisions leading up to the construction of the Wall, see Michael Lemke, *Die Berlinkrise 1958 bis 1963. Interessen und Handlungsspielräume der SED im Ost–West Konflikt* (Berlin: Akademie-Verlag, 1995); André Steiner, 'Politische Vorstellungen und ökonomische Probleme im Vorfeld der Errichtung der Berliner Mauer. Briefe Walter Ulbrichts an Nikita Chruschtschow', in H. Mehringer (ed.), *Von der SBZ zur DDR*, pp. 233–68; Hope Harrison, 'Ulbricht and the Concrete "Rose": New Archival Evidence on the Dynamics of Soviet–East German Relations and the Berlin Crisis 1958–1961', in *Cold War International History Project Working Paper*, no. 5 (May 1993).
2 SAPMO-BA DY30/JIV2/202/30, letter from Ulbricht to Kruschev, 4 Aug. 1961, reprinted in André Steiner, 'Politische Vorstellungen und ökonomische Probleme im Vorfeld der Errichtung der Berliner Mauer. Briefe Walter Ulbrichts an Nikita Chruschtschow', in H. Mehringer (ed.), *Von der SBZ zur DDR*, pp. 233–68, letter pp. 254–68.
3 *Ibid.*, pp. 263–5.

12 The grass-roots effects of the Berlin Wall

1 SAPMO-BA DY30/6.11/65, bl. 294.
2 SAPMO-BA DY30/IV2/5/433, 'Kurzinformation Nr. 5 über die Lage in der Zeit von 15.15–20.15 Uhr', 13 Aug. 1961, pp. 2.
3 SAPMO-BA DY30/IV2/5/433, '2. Kurzinformation über die Lage in der Zeit von 9.30 Uhr bis 11.30 Uhr', 13 Aug. 1961, pp. 1–2.
4 *Ibid.*; also '3. Kurzinformation', '5. Kurzinformation'. Such was reportedly the case at Brunnenstraße, Eberswalderstraße and the Brandenburg Gate. Similar 'provocations' were also organized in front of the district party headquarters in Berlin-Mitte.
5 SAPMO-BA DY30/IV2/5/433, 'Kurzinformation über die ersten Maßnahmen und Stimmungen zur Durchführung des Ministerratbeschlusses vom 12.8.61', 13 Aug. 1961, p. 3.
6 Heinz Niemann, *Meinungsforschung in der DDR. Die geheimen Berichte des Instituts für Meinungsforschung an das Politbüro der SED* (Cologne: Bund-Verlag, 1993), p. 66.
7 SAPMO-BA DY30/IV2/611/65, bl. 226.
8 See, for example, M. Fulbrook, *Anatomy*.

9 Despite isolated instances of drunkenness, hesitations about firing on would-be illegal emigrants and cross-border fraternizing with western police, most reports speak of an 'exemplary readiness' on the part of the police force deployed to guard the border. Cf. BAB DO1/11/322.

10 Patrick Major, '"Mit Panzern kann man doch nicht für den Frieden sein". Die Stimmung der DDR-Bevölkerung zum Bau der Berliner Mauer am 13 August 1961 im Spiegel der Parteiberichte der SED', in *JHK* (Berlin, 1995), pp. 208–23. The figures for 1953 are taken from T. Diedrich, *Der 17 Juni*, p. 300.

11 F. Werkentin, *Politische Strafjustiz*, pp. 256, 268. There were over 18 000 convictions of 'state crimes' in the second half of 1961. This was as many as in all of 1960, which itself was the year of forced agricultural collectivization.

12 SAPMO-BA DY30/9.02/6, 'Argumente, die besonders in der Intelligenz auftreten', 24 Aug. 1961, p. 8.

13 For the latter, see Laurence McFalls, *Communism's Collapse, Democracy's Demise?: The Cultural Context and Consequences of the East German Revolution* (London: Macmillan, 1995), pp. 31–2.

14 SAPMO-BA DY30/9.02/6, 'Argumente, die besonders in der Intelligenz auftreten', 24 Aug. 1961, p. 8.

15 SAPMO-BA DY34/22232, 'Information', 14 Aug. 1961, p. 2; 'Information', 16 Aug. 1961, p. 2; 'Information', 17 Aug. 1961, p. 3.

16 Up until 26 August, shops in *Bezirk* Cottbus reported 8 to 10 times the normal turnover, and banks reported 10 times the normal rate of savings withdrawals. SAPMO-BA DY34/23769, 'Informationsbericht', 1 Sept. 1961. See also the series of reports in DY34/22232, 22677.

17 SAPMO-BA DY34/22677, 'Informationsbericht von 8 Uhr', pp. 6–7.

18 SAPMO-BA DY30/IV2/12/107, 'Information über die Tätigkeit der POen und über die Stimmung der Bevölkerung zu den Maßnahmen des Ministerrates', 18 Aug. 1961, p. 6.

19 These quotes taken from SAPMO-BA DY30/IV2/5/433, '2. Kurzinformation über die Lage in der Zeit von 9.30 Uhr bis 11.30 Uhr', 13 Aug. 1961, p. 2; 'DY34/22677, 'Informationsbericht Nr. 3', 15 Aug. 1961; DY30/ IV2/12/107, 'Information über die Tätigkeit der POen und über die Stimmung der Bevölkerung . . .', 18 Aug. 1961, pp. 3–4.

20 SAPMO-BA DY34/22677, 'Informationsbericht Nr. 6', 16 Aug. 1961.

21 For the appeal by the Lichtenberg brigade, see LAB C Rep. 900, IV-2/6/ 843–4.

22 SAPMO-BA DY34/22677, '5. Information über Ergebnisse bei der weiteren Durchsetzung des Produktionsaufgebotes', 21 Oct. 1961; SAPMO-BA DY30/ IV2/5/425, report from BL Potsdam, undated.

23 SAPMO-BA DY34/23769, 'Information', 13 Oct. 1961; DY34/22232, 'Information über den Stand bei der Organisierung des Produktionsaufgebotes in Berlin', 19 Oct. 1961; BLHA Bez. Pdm. Rep. 530, Nr. 1218, 'Anlage: Schwerpünkte des Bezirksvorstandes FDGB zur Weiterführung des Produktionsaufgebot', undated, mid-Oct. 1961, unpag.

24 SAPMO-BA DY30/IV2/6.11/66, 'Analyse über Arbeitskonflikte, die zu Arbeitsniederlegungen führten, und über klassenfeindliche Tätigkeit im Jahre 1961', 1 Feb. 1962, bl. 34; also bl. 267.

25 It should be noted that this was not new or unique to the GDR, but rather must be seen as a continuation of the breakdown of broad networks of working-class solidarity since the 1920s. A number of studies on worker protest and resistance in the Third Reich have emphasized the divisions within the working-class that developed as a result of mass unemployment, the Nazi destruction of the workers' movement, the individualistic wage system during the armaments boom as well as the other factors that I have mentioned. See esp. Tim Mason's influential essay, 'The containment of the working class in Nazi Germany', in *Nazism, Fascism and the Working Class* (Cambridge: Cambridge University Press, 1995), pp. 231–73. Similar tendencies were also observed in the Federal Republic in the 1950s. See Detlev Peukert, *Inside Nazi Germany*, pp. 114–17.

26 According to official statistics, in 1962 wages were indeed down to 99.5 per cent of the previous year, but levelled off again in 1963 and already in 1964 reached 104 per cent of the previous year. *StJB* 1965, p. 227.

27 SAPMO-BA DY30/IV2/6.11/39, FDGB analysis of 'Feindtätigkeit' in third quarter 1961, bl. 478–82.

28 SAPMO-BA DY30/IV2/6.11/65, bl. 294.

29 LAB C Rep. 900, IV/4/03–135, 'Arbeit mit dem Produktionsaufgebot im BEV Druckwalzen und Gummiwaren', 13 Dec. 1961, p. 3.

30 LAB C Rep. 900, IV/4/03–135, 'Betr.: Produktionsaufgebot VEB Wälzlagerfabrik "Josef Orlopp"', 15 Sept. 1961, unpag.; BLHA Bez. Pdm. Rep. 530, Nr. 1218, 'Betr.: Argumentation im BTW', 28 Oct. 1961, unpag.

31 LAB C Rep. 900, IV/4/07–159, 'Informationsbericht', 9 Sept. 1961, p. 24; see also IV/4/03–106, Bericht der KPKK über die Arbeit mit den Grenzgängern in einigen Lichtenberger Großbetrieben', 21 Dec. 1961, p. 1.

32 SAPMO-BA DY34/23770, 'Informationsbericht', 5 June 1962, p. 9; 'Informationsbericht', 25 April 1962, p. 8; 'Informationsbericht', 24 Aug. 1962, p. 6.

33 BLHA Bez. Ctb. Rep. 931, '3. Kreisdelegiertenkonferenz', Beitrag Menzeln, 16 May 1962, cited in Soldt, p. 95.

34 Labour fluctuation remained an aggravating problem for state planners in the 1960s, so much so that it soon became a field of sociological study in its own right. It has been calculated that labour fluctuation cost the GDR economy some DM 1 billion in production-losses during the early 1960s. Cf. Dieter Voigt, 'Die Fluktuation von Arbeitskräften als Forschungsgegenstand in der DDR', in *DA*, vol. 3 (1970), no. 11, p. 1207ff; Katharina Belwe, 'Zu den Hintergründen der Fluktuation in der DDR', in *DA*, vol. 13 (1980), no. 6, pp. 601–11.

35 SAPMO-BA DY34/22677, '1. Information über die ersten Ergebnisse, den Inhalt und den Stand der Durchsetzung des Produktionsaufgebotes', 19 Sept. 1961; '4. Information über den Stand, Inhalt und die Ergebnisse des Produktionsaufgebotes', 9 Oct. 1961; SAPMO-BA DY34/23769, 'Information', 13 Oct. 1961.

36 LAB C Rep. 900, IV/4/03–135, 'Einschätzung der politischen Arbeit im VEB LTA beim Produktionsaufgebot für den Friedensvertrag', 26 Sept. 1961, p. 2; 'Bericht über den Stand des Produktionsaufgebotes im VEB

Volksbau', 26 Sept. 1961, p. 3; 'Bericht über den Stand des Produktionsaufgebotes im VEB Elektroprojekt Berlin', 27 Sept. 1961, p. 1; SAPMO-BA DY34/23769, 'Informationsbericht', *Bezirk* Cottbus, 13 Oct. 1961, p. 2.

37 SAPMO-BA DY34/22677, '1. Information über die ersten Ergebnisse, den Inhalt und den Stand der Durchsetzung des Produktionsaufgebotes', 19 Sept. 1961; '4. Information über den Stand, Inhalt und die Ergebnisse des Produktionsaufgebotes', 9 Oct. 1961; SAPMO-BA DY34/23769, 'Information', 13 Oct. 1961.

38 SAPMO-BA DY30/IV2/6.11/65, 'Information Nr. 54/1961', 21 Nov. 1961, bl. 336–8.

39 *Ibid.*

40 SAPMO-BA DY34/22677, '1. Information über die ersten Ergebnisse, den Inhalt und den Stand der Durchsetzung des Produktionsaufgebotes', 19 Sept. 1961; '4. Information über den Stand, Inhalt und die Ergebnisse des Produktionsaufgebotes', 9 Oct. 1961; SAPMO-BA DY34/23769, 'Information', 13 Oct. 1961.

41 SAPMO-BA DY30/IV2/5/425, report from BL Potsdam, 4 Oct. 1961.

42 SAPMO-BA DY34/22677, '4. Information über den Stand, Inhalt und die Ergebnisse des Produktionsaufgebotes', 9 Oct. 1961.

43 LAB C Rep. 900, IV/4/03/135, 'Arbeit mit dem Produktionsaufgebot im VEB Lederverarbeitung', 12 Dec. 1961, p. 2.

44 BLHA Bez. Pdm. Rep. 530, Nr. 1218, 'Anlage: Schwerpünkte des Bezirksvorstandes FDGB zur Weiterführung des Produktionsaufgebotes', undated, mid-Oct. 1961, unpag.

45 *Ibid.*

46 *Ibid.*; also LAB C Rep. 900, IV/4/03/135, 'Information über den Stand des Produktionsaufgebotes im Kreis Lichtenberg', 19 July 1962, p. 5; SAPMO-BA DY34/23770, 'Informationsbericht', 15 Mar. 1962, p. 14.

47 The *Berliner Zeitung* reported his trial on 30 August under the headline 'No Place for Loafers'; the National Front even prepared a flyer to publicize the verdict. Cf. F. Werkentin, *Politische Strafjustiz*, pp. 106–7.

48 SAPMO-BA DY30/IV2/7/401, 'Die Lage der Landwirtschaft im Bezirk Potsdam', report compiled by MfS and *Volkspolizei*, 1 Dec. 1961, bl. 187–207.

49 See, for example, the otherwise convincing study by F. Werkentin, *Politische Strafjustiz*, p. 92ff.; also A. Mitter and S. Wolle, *Untergang auf Raten*, p. 305ff.

50 SAPMO-BA DY30/IV2/7/401, 'Die Lage der Landwirtschaft im Bezirk Potsdam', bl. 188–90.

51 See esp. SAPMO-BA DY30/IV2/7/401.

52 These quotes from SAPMO-BA DY30/IV2/5/433, 'Kurzinformation über die ersten Maßnahmen und Stimmungen zur Durchführung des Ministerratbeschlusses vom 12.8.61', 13 Aug. 1961; DY34/22677, 'Informationsbericht Nr. 7', 16 Aug. 1961, p. 4.

53 The losses were particularly drastic in East Berlin and *Bezirk* Potsdam, the regions bordering West Berlin. See Dorle Zilch, *Millionen unter der blauen Fahne* (Rostock: Norddt. Hochschulschriften-Verlag, 1994), p. 53.

54 SAPMO-BA DY30/IV2/905/27, 'Bericht über die Vorkommnisse an der Erweiterten Oberschule Jüterbog', 4 Oct. 1961.

55 BLHA Bez. Pdm. Rep. 530, Nr. 1765, 'Bericht über die Lage auf dem

Gebiet der Volksbildung im Kreis Jüterbog', 14 Nov. 1961, bl. 90–7.
56 BLHA Bez. Pdm. Rep. 530, Nr. 1712, 'Bericht über die Parteiaktivtagung in Jüterbog', 26 Oct. 1961, bl. 55–7.
57 BLHA Bez. Pdm. Rep. 530, Nr. 1712, 'Bericht über die Vorkommnisse an der EOS Oranienburg', 15 Nov. 1961, bl. 69–71.
58 BLHA Bez. Pdm. Rep. 530, Nr. 1712, 'Zu den Vorkommnissen an der erw. Oberschule 4 Potsdam, Klasse 10 b 2', 2 Nov. 1961, bl. 60–3.
59 SAPMO-BA DY30/IV2/905/27, 'Betr.: Reaktionäre Vorgänge in der Erweiterten Oberschule in Anklam Bezirk Neubrandenburg', 26 Sept. 1961. The incident is recounted at greater length in Dorothee Wierling, 'Die Jugend als innerer Feind. Konflikte in der Erziehungsdiktatur der sechziger Jahre', in Kaelble *et al.*, *Sozialgeschichte*, pp. 405–8, and M. Fulbrook, *Anatomy*, pp. 1–3.
60 I have discussed this in greater detail in '"What about peace and bread?" East Germans and the Remilitarization of the GDR, 1952–1962', in *Militärgeschichtliche Mitteilungen*, vol. 58 (1999), no. 1. There had been nagging fears of being unable to sustain troop levels because of the dwindling birth-rate during the war. The plan for 1961–65 was to raise the number of recruits over this period from 193 000 to 275 000. Taken together, the smaller cohorts and higher number of recruits meant that whereas 1 in 5 young males between the ages of 18 and 24 had to be recruited from 1956 to 1960, between 1961 and 1965 the ratio would skyrocket to 2 in 3.
61 SAPMO-BA DY30/IV2/12/58, 'Bericht über die Werbung von Jugendlichen für die bewaffneten Kräfte der DDR 1961', undated, bl. 270.
62 SAPMO-BA DY30/IV2/12/58, 'Überspitzungen bei der Gewinnung von Jugendlichen für den Dienst in den bewaffneten Kräften der DDR im Kreis Oranienburg', 14 Oct. 1961, bl. 274–6.
63 SAPMO-BA DY30/IV2/12/58, bl. 270.
64 SAPMO-BA DY30/IV2/12/58, report of 24 Oct. 1961, bl. 134–5.
65 SAPMO-BA DY30/IV2/12/58, letter from Mückenberger to SED-ZK, 19 Dec. 1961, bl. 136–7.
66 SAPMO-BA DY30/IV2/12/57, 'Information: Stimmung zum Gesetz über die allgemeine Wehrpflicht', 25 Jan. 1962, bl. 8. Similar findings are reported in BAB DO1/11/1120, '1. Bericht über Stimmungen und Meinungen der Bevölkerung sowie der Tätigkeit des Gegners zum Gesetz der allgemeinen Wehrpflicht', 27 Jan. 1962, bl. 4; SAPMO-BA DY34/22233, 'Information', 25 Jan. 1962.
67 LAB C Rep. 900, IV/4/06–380, 'Stimmungen zum Wehrpflichtgesetz', 25 Jan. 1962, unpag.
68 SAPMO-BA DY34/22233, 'Information', 25 Jan. 1962, unpag.
69 See SAPMO-BA DY30/IV2/14/36, bl. 24–5.
70 BAB DO1/11/1120, 1. Bericht über Stimmungen . . .', 27 Jan. 1962, p. 6.
71 SAPMO-BA DY30/IV2/12/57, bl. 30–2, 35–9, 56–7. The strike took place on 23 January in the Gustav Thiele factory in Löbau, where ten youths of conscription age downed tools for two hours and categorically refused to resume work because conscription was being introduced. The incident was quickly cleared up, however, by union officials and 'state organs'. SAPMO-BA DY30/IV2/6.11/66, bl. 22.

72 BAB DO1/11/1120, '1. Bericht über Stimmungen und Meinungen der Bevölkerung sowie der Tätigkeit des Gegners zum Gesetz der allgemeinen Wehrpflicht', 27 Jan. 1962, p. 8; *ibid.*, '2. Bericht über Stimmungen...', 30 Jan. 1962, p. 4; SAPMO-BA DY30/IV2/12/57, 'Information über Feindarbeit, die zum Gesetz...', 23 Feb. 1962, bl. 31.

73 BAB DO1/11/1120, '1. Bericht über Stimmungen...', 27 Jan. 1962, p. 8; SAPMO-BA DY30/IV2/12/57, 'Information für den Genossen Honecker über Stimmungen und Argumente aus dem Bereich der Nationalen Volksarmee zur Einführung des Wehrpflichtgesetzes für die Zeit vom 22.01–25.01.1962', bl. 13–15.

74 Church efforts to place the question of conscientious objection on the agenda for political discussion, which were eventually successful in gaining conscientious objectors the status of *Bausoldaten*, or 'construction soldiers' in 1964, was on behalf of only a handful of committed individuals, no more than 1–1.5 per cent of eligible conscripts after 1964. This statistic from Rüdiger Wenzke, 'Die Wehrpflicht im Spiegel der marxistisch–leninistischen Theorie in der DDR', in Roland Foerster (ed.), *Die Wehrpflicht* (Munich: Oldenbourg, 1994), pp. 119–32. On conscientious objection in the GDR generally, see Uwe Koch and Stephan Eschler, *Zähne hoch Kopf zusammenbeißen: Dokumente zur Wehrdienstverweigerung in der DDR von 1962–1990* (Kückenshagen: Scheunen-Verlag, 1994).

75 BAB DO1/11/1120, '1. Bericht über Stimmungen und Meinungen der Bevölkerung sowie der Tätigkeit des Gegners zum Gesetz der allgemeinen Wehrpflicht', 27 Jan. 1962, pp. 7–8; '2. Bericht über Stimmungen...', 30 Jan. 1962, p. 12; SAPMO-BA DY30/IV2/12/57, bl. 99. Over the two days following the introduction of conscription on 24 January, a record 16 youths enquired about enlisting at police headquarters in Magdeburg, all of whom were sent to the local army recruiting board.

76 BLHA Bez. Ffo. Rep. 730, Nr. 1100, 'Auszug aus der Einschätzung über den Verlauf der Musterung in der Zeit vom 03.09.62–15.09.62', unpag.

77 SAPMO-BA DY30/IV2/12/57, 'Information über die durchgeführte Musterung in der Zeit vom 3.9.62–26.9.62', bl. 95–102; 'Abschlußbericht über die durchgeführte Musterung in der Zeit vom 15–31.03.1962', bl. 73–9.

78 For a personal view, see Thomas Spanier, 'In Erinnerung an meine Dienstzeit. 18 Monate als Wehrpflichtiger in der NVA', in Manfred Backerra (ed.), *NVA. Ein Rückblick für die Zukunft* (Cologne: Markus, 1992), p. 27 ff.

79 SAPMO-BA DY30/IV2/12/57, 'Information über die durchgeführte Musterung der Wehrpflichtigen 1962', undated, bl. 42–9.

13 Integration, scepticism and pragmatism

1 On this, see H. Niemann, *Meinungsforschung in der DDR*.

2 BLHA Bez. Pdm. Rep. 530, Nr. 1218, 'Anlage: Schwerpünkte des Bezirksvorstandes FDGB zur Weiterführung des Produktionsaufgebotes', undated, mid-Oct. 1961, unpag.

3 BLHA, Bez. Pdm. Rep. 530 Nr. 2863, 'Bericht über den Massenwettbewerb...', 17 May 1963, pp. 11–12.

4   It has been calculated that there were 1473 different tariff levels in the mid-1960s. See A. Bust-Bartels, *Herrschaft*, p. 105.

5   BLHA, Bez. Pdm. Rep. 530 Nr. 2863, 'Bericht über den Massenwettbewerb...', 17 May 1963, p. 12.

6   BLHA, Bez. Pdm. Rep. 530 Nr. 2863, 'Bemerkungen zur Berichterstattung des Sekretariats der KL', 11 June 1963, p. 5.

7   P. Hübner, *Konsens*, pp. 84–6.

8   LAB C Rep. 900, IVA4/03/088, 'Einschätzung der Bewußtseinsentwicklung in der Arbeiterklasse und bei den Bürgern der verschiedenen Schichten der Bevölkerung im Stadtbezirk Lichtenberg', 23 Sept. 1963, pp. 1–3.

9   SAPMO-BA DY34/22235, 'Information 34/63', 12 Nov. 1963.

10   SAPMO-BA DY30/IVA2/5/22, 'Information über die Stimmung unter der Arbeiterklasse und der technischen Intelligenz in den Betrieben des Chemieanlagebaus und des Bauwesens im Bezirk Magdeburg', 4 Dec. 1964, pp. 1–3.

11   *Ibid.*

12   LAB C Rep. 900, IVA4/06/098, 'Bericht für das Sekretariat der BL: Analyse des Bewußtseins der Bevölkerung des Stadtbezirkes Prenzlauer Berg', 16 Nov. 1964, pp. 5–6.

13   *Ibid.*

14   This was clearly reflected in the changing structure of LPG farming during the 1960s. Whereas in 1960 the average size of LPGs was 300 hectares and two-thirds of all LPGs were Type I; by 1970 the average LPG size had doubled to around 600 hectares and two-thirds had either transformed or were integrated into Type III LPGs. *DDR-Handbuch*, 2nd edn, vol. 1, p. 804.

15   SAPMO-BA IVA2/7/41a, 'Analyse über die Entwicklung der Parteiarbeit in den sozialistischen Landwirtschaftsbetrieben', 26 Feb. 1963, p. 4.

16   Rolf Badstübner *et al.*, *DDR – Werden und Wachsen. Zur Geschichte der DDR* (Berlin, 1974), p. 427.

17   BLHA, Bez. Pdm. Rep. 530, Nr. 3146, 'Einige Bemerkungen zur Trennung von großen LPG im Kreis Pritzwalk', 22 July 1963; see also 'Einschätzung der Lage in den POen der sozialistischen Landwirtschaftsbetrieben im Kreis Nauen', 4 Jan. 1963.

18   BLHA, Bez. Pdm. Rep. 530, Nr. 2863, report of 17 May 1963.

19   BLHA, Bez. Pdm. Rep. 530, Nr. 2867, report of 10 Feb. 1964 on preparation for the Eighth Farmers' Congress; also Nr. 2868, report of 25 Sept. 1964.

20   SAPMO-BA DY30/IVA2/7/7, 'Information über Meinungen, Fragen und Unklarheiten die in 6 LPGen des Kreises Nauen auftraten', 14 Aug. 1964.

21   SAPMO-BA DY30/IV2/7/359, bl. 99–101.

22   As one report put it: 'Among the men – especially also among many functionaries in the villages, there is the opinion that it is enough if they are members, the women should run the household and rear the children, and can simply help during peak times'. SAPMO-BA DY30/IV2/7/359, 'Einschätzung über die Arbeit mit den Bäuerinnen in Auswertung des Kommuniques "Die Frau – der Frieden und der Sozialismus"', 29 June 1962, bl. 328; See also SAPMO-BA DY30/902/6, 'Argumente aus den Blockparteien', 2 Mar. 1962; SAPMO-BA FDGB-ZV Land- und Forstwirtschaft 10/356/7927, reports of 4 Jan. 1964, 7 Feb. 1964.

23 SAPMO-BA IVA2/7/7, 'Information über Meinungen, Fragen und Unklarheiten die in 6 LPGen des Kreises Nauen auftraten', 14 Aug. 1964, pp. 7, 10, 14, 15, 16.

24 BLHA, Bez. Pdm. Rep. 530, Nr. 3150, 'Auszug aus dem Material zur Perspektivplanung', 12 Nov. 1964; SAPMO-BA FDGB-ZV Land- und Forstwirtschaft 10/356/7927, 'Informationsbericht der Arbeitsgruppe Landwirtschaft', 29 May 1964.

25 SAPMO-BA IVA2/7/7, 'Information über Meinungen, Fragen und Unklarheiten die in 6 LPGen des Kreises Nauen auftraten', 14 Aug. 1964, pp. 12, 17–18.

26 BLHA, Bez. Pdm. Rep. 530, Nr. 2865, 'Bericht zum 9.10.1963 über die bisherige Ergebnisse des Wahlkampfes'; see also 'Bericht zum 10.9.63' on the preparations for the elections in rural areas.

27 SAPMO-BA IVA2/7/41a, 'Einige Probleme der Führungstätigkeit der Bezirks- und Kreisleitungen', Instrukteurbericht to Abt. Landwirtschaft, 6 Aug. 1963.

28 SAPMO-BA IVA2/7/41a, 'Einige Probleme der Parteiarbeit für die Beratung mit den Leitern der Büros für Landwirtschaft der Bezirks- und Kreisleitungen', Instrukteurbericht to Abt. Landwirtschaft, 9 Jan. 1964; IVA2/7/7, 'Information über Meinungen, Fragen und Unklarheiten die in 6 LPGen des Kreises Nauen auftraten', 14 Aug. 1964, pp. 10–11.

29 SAPMO-BA IVA2/7/7, 'Information über Meinungen, Fragen und Unklarheiten die in 6 LPGen des Kreises Nauen auftraten', 14 Aug. 1964, pp. 14, 18.

30 BLHA, Bez. Pdm. Rep. 530, Nr. 3139, 'Analyse des Standes der Bewußtseinsentwicklung in der LPG Typ III in Dreetz, Kreis Kyritz', 2 Feb. 1965.

31 See Detlef Pollack, 'Von der Volkskirche zur Minderheitskirche. Zur Entwicklung von Religiosität und Kirchlichkeit in der DDR', in Kaelble *et al.*, *Sozialgeschichte*, pp. 271–94.

32 See A. Bauerkämper, 'Transformation'; see also BLHA Rep. 401, Nr. 4276, on the June 1962 Council of Ministers resolution for the further qualification of agricultural cadre.

33 BLHA Bez. Pdm. Rep. 401, Nr. 4343, unpag.

34 This and the following paragraph are based on D. Wierling, 'Die Jugend als innerer Feind'.

35 See Karen Henderson, 'The Search for Ideological Conformity: Sociological Research on Youth in Honecker's GDR', in *German History*, vol. 10, no. 3 (Oct. 1992), pp. 318–34.

36 For a statistical overview of some of the demographic changes this involved, see Heike Solga, *Auf dem Weg in eine klassenlose Gesellschaft? Klassenlagen und Mobilität zwischen Generationen in der DDR* (Berlin: Akademie-Verlag, 1995).

37 In 1961, the percentage of former refugees in the FRG possessing a higher degree was 7.2 per cent for men and 2.1 per cent for women, compared to only 3.4 per cent and 1.0 per cent possessing higher degrees in the West German populace as a whole. Likewise, students comprised 0.7 per cent of all refugees from 1952–61 but only 0.34 per cent of the entire GDR population over the same period. Figures from H. Heidemeyer, *Flucht und Zuwanderung*, p. 50.

38 According to official East German statistics, the proportion of the populace in higher education rose from 17.2 per 10 000 in 1951 to 59.0 per 10 000 by 1960. *StJB* 1973, p. 363.

39 In fact, interviewers found it difficult in 1987 to find a man over 60 from a skilled working-class background who had remained a manual labourer. Cf. L. Niethammer *et al.*, *Volkseigene Erfahrung*, pp. 44–5; also L. Niethammer, 'Erfahrungen und Strukturen. Prolegomena zu einer Geschichte der Gesellschaft der DDR', in Kaelble *et al.*, *Sozialgeschichte*, pp. 99–105.

40 For an overview, see Dieter Voigt *et al.*, *Sozialstruktur der DDR, eine Einführung* (Darmstadt: Wissenschaftliche Buchgesellschaft, 1987); also H. Solga, *Auf dem Weg*.

41 See generally J. Kopstein, *The Politics*.

42 Whereas 21.6 per cent (1 774 747) of the working populace were in agriculture and forestry in 1955, by 1965 this had decreased to 16.3 per cent (1 249 011). *StJB* 1956, p. 166; *StJB* 1966, pp. 59–60.

43 SAPMO-BA DY30/IVA2/2021/370, 'Kurzfassung über Probleme und Folgerungen zur Bewußtseinsentwicklung Jugendlicher in der DDR, die vom Zentralinstitut für Jugendforschung anläßlich der "Umfrage 69" vorgelegt wurden', pp. 11–12.

44 *Ibid.*

45 A. Hirschman, *Exit, Voice and Loyalty*, p. 82.

46 LAB C Rep. 900, IVA4/08/096, 'Einschätzung des Entwicklungsstandes des sozialistischen Bewußtseins im Stadtbezirk Weißensee', 10 Jan. 1967, pp. 7–8; underline in the original.

14 Conclusions

1 E. Jesse, 'War die DDR totalitär?', p. 12.

2 For overviews, see Wolfgang Wippermann, *Totalitarismustheorien: die Entwicklung der Diskussion von den Anfängen bis heute* (Darmstadt: Primus-Verlag, 1997); Alfons Söllner (ed.), *Totalitarismus: eine Ideengeschichte des 20 Jahrhunderts* (Berlin: Akademie-Verlag, 1997). Somewhat less convincing, but with a useful bibliography is Eckard Jesse (ed.), *Totalitarismus im 20 Jahrhundert: eine Bilanz der internationalen Forschung* (Baden-Baden: Nomos, 1996). See also *idem*, 'Die Totalitarismusforschung und ihre Repräsentanten', in *APuZG*, B20/98, pp. 3–18. On totalitarianism and *Diktaturenvergleich*, see esp. Jürgen Kocka, *Vereinigungskrise. Zur Geschichte der Gegenwart* (Göttingen: Vandenhoeck & Ruprecht, 1995), pp. 91–101; also Hans Maier (ed.), *'Totalitarismus' und 'politische Religionen': Konzepte des Diktaturenvergleichs* (Paderborn: F. Schöningh, 1996). Highly polemical and rather unconvincing are Klaus Schroeder and Jochen Staadt, 'Der diskrete "Charme des Status-quo": DDR-Forschung in der Ära der Entspannungspolitik', in Klaus Schroeder (ed.), *Geschichte und Transformation*, pp. 309–46; and in the same volume, *idem*, 'Die Kunst des Aussitzens', pp. 347–54; see also K. Schroeder, *Totalitarismustheorien: Begründung und Kritik* (Berlin: Forschungsverbund SED-Staat, 1994).

3 Arnold Sywottek has tested the classic 'six-point' definition of Friedrich

and Brzezinski for the GDR, and concludes that its utility is very limited. See *idem*, '"Stalinismus" und "Totalitarismus" in der DDR-Geschichte', in *Deutsche Studien*, vol. 30 (1993), no. 117/118, pp. 25–38.

4 See especially the critique and discussion in Ralph Jessen, 'DDR-Geschichte und Totalitarismustheorie', in *Berliner Debatte Initial*, vol. 5 (1995), no. 4, pp. 17–24.

5 K. Schroeder, *Der SED-Staat*, p. 630.

6 S. Meuschel, 'Überlegungen'; *idem*, *Legitimation und Parteiherrschaft*.

7 See, for instance, D. Staritz, *Geschichte der DDR*, pp. 61–2; H. Weber, *DDR, Grundriß der Geschichte 1945–1990*, pp. 60–1; K. Schroeder, *Der SED-Staat*, p. 416ff.

8 My thinking on this has benefitted greatly from talks with Sebastian Simsch, who argues this point at length in his doctoral dissertation (FU-Berlin, 1999) originating from his research project 'Arbeiterschaft und Arbeiterorganisationen in zwei deutschen Diktaturen. Unterschiede, Ähnlichkeiten und Kontinuitäten in Sachsen, 1933–1961'.

9 Gert-Joachim Glaeßner, 'Vom "realen Sozialismus" zur Selbstbestimmung: Ursachen und Konsequenzen der Systemkrise in der DDR', *APuZG*, 1–2/90 (5 Jan. 1990), p. 3.

10 C. Maier, *Dissolution: The crisis of Communism and the end of East Germany* (Princeton: Princeton University Press, 1997), p. 53.

11 Günter Gaus, *Wo Deutschland liegt* (Munich: Deutscher Taschenbuch Verlag, 1983).

12 Ralph Jessen, 'Die Gesellschaft im Sozialismus. Probleme einer Sozialgeschichte der DDR', in *GG*, vol. 21 (1995), p. 106.

13 Merle Fainsod, *Smolensk under Soviet Rule* (London: Macmillan, 1958), p. 450.

14 Martin Broszat, 'Resistenz und Widerstand. Eine Zwischenbilanz des Forschungsprojektes', in M. Broszat, E. Fröhlich and A. Grossmann (eds), *Bayern in der NS-Zeit*, vol. 4 (Munich: Oldenbourg, 1981), pp. 691–709.

15 Charles Maier, 'Geschichtswissenschaft und "Ansteckungsstaat"', in *GG*, vol. 20 (1994), pp. 616–24.

Sources and Bibliography

Archives

BAB   *Bundesarchiv, Abteilung Berlin-Lichterfelde.* German Federal State
         Archives: East German state ministries, police.
BA-MA   *Bundesarchiv, Militärarchiv.* HVA, KVP, NVA.
BLHA   *Brandenburgisches Landeshauptarchiv.* Brandenburg State Archive:
         regional and district SED, police and mass organizations; large
         VEBs.
LAB   *Landesarchiv Berlin.* Berlin State Archive: regional and district
         SED, police and mass organizations; large VEBs.
SAPMO-BA   *Stiftung Archiv der Parteien und Massenorganisationen der DDR
         im Bundesarchiv.* SED Central Party Archive, central archives
         of mass organizations.

Select bibliography of published sources

Ackermann, V. (1995) *Der 'echte' Flüchtling: Deutsche Vertriebene und Flüchtlinge aus der DDR 1945–1961* (Osnabrück: Universitätsverlag Rasch).

Arendt, H. (1951) *The Origins of Totalitarianism* (London: Secker & Warburg).

Augustine, D. (1996) 'Frustrierte Technokraten. Zur Sozialgeschichte des Ingenieurberufs in der Ulbricht Ära', in Bessel and Jessen, *Die Grenzen*, pp. 49–75.

Backerra, M. (ed.) (1992) *NVA. Ein Rückblick für die Zukunft* (Cologne: Markus).

Bauerkämper, A. (ed.) (1996) *'Junkerland in Bauernhand'? Durchführung, Auswirkungen und Stellenwert der Bodenreform in der Sowjetischen Besatzungszone* (Stuttgart: Franz Steiner).

— (1994) 'Von der Bodenreform zur Kollektivierung. Zum Wandel der ländlichen Gesellschaft in der Sowjetischen Besatzungszone Deutschlands und DDR 1945–1952', in Kaelble *et al.*, *Sozialgeschichte*, pp. 119–43.

— (1994) 'Strukturumbruch ohne Mentalitätenwandel. Auswirkungen der Bodenreform auf die ländliche Gesellschaft in der Provinz Mark Brandenburg 1945–1949', in *idem*, *Junkerland*, pp. 67–86.

— (1996) 'Die Neubauern in der SBZ/DDR 1945–1952. Bodenreform und politisch induzierter Wandel der ländlichen Gesellschaft', in R. Bessel and R. Jessen, *Die Grenzen*, pp. 108–36.

— (1997) 'Transformation or Transition? Rural Elites under the Impact of Land Reform and Collectivisation in the GDR', manuscript.

— (1997) 'Die tabuisierte Elite. Problembereiche, Fragen und Hypothesen der Zeithistorischen Forschung über Führungsgruppen in der DDR', in *Potsdamer Bulletin für Zeithistorische Studien*, no. 9 (April), pp. 19–33.

Baylis, T. (1974) *The Technical Intelligentsia and the East German Elite* (Berkeley: University of California Press).

Bell, W. (1992) *Enteignungen in der Landwirtschaft der DDR nach 1949 und deren politische Hintergründe. Analyse und Dokumentation* (Münster: Landwirtschafts-Verlag).

Bessel, R. and Jessen, R. (eds) (1996) *Die Grenzen der Diktatur: Staat und Gesellschaft in der SBZ/DDR* (Göttingen: Vandenhoeck & Ruprecht).

Bessel, R. (1996) 'Grenzen des Polizeistaates. Polizei und Gesellschaft in der SBZ und frühen DDR, 1945–1953', in R. Bessel and R. Jessen (eds), *Die Grenzen der Diktatur*, pp. 224–52.

Blücher, V.G. (1959) *Industriearbeiterschaft in der Sowjetzone* (Stuttgart: Enke).

Braun, G. (1986) 'Determinanten der Wahlentscheidungen in der Sowjetischen Besatzungszone 1946. Problemskizze', in *Deutsche Studien*, vol. 24, pp. 346–54.

Broszat, M. (1981) 'Resistenz und Widerstand. Eine Zwischenbilanz des Forschungsprojektes', in M. Broszat, E. Fröhlich and A. Grossmann (eds), *Bayern in der NS-Zeit*, vol. IV (Munich: Oldenbourg), pp. 691–709.

— and Weber, H. (eds) (1993) *SBZ-Handbuch*, 2nd edn (Oldenbourg: Munich).

Buddrus, M. (1994) *Die Organisation 'Dienst für Deutschland'* (Weinheim: Juventa).

— '"Kaderschmiede für den Führungsnachwuchs"? Die Kadettenschule der nationalen Volksarmee in Naumburg 1956–1961. Ein Beitrag zur Geschichte der Militärund Jugendpolitik der SED', in H. Mehringer (ed.), *Von der SBZ zur DDR*, pp. 167–232.

Bundesministerium für gesamtdeutsche Fragen (1961) *Die Flucht aus der Sowjetzone und die Sperrmaßnahmen des kommunistischen Regimes vom 13 August 1961* (Bonn/Berlin).

Bundesministerium für Vertriebene, Flüchtlinge und Kriegsgeschädigte (1964) *Flucht aus der Sowjetzone* (Bonn/Berlin).

Bust-Bartels, A. (1980) *Herrschaft und Widerstand in den DDR-Betrieben. Leistungsentlohnung, Arbeitsbedingungen, innerbetriebliche Konflikte und technologische Entwicklung* (Fr./Main: Campus-Verlag).

Cerny, J. (ed.) (1990) *Brüche, Krisen, Wendepunkte. Neubefragung von DDR-Geschichte* (Leipzig: Urania).

Christopeit, G. (1993) 'Die Herkunft und Verteilung der Evakuierten, Flüchtlinge und Vertriebenen in der Provinz Mark Brandenburg und ihr Verhältnis zu der einheimischen Bevölkerung', in M. Wille *et al.*, *Sie hatten alles verloren*, pp. 86–109.

Connelly, J. (1994) 'Zur "Republikflucht" von DDR-Wissenschaftlern in den fünfziger Jahren, Dokumentation', in *ZfG*, vol. 42, no. 4, pp. 331–52.

Conquest, R. (1986) *Harvest of Sorrow: Soviet Collectivization and the Terror-Famine* (London: Hutchinson).

Dähn, H. (1982) *Konfrontation oder Kooperation? Das Verhältnis von Staat und Kirche in der SBZ/DDR 1945–1980* (Opladen: Westdeutscher Verlag).

Dahrendorf, R. (1961) *Gesellschaft und Freiheit* (Munich: R. Piper).

Diedrich, T., Ehlert, H. and Wenzke, R. (eds) (1998) *Im Dienste der Partei. Handbuch der bewaffneten Organe der DDR* (Berlin: Ch. Links).

Diedrich, T. (1991) *Der 17. Juni in der DDR. Bewaffnete Gewalt gegen das Volk* (Berlin: Dietz).

Dokumente der SED, vols. 1–6 (Berlin, 1952–1958).

Eberle, H. (1996) 'Weder Gegnerschaft noch Abwerbung. Zu den Motiven republikflüchtiger SED-Mitglieder aus dem Bezirk Halle im Jahr 1961', in

Heiner Timmermann (ed.) *Diktaturen in Europa im 20. Jahrhundert*, pp. 449–60.

Eisenfeld, B. (1996) 'Zur politischen Wirkung der Bausoldaten in der DDR', in *DA*, vol. 29, no. 2, pp. 3–17.

Erbe, G. (1982) *Arbeiterklasse und Intelligenz in der DDR* (Opladen: Westdeutscher Verlag).

Ernst, A.-S. (1996) 'Von der bürgerlichen zur sozialistischen Profession? Ärzte in der DDR 1945–1961', in R. Bessel and R. Jessen, *Die Grenzen*, pp. 25–48.

Ewers, K. (1981) 'Aktivisten in Aktion. Adolf Hennecke und der Beginn der Aktivistenbewegung 1948/49', in *DA*, vol. 14, no. 9 (September), pp. 947–70.

Fainsod, M. (1958) *Smolensk under Soviet Rule* (London: Macmillan).

Fischer, A. (ed.) (1993) *Studien zur Geschichte der SBZ/DDR* (Berlin: Duncker & Humblot).

Forster, T. (1983) *Die NVA* (Cologne: Markus-Verlag).

Friedrich, C. and Brzezinski, Z. (1956) *Totalitarian Dictatorship and Autocracy* (Cambridge, MA: Harvard University Press).

Fulbrook, M. (1995) *Anatomy of a Dictatorship: Inside the GDR 1949–1989* (Oxford: Oxford University Press).

Gaus, G. (1983) *Wo Deutschland liegt* (Munich: Deutscher Taschenbuch Verlag).

Gillis, J. (ed.) (1989) *The Militarization of the Western World* (London: Rutgers University Press).

Glaeßner, G.-J. (1990) 'Vom "realen Sozialismus" zur Selbstbestimmung: Ursachen und Konsequenzen der Systemkrise in der DDR', *APuZG*, 1–2/90 (5 January).

Goeckel, R. (1990) *The Lutheran Church and the East German State* (Ithaca, NY: Cornell University Press).

Goerner, M.G. (1997) *Die Kirche als Problem der SED* (Berlin: Akademie-Verlag).

Grünberg, K. *et al.* (1951) *Helden der Arbeit: Aus Ihrem Leben und Wirken* (Berlin).

Häder, S. (1993) 'Von der "demokratischen Schulreform" zur Stalinisierung des Bildungswesens – Der 17 Juni 1953 in Schulen und Schulverwaltungen Ost-Berlins', in J. Kocka, *Historische DDR-Forschung*, pp. 191–214.

Hagen, M. (1992) *DDR – Juni '53; die erste Volkserhebung im Stalinismus* (Stuttgart: Franz Steiner).

Harrison, H. (1993) 'Ulbricht and the Concrete "Rose": New Archival Evidence on the Dynamics of Soviet-East German Relations and the Berlin Crisis 1958–1961', in *Cold War International History Project Working Paper*, no. 5 (May).

Heidemeyer, H. (1994) *Flucht und Zuwanderung aus der SBZ/DDR 1945/1949–1961. Die Flüchtlingspolitik der Bundesrepublik Deutschland bis zum Bau der Berliner Mauer* (Düsseldorf: Droste).

Hennecke, A. (1975) 'Der Durchbruch aus dem Teufelskreis', in Erwin L. *et al.* (eds) *Aufbruch in unsere Zeit: Erinnerungen an die Tätigkeit der Gewerkschaften von 1945 bis zur Gründung der Deutschen Demokratischen Republik*, 2nd ed. (Berlin).

Hirschmann, A. (1970) *Exit, Voice and Loyalty: Responses to Decline in Firms, Organizations and States* (Cambridge, MA: Harvard University Press).

Hohmann, J. (1997) ' "Wenn Sie dies lesen, bin ich schon auf dem Weg in den Westen". "Republikflüchtige" DDR-Lehrer in den Jahren 1949–1961', in *ZfG*, vol. 45, no. 4, pp. 311–30.

Hohlfeld, B. (1992) *Die Neulehrer in der SBZ/DDR 1945–1953: Ihre Rolle bei der Umgestaltung von Gesellschaft und Staat* (Weinheim: Deutsche Studien-Verlag).

Holzweißig, G. (1985) *Militärwesen in der DDR* (Berlin: Verlag Gebr. Holzapfel).

Hübner, P. (1995) *Konsens, Konflikt, Kompromiß. Soziale Arbeiterinteressen und Sozialpolitik in der SBZ/DDR 1945–1970* (Berlin: Akademie-Verlag).

— (ed.) (1995) *Niederlausitzer Industriearbeiter 1935 bis 1970. Studien zur Sozialgeschichte* (Berlin: Akademie-Verlag).

— (1996) '"Sozialistischer Fordismus?" Oder: Unerwartete Ergebnisse eines Kopiervorganges. Eine Geschichte der Produktionsbrigaden in der DDR', in A. Lüdtke, I. Marßolek and A. von Saldern (eds), *Amerikanisierung*, pp. 96–115.

— (1995) 'Syndikalistische Versündigungen? Versuche unabhängiger Interessenvertretung für die Industriearbeiter der DDR um 1960', in *JHK* (Berlin), pp. 100–17.

— (1994) 'Die Zukunft war gestern: Soziale und mentale Trends in der DDR-Industriearbeiterschaft', in Kaelble *et al.*, *Sozialgeschichte der DDR*, pp. 171–87.

— (1993) '"Wir wollen keine Diktatur mehr..." Aspekte des Diktatureinvergleichs am Beispiel einer Sozialgeschichte der Niederlausitzer Industriearbeiterschaft 1936 bis 1965', in J. Kocka, *Historische DDR-Forschung*, pp. 215–32.

— (1993) 'Balance des Ungleichgewichtes. Zum Verhältnis von Arbeiterinteressen und SED-Herrschaft', in *GG*, vol. 19, pp. 15–28.

— (1995) 'Arbeitskonflikte in Industriebetrieben der DDR nach 1953. Annäherungen an eine Struktur und Prozeßanalyse', in U. Poppe, R. Eckert and I.-S. Kowalczuk (eds), *Zwischen Selbstbehauptung und Anpassung*, pp. 178–91.

— (1993) 'Umworben und bedrängt: Industriearbeiter in der SBZ', in A. Fischer (ed.), *Studien zur Geschichte der SBZ/DDR*, pp. 195–209.

— (ed.) (1999) *Eliten im Sozialismus. Studien zur Sozialgeschichte der DDR* (Cologne: Böhlau-Verlag).

Infratest GmbH (1957) *Jugendliche Flüchtlinge aus der SBZ* (Munich: Infratest-Verlag).

— (1958) *Angestellten in der Sowjetzone Deutschlands: Verhaltensweise und gesellschaftliche Einordnung der mitteldeutschen Angestellten* (Munich: Infratest-Verlag).

— (1960) *Die Intelligenzschicht in der Sowjetzone Deutschlands, Band III: Ideologische Haltungen und politische Verhaltensweisen* (Munich: Infratest-Verlag).

Jesse, E. (ed.) (1996) *Totalitarismus im 20. Jahrhundert: eine Bilanz der internationalen Forschung* (Baden-Baden: Nomos).

— (1994) 'War die DDR totalitär?', in *APuZG*, B40/94, pp. 12–23.

— (1998) 'Die Totalitarismusforschung und ihre Repräsentanten', in *APuZG*, B20/98, pp. 3–18.

Jessen, R. (1997) 'Diktatorische Herrschaft als kommunikative Praxis. Überlegungen zum Zusammenhang von "Bürokratie" und Sprachnormierung in der DDR-Geschichte', in A. Lüdtke, P. Becker, *Akten. Eingaben. Schaufenster*, pp. 57–75.

— (1995) 'Die Gesellschaft im Sozialismus. Probleme einer Sozialgeschichte der DDR', in *GG*, vol. 21.

— (1995) 'DDR-Geschichte und Totalitarismustheorie', in *Berliner Debatte Initial*, vol. 5, no. 4, pp. 17–24.

Kaelble, H., Kocka, J. and Zwahr, H. (eds) (1994) *Sozialgeschichte der DDR* (Stuttgart: Klett-Cotta).

Karlsch, R. (1994) '"Arbeiter, schützt Euere Betriebe!" Widerstand gegen Demontagen in der SBZ', in *Internationale wissenschaftliche Korrespondenz zur Geschichte der deutschen Arbeiterbewegung*, vol. 30, no. 3, pp. 380–404.

Klein, J. (1955) 'Ursachen und Motiven der Abwanderung aus der Sowjetzone Deutschlands', in *APuZG*, B 24/55 (15 June), pp. 361–83.

Kleßmann, C. (1994) 'Relikte des Bildungsbürgertums in der DDR', in Kaelble, *et al.*, *Sozialgeschichte der DDR*, pp. 254–70.

— (1996) 'Opposition und Resistenz in zwei Diktaturen in Deutschland', in *Historische Zeitschrift*, vol. 262, no. 2, pp. 453–79.

— (1993) 'Zur Sozialgeschichte des protestantischen Milieus in der DDR', in *GG*, vol. 19, pp. 29–53.

Kluttig, T. (1997) *Parteischulung und Kaderauslese in der Sozialistischen Einheitspartei Deutschlands 1945–1961* (Berlin: Berlin-Verlag).

Koch, U. and Eschler, S. (1994) *Zähne hoch Kopf zusammenbeißen: Dokumente zur Wehrdienstverweigerung in der DDR von 1962–1990* (Kückenshagen: Scheunen-Verlag).

Kocka, J. (ed.) (1993) *Historische DDR-Forschung: Aufsätze und Studien* (Berlin: Akademie-Verlag).

— (1995) *Vereinigungskrise. Zur Geschichte der Gegenwart* (Göttingen: Vandenhoeck & Ruprecht).

Koop, V. (1997) *Armee oder Freizeitclub? Die Kampfgruppen der Arbeiterklasse in der DDR* (Bonn: Bouvier).

Kopstein, J. (1997) *The Politics of Economic Decline in East Germany, 1945–1989* (Chapel Hill: University of North Carolina Press).

— (1996) 'Chipping Away at the State. Workers' Resistance and the Demise of East Germany', in *World Politics*, vol. 48 (April), pp. 391–423.

Kowalczuk, I.-S., Mitter, A. and Wolle, S. (eds) (1995) *Der Tag X – 17. Juni 1953. Die 'Innere Staatsgründung' der DDR als Ergebnis der Krise 1952/54* (Berlin: Ch. Links).

Krebs, C. (1989) *Der Weg zur industriemäßigen Organisation der Agrarproduktion in der DDR. Die Agrarpolitik der SED 1945–1960* (Bonn: Forschungsgesellschaft für Agrarpolitik u. Agrarsoziologie).

Kuromiya, H. (1988) *Stalin's Industrial Revolution: Politics and Workers, 1928–1932* (Cambridge: Cambridge University Press).

Lewin, M. (1968) *Russian Peasants and Soviet Power* (New York: Norton).

Lindenberger, T. (1999) *Herrschaft und Eigen-Sinn in der Diktatur. Studien zur Gesellschaftsgeschichte der DDR* (Cologne: Böhlau-Verlag).

— (1999) 'Der ABV als Landwirt. Zur Mitwirkung der Deutschen Volkspolizei an der Kollektivierung der Landwirtschaft, 1952–1960', in *idem* (ed.), *Herrschaft und Eigen-Sinn*.

Lüdtke, A. (1993) *Eigen-Sinn. Fabrikalltag, Arbeitererfahrungen und Politik vom Kaiserreich bis in den Faschismus. Ergebnisse* (Hamburg: Ergebnisse-Verlag).

— (ed.) (1991) *Herrschaft als sozialer Praxis. Historische und sozio-anthropologische Studien* (Göttingen: Vandenhoeck & Ruprecht).

— (1994) '"Helden der Arbeit" – Mühe beim Arbeiten. Zur mißmutigen Loyalität von Industriearbeitern in der DDR', in Kaelble, *et al.*, *Sozialgeschichte der DDR*, op. cit., pp. 188–213.

— (1998) 'Die DDR als Geschichte. Zur Geschichtsschreibung über die DDR', in *APuZG*, B36/1998, pp. 3–16.

— (1996) Marßolek, Inge and von Saldern, Adelheid (eds), *Amerikanisierung: Traum und Alptraum im Deutschland des 20. Jahrhunderts* (Stuttgart: Franz Steiner).

— and Becker, P. (eds) (1997) *Akten. Eingaben. Schaufenster. Die DDR und ihre Texte* (Berlin: Akademie-Verlag).

Ludz, P.C. (1972) *The Changing Party Elite in East Germany* (Cambridge, MA: Harvard University Press).

Mählert, U. (1995) *Die Freie Deutsche Jugend 1945–1949. Von den 'Antifaschistischen Jugendausschüssen' zur SED-Massenorganisation: Die Erfassung der Jugend in der Sowjetischen Besatzungszone* (Paderborn: F. Schöningh).

Maier, C. (1997) *Dissolution: The crisis of Communism and the end of East Germany* (Princeton: Princeton University Press).

— (1994) 'Geschichtswissenschaft und "Ansteckungsstaat"', in *GG*, vol. 20, pp. 616–24.

Maier, H. (ed.) (1996) *'Totalitarismus' und 'politische Religionen': Konzepte des Diktaturenvergleichs* (Paderborn: F. Schöningh).

Major, P. (1995) '"Mit Panzern kann man doch nicht für den Frieden sein". Die Stimmung der DDR-Bevölkerung zum Bau der Berliner Mauer am 13. August 1961 im Spiegel der Parteiberichte der SED', in *JHK* (Berlin), pp. 208–23.

Mason, T. (1995) *Nazism, Fascism and the Working Class* (Cambridge: Cambridge University Press).

McFalls, L. (1995) *Communism's Collapse, Democracy's Demise?: The Cultural Context and Consequences of the East German Revolution* (London: Macmillan).

Mehringer, H. (ed.) (1995) *Von der SBZ zur DDR. Studien zum Herrschaftssystem in der Sowjetischen Besatzungszone und in der Deutschen Demokratischen Republik* (Munich: Oldenbourg).

Meuschel, S. (1992) *Legitimation und Parteiherrschaft. Zum Paradox von Stabilität und Revolution in der DDR 1945–1989* (Fr./Main: Suhrkamp).

— (1993) 'Überlegungen zu einer Herrschaftsund Gesellschaftsgeschichte der DDR', in *GG*, vol. 19, pp. 5–14.

— (1993) 'Auf der Suche nach der versäumten Tat. Kommentar zu Klaus Schroeders und Jochen Staadts Kritik an der bundesdeutschen DDR-Forschung', in *Leviathan*, vol. 21, pp. 407–23.

Mitter, A. and Wolle, S. (1993) *Untergang auf Raten: Unbekannte Kapitel der DDR-Geschichte* (Munich: Bertelsmann).

— (1995) *Der Tag X: Quellen und Forschungen zum 17. Juni 1953* (Berlin: Ch. Links).

Morsch, G. (1988) 'Die kalkulierte Improvisation. Streiks und Arbeitsniederlegungen im "Dritten Reich"', in *Vierteljahreshefte für Zeitgeschichte*, vol. 36, no. 4, pp. 649–89.

Mühlberg, F. (1996) 'Konformismus oder Eigensinn?' Eingaben als Quelle zur Erforschung der Alltagsgeschichte der DDR', in *Mitteilungen aus der kulturwissenschaftlichen Forschung*, vol. 19, no. 37 (February), pp. 331–45.

Müller, K. (1962) *Die Manager in der Sowjetzone* (Cologne: Westdeutscher-Verlag).

Naimark, N. (1995) *The Russians in Germany: A History of the Soviet Zone of Occupation, 1945–1949* (Cambridge, MA: Harvard University Press).

Nawrocki, J. (1967) *Das geplante Wunder: Leben und Wirtschaften im anderen Deutschland* (Hamburg: Wegner).

Nehrig, C. (1993) 'Zur sozialen Entwicklung der Bauern in der DDR 1945–1960', in *Zeitschrift für Agrargeschichte und Agrarsoziologie*, vol. 41, pp. 66–76.

— (1993) 'Bauern zwischen Hoffnung und Wirklichkeit. Die modifizierte Agrarpolitik von 1950/51', in E. Scherstjanoi (ed.), *Provisorium für längstens ein Jahr*, pp. 236–42.

Neubert, E. (1997) *Geschichte der Opposition in der DDR 1949–1989* (Berlin: Ch. Links).

Niemann, H. (1993) *Meinungsforschung in der DDR. Die geheimen Berichte des Instituts für Meinungsforschung an das Politbüro der SED* (Cologne: Bund-Verlag).

Niethammer, L., Wierling, D. and von Plato, A. (1991) *Die Volkseigene Erfahrung. Eine Ärchaeologie des Lebens in der Industrieprovinz der DDR* (Berlin: Rowohlt).

Niethammer, L. (1994) 'Erfahrungen und Strukturen. Prolegomena zu einer Geschichte der Gesellschaft der DDR', in Kaelble *et al.*, *Sozialgeschichte*, pp. 99–105.

Osmond, J. (1996) 'Kontinuität und Konflikt in der Landwirtschaft der SBZ/DDR zur Zeit der Bodenreform und der Vergenossenschaftlichung, 1945–1961', in R. Bessel and R. Jessen, *Die Grenzen*, pp. 137–69.

— (1996) 'Geschlectsspezifische Folgen der Bodenreform in der Sowjetischen Besatzungszone: Gutsbesitzerinnen, Bäuerinnen und Landarbeiterinnen nach 1945', in A. Bauerkämper, *Junkerland*, pp. 153–68.

Peukert, D. (1982) *Volksgenossen und Gemeinschaftsfremde. Anpassung und Aufbegehren unter dem Nationalsozialismus* (Cologne: Bund-Verlag).

Piskol, J. (1995) 'Zum Beginn der Kollektivierung der Landwirtschaft der DDR im Sommer 1952', in *Beiträge zur Geschichte der Arbeiterbewegung*, vol. 37, no. 3, pp. 19–26.

— (1991) 'Zur sozialökonomischen Entwicklung der Großbauern in der DDR 1945 bis 1960', in *ZfG*, vol. 39, pp. 419–33.

Poiger, U. (1997) 'Amerikanischer Jazz und (ost)deutsche Respektabilität', in A. Lüdtke, P. Becker (eds), *Akten. Eingaben. Schaufenster*, pp. 119–36.

— (1996) 'Rock 'n' Roll, Female Sexuality and the Cold War Battle over German Identities', in *Journal of Modern History*, vol. 68 (September).

Pollack, D. (1994) 'Von der Volkskirche zur Minderheitskirche. Zur Entwicklung von Religiosität und Kirchlichkeit in der DDR', in Kaelble *et al.*, *Sozialgeschichte*, pp. 271–94.

Poppe, U., Eckert, R. and Kowalczuk, I.-S. (eds) (1995) *Zwischen Selbstbehauptung und Anpassung. Formen des Widerstandes und der Opposition in der DDR* (Berlin: Ch. Links).

Prokop, S. (1993) *Unternehmen 'Chinesischer Wall' – Die DDR im Zwielicht der Mauer*, 2nd ed. (Fr./Main: R.G. Fischer).

Protokoll der Verhandlungen der II. Parteikonferenz der SED (Berlin, 1952).

Richert, E. (1964) *Das zweite Deutschland* (Gütersloh: Mohn).

Roesler, J. (1994) 'Die Produktionsbrigaden in der Industrie der DDR'. Zentrum der Arbeitswelt?', in Kaelble *et al.*, *Sozialgeschichte der DDR*, pp. 144–70.

— (1996) 'Gewerkschaften und Brigadebewegung in der DDR, Ende der 40er bis Anfang der 60er Jahre', in *Beiträge zur Geschichte der Arbeiterbewegung*, vol. 38, no. 3, pp. 3–26.

— (1997) 'Probleme des Brigadealltags: Arbeitsverhältnisse und Arbeitsklima in volkseigenen Betrieben', in *APuZG*, vol. 47, no. 38, pp. 3–17.

— (1997) 'Zur Rolle der Arbeitsbrigaden in der betrieblichen Hierarchie der VEB: eine politikund sozialgeschichtliche Betrachtung', in *DA*, vol. 30, pp. 737–50.

Schelsky, H. (1957) *Die skeptische Generation. Eine Soziologie der deutschen Jugend* (Düsseldorf: Diedrichs).

Scherstjanoi, E. (ed.) (1993) *'Provisorium für längstens ein Jahr'. Protokoll des Kolloquiums Die Gründung der DDR* (Berlin: Akademie-Verlag).

— (1994) 'Die DDR im Frühjahr 1952: Sozialismuslosung und Kollektivierungsbeschluß in sowjetischer Perspektive', in *DA*, vol. 27, no. 4, pp. 354–63.

Schraut, S. and Grosser, T. (eds) (1996) *Die Flüchtlingsfrage in der deutschen Nachkriegsgesellschaft* (Mannheim: Palatium-Verlag).

Schroeder, K. (ed.) (1994) *Geschichte und Transformation des SED-Staates. Beiträge und Analyse* (Berlin: Akademie-Verlag).

— (1994) *Totalitarismustheorien: Begründung und Kritik* (Berlin: Forschungsverbund SED-Staat).

— (1998) *Der SED-Staat. Partei, Staat und Gesellschaft 1949–1990* (Munich: C. Hanser).

Schulz, D. (1990) 'Ruhe im Dorf? Die Agrarpolitik von 1952/53 und ihre Folgen', in Jochen Cerny (ed.), *Brüche, Krisen, Wendepunkte*, pp. 103–109.

Schulz, F. (1995) 'Elitenwandel in der Leipziger Wirtschaftsregion 1945–1948. Von den Leipziger "sächsischen Industriefamilien" zu Kadern aus dem Leipziger Arbeitermilieu', in *Comparativ*, vol. 5, no. 4, pp. 112–26.

Schulze, E. (ed.) (1995) *DDR-Jugend: ein statistisches Handbuch* (Berlin: Akademie-Verlag).

Schulze, R., von der Brelie-Lewien, D. and Grebing, H. (eds) (1987) *Flüchtlinge und Vertriebene in der westdeutschen Nachkriegsgeschichte* (Hildesheim: A. Lax).

Scott, J. (1985) *Weapons of the Weak* (New Haven: Yale University Press).

Semmelmann, D. (1993) 'Zeitzeugen über ihren 17. Juni 1953 in Berlin', in *hefte zur ddr-geschichte*, no. 7, Berlin, pp. 26–55.

— (1993) *Schauplatz Stalinstadt/EKO. Erinnerungen an den 17. Juni 1953* (Potsdam).

Siegelbaum, L. (1988) *Stakhanovism and the Politics of Productivity in the USSR, 1935–1941* (Cambridge: Cambridge University Press).

Simsch, S. (1999) '". . . was zeigt, daß sie ideologisch zurückgeblieben sind." Personelle Grenzen der frühen DDR-Diktatur am Beispiel der FDGB-Funktionäre in und um Dresden, 1945–1951', in P. Hübner (ed.), *Eliten im Sozialismus*.

Söllner, A. (ed.) (1997) *Totalitarismus: eine Ideengeschichte des 20. Jahrhunderts* (Berlin: Akademie-Verlag).

Solga, H. (1995) *Auf dem Weg in eine klassenlose Gesellschaft? Klassenlagen und Mobilität zwischen Generationen in der DDR* (Berlin: Akademie-Verlag).

Spix, B. (1997) *Die Bodenreform in Brandenburg 1945–47: Konstruktion einer Gesellschaft am Beispiel der Kreise West- und Ostprignitz* (Münster).

Staritz, D. (1978) *Sozialismus in einem halben Lande* (Berlin: Wagenbach).

— (1985) *Geschichte der DDR 1949–1985* (Fr./Main: Suhrkamp).

— (1996) *Geschichte der DDR, Erweiterte Neuausgabe* (Fr./Main: Suhrkamp).

Statistisches Jahrbuch der DDR (Berlin, 1955–1990).

Steiner, A. (1995) 'Politische Vorstellungen und ökonomische Probleme im Vorfeld der Errichtung der Berliner Mauer. Briefe Walter Ulbrichts an Nikita Chruschtschow', in Hartmut Mehringer (ed.), *Von der SBZ zur DDR*, pp. 233–68.

Stöckigt, R. 'Direktiven aus Moskau, Sowjetische Einflußnahme auf DDR-Politik 1952/1953', in Jochen Cerny (ed.), *Brüche, Krisen, Wendepunkte*, pp. 81–7.

Storbeck, D. (1963) 'Flucht oder Wanderung?', in *Soziale Welt*, vol. 14, pp. 153–71.

— (1961) *Arbeitskraft und Beschäftigung in Mitteldeutschland* (Cologne: Westdeutscher-Verlag).

Suckut, S. (1982) *Die Betriebsrätebewegung in der Sowjetisch Besetzten Zone Deutschlands, 1945–1948* (Fr./Main: Haag & Herchen).

Sywottek, A. (1993) '"Stalinismus" und "Totalitarismus" in der DDR-Geschichte', in *Deutsche Studien*, vol. 30, no. 117/118, pp. 25–38.

Ther, P. (1995) 'Die Vertriebenenpolitik in der SBZ/DDR 1945–1953 am Beispiel des Kreises Calau-Senftenberg', in *Jahrbuch für brandenburgische Landesgeschichte*, vol. 46, pp. 155–72.

Thoß, B. (ed.) (1994) *Volksarmee schaffen – ohne Geschrei! Studien zu den Anfängen einer 'verdeckten Aufrüstung' in der SBZ/DDR 1947–1952* (Munich: Oldenbourg).

Timmermann, H. (ed.) (1996) *Diktaturen in Europa im 20. Jahrhundert – der Fall DDR* (Berlin: Duncker & Humblot).

Voigt, D. (1973) *Montagearbeiter in der DDR* (Darmstadt: Luchterhand).

— (1987) *et al.*, *Sozialstruktur der DDR, eine Einführung* (Darmstadt: Wissenschaftliche Buchgesellschaft).

Volks- und Berufszählung der DDR (Berlin, 1964).

Weber, H. (1993) *Die DDR 1945–1990*, 2nd ed. (Munich: Oldenbourg).

Wegner, H. (1958) 'Die Kollektivierung wird vorangetrieben', in *SBZ-Archiv*, p. 354.

Wenzke, R. (1994) 'Auf dem Weg zur Kaderarmee. Aspekte der Rekrutierung, Sozialstruktur und personellen Entwicklung des entstehenden Militärs in der SBZ/DDR 1947–1952', in Bruno T. (ed.), *Volksarmee*, pp. 205–72.

— (1994) 'Die Wehrpflicht im Spiegel der marxistisch-leninistischen Theorie in der DDR', in Roland Foerster (ed.), *Die Wehrpflicht* (Munich: Oldenbourg), pp. 119–32.

Werkentin, F. (1995) *Politische Strafjustiz in der Ära Ulbricht* (Berlin: Ch. Links).

Wette, W. (ed.) (1992) *Der Krieg des kleinen Mannes. Eine Militärgeschichte von unten* (Munich: R. Piper).

Wierling, D. (1993) 'Die Jugend als innerer Feind. Konflikte in der Erziehungsdiktatur der sechziger Jahre', in Kaelble *et al.*, *Sozialgeschichte*, pp. 404–25.

Wille, M., Hoffmann, J. and Meinicke, W. (eds) (1993) *Sie hatten alles verloren.*

Flüchtlinge und Vertriebene in der sowjetischen Besatzungszone Deutschlands (Wiesbaden: Harrassowitz).

Wippermann, W. (1997) *Totalitarismustheorien: die Entwicklung der Diskussion von den Anfängen bis heute* (Darmstadt: Primus-Verlag).

Wollweber, E. (1990) 'Aus Erinnerungen. Ein Porträt Walter Ulbrichts', in *Beiträge zur Geschichte der Arbeiterbewegung*, no. 3. pp. 350–78.

Zank, W. (1987) *Wirtschaft und Arbeit in Ostdeutschland 1945–1949. Probleme des Wiederaufbaus in der Sowjetischen Besatzungszone Deutschlands* (Munich: Oldenbourg).

Zatlin, J. (1997) 'Ausgaben und Eingaben: Das Petitionsrecht und der Untergang der DDR', in *ZfG*, vol. 45, no. 10, pp. 902–17.

Zilch, D. (1994) *Millionen unter der blauen Fahne* (Rostock: Norddt. Hochschulschriften-Verlag).

Zimmermann, H. (1993) 'Überlegungen zur Geschichte der Kader und der Kaderpolitik in der SBZ/DDR', in Kaelble *et al.*, *Sozialgeschichte*, pp. 322–56.

— (1985) *et al.*, *DDR-Handbuch*, 3rd ed., 2 vols. (Cologne: Verlag Wissenschaft und Politik).

Index